Hand

THE MUSIC MEN

THE MUSIC

SMITHSONIAN INSTITUTION PRESS

Washington, D.C., London

MEN

AN ILLUSTRATED HISTORY OF BRASS BANDS IN AMERICA, 1800–1920

by Margaret Hindle Hazen

and Robert M. Hazen

Library of Congress Cataloging-in-Publication Data

Hazen, Margaret Hindle.
  The music men.
    Bibliography: p.
    Includes index.
    1. Brass bands—United States—History. I. Hazen,
Robert M., 1948–   . II. Title.
ML1311.H3 1987   785'.06'70973   86-20376
ISBN 0-87474-546-2 (alk. paper)
ISBN 0-87474-547-0 (pbk. : alk. paper)

British Library Cataloguing-in-Publication Data is available.

The paper used in this publication meets the minimum requirements of the American National Standard for Permanence of Paper for Printed Library Materials Z39.48-1984.

Front Cover. Program cover for Sousa's "New Marine Band," November 1892. Courtesy of Lillian and Stuart Caplin, Center for Musical Antiquities, New York.

Back cover. Poster of Patrick Gilmore, issued by C. G. Conn Company, ca. 1890. From the band ephemera collection at the National Museum of American History, Smithsonian Institution.

Note. The instrument shown on the front cover and used throughout as a text ornament is an Elegant Artist B-flat Gold Cornet. From a catalog of the Charles Missenharter Company, ca. 1895.

This book was designed by Janice Wheeler, edited by Ruth W. Spiegel and Jeanie J. Kim, and proofed by Jan S. Danis.

To R. E. S., the bandmaster

The quintessential American band at the quintessential American landmark: Henry's United Silver Cornet Band posed ca. 1855 at Niagara Falls. This type of instrumental ensemble abounded in the United States from the mid-nineteenth century through the First World War. The Library Company of Philadelphia.

CONTENTS

LIST OF ILLUSTRATIONS

Unless otherwise attributed, illustrations are from the collection of band ephemera, including photographs, concert programs, and instrument manufacturers' literature, assembled by Margaret and Robert Hazen. This collection now forms the nucleus of an archive of American band history at the Smithsonian Institution, National Museum of American History.

PREFACE

Several years ago the Smithsonian Institution's National Museum of American History celebrated the Fourth of July with a joyful reenactment of a nineteenth-century band concert. The highlight of the occasion was the inauguration of an ornate Victorian bandstand that had been moved, piece by piece, from Jacksonville, Illinois, to its new home on the museum's west grounds. There, amidst flags and bunting, ten red-jacketed musicians gathered with saxhorns in hand and keppies on head. As was customary a century ago, the Declaration of Independence was read and a short oration delivered. Then, in the deepening twilight, as children tumbled on a grassy hillside and parents reclined on blankets and chairs, the band rendered such old favorites as "Hail, Columbia" and Stephen Foster's "Maggie by My Side." For a few hours the past was revived.

Across the street, in stark contrast, another concert was taking place at precisely the same time. This celebration, thoroughly modern in concept and execution, featured extravagantly amplified country-western music directed toward a crowd numbering in the hundreds of thousands congregated near the Washington Monument. Most of that audience, unable to catch even a glimpse of the performers, milled about while helicopters chopped overhead and police cars cruised the adjacent city streets.

The juxtaposition of these two Independence Day scenes exemplifies the transformation of American society and musical taste over the past one hundred years. Although many American town bands still present open-air concerts of patriotic and nostalgic selections, the modern music scene in America is but distantly related to the band movement so familiar to our pioneering, nineteenth-century forebears. For almost three-quarters of a century—from about 1850 until after World War I—bands such as the one recreated at the Smithsonian were a pervasive aspect of American life. At one time as many as twenty thousand bands, representing virtually every geographic, ethnic, occupational, social, and age grouping, were active in America. Almost every town and village of a few hundred population or more had its band of ten or twenty musicians who performed for almost all public gatherings: concerts, parades, dances, picnics, weddings, funerals. In most communities the town band provided the only instrumental concert music other than church and parlor music. And bands were by no means restricted to towns; ensembles were formed in prisons, leper colonies, insane asylums, orphanages, and veterans hospitals. Bands composed of Blacks, Native Americans, Hawaiians, Eskimos, as well as settlers from Germany, Italy, Norway, Poland, and many other countries, were formed following the Civil War. Occupational bands represented miners, farmers, factory workers, cowboys, newsboys, and dentists. Women's bands, boys' bands, girls' bands, and family bands evoked much comment, while men's club bands representing Eagles, Odd Fellows, Elks, Masons, and others gained great popularity around the turn of the century. The band movement thus provides an unparalleled mirror of American society.

The Music Men focuses on the evolution of the American band movement from its origins early in the nineteenth century, through the golden age of the late nineteenth century, to the end of the First World War. Utilizing original band records, contemporary newspaper accounts, hundreds of band programs, and thousands of pictorial records, we have sought to profile the musicians, amateur as well as professional, who contributed to the movement. The many occasions and celebrations that featured band performances, the evolution of band instruments and music during the nineteenth century, the influence of military music traditions, and the relationship between the music business and band development, are but a few of the themes central to an understanding of the band movement. Unlike many music scholars who tend to view bands only as they relate to the development of "high art" music in America, we attempt to present the subject in the context of American society at large. What may emerge is a more complete picture of America's vital and vibrant bands, the musical ensembles of the people.

Our research focused initially on materials in our own large collection of band photographs, programs, and other ephemera. A principal objective of our research was the transfer of this collection to the Smithsonian and the establishment of an American band archive at the Division of Musical Instruments of the National Museum of American History, Smithsonian Institution. That archive, which now includes originals and copies of more than two thousand documents, programs, photographs, and other ephemera relating to American bands, forms the basis for this illustrated history. *Unless otherwise attributed, the illustrations in this book come from that collection.*

This project would not have been possible without the support and encouragement of many individuals. Librarians and archivists from more than three hundred institutions were generous in providing copies of programs, photographs, articles, and other sources on American bands and bandsmen. Of special note are the following individuals who rendered assistance beyond the call of duty: Dorothy B. Bailey, Brown County Historical Society, Nashville, Indiana; Dorothy B. Ballantyne and Elin Christianson, Hobart (Indiana) Historical Society; Lance J. Bauer, Providence (Rhode Island) Public Library; Raoul F. Camus, Queensborough Community College; Donna N. Carlson, Historical Museum of the Darwin R. Baker Library, Fredonia, New York; Marilyn R. Cook, Navarre-Bethlehem Township (Pennsylvania) Historical Society, Inc.; Carl E. W. Hauger and Robert H. Hill, Fort Delaware Society; Frank B. Holt, Historian, Stonewall Brigade Band, Staunton, Virginia; Greg Koos, McClean County (Illinois) Historical Society; Jon Newsom, Library of Congress; Susan Oyama, The Library Company of Pennsylvania; Arnold D. Roggman, Garnavillo (Iowa) Historical Society; Betty Salomon, Hope Valley (Rhode Island) Historical Society; Stephen Trent Seames, Maine Historical Society; Pearl Tobiash, American Bandmasters' Association Research Center, University of Maryland, College Park, Maryland; and Commander Gifford Wilcox, U.S.N.R., Tallmadge (Ohio) Historical Society.

Numerous individuals contributed resources from their private collections. Photographs, band ephemera, or research notes were lent by Hope Andrews, Christopher Banner, Helen Ducommun, Ralph Dudgeon, Richard Dundas, Mark Elrod, Lloyd Farrar, Loren Geiger, Peter A. Greene, William T. Hassett, Jr., James Kimball, Johnny Maddox, Robert Multhauf, Will Scarlett, Robb Stewart, and John Waldsmith. We are especially grateful to bookseller Ken Leach of Brattleboro, Vermont, who donated important Vermont photographs and an early band broadside to the Smithsonian collections, and Lillian and Stuart Caplin of the Center for Musical Antiquities, New York, who discovered and provided access to many important items relating to American bands.

We have benefited immeasurably from the expertise of American musical scholars. Paul Bierley, professional bandsman and biographer of John Philip Sousa, generously shared his knowledge and enthusiasm for American band history. S. Frederick Starr of Oberlin College reviewed the manuscript and not only offered his thoughts on the relationships between bands and jazz, but also discussed with us his valuable ideas on the importance of bands as social institutions. Robert Eliason, former curator of musical instruments at the Henry Ford Museum,

also reviewed the manuscript and contributed helpful additions and corrections.

Throughout the research and writing of *The Music Men* we have enjoyed the benefits of association with staff members of the Division of Musical Instruments, National Museum of American History, Smithsonian Institution. Cynthia A. Hoover first suggested that we pursue our research in conjunction with the Smithsonian, and she has provided continuing support. John Hasse provided numerous specific references as well as general comments based on his broad knowledge of American music. John Fesperman, Gary Sturm, and Minnie Krantz contributed time and energy to aspects of our American band research. Thanks are also due to Carl H. Scheele of the Smithsonian's Division of Community Life for his insights on the Jacksonville Bandstand.

Our greatest debt is to Robert E. Sheldon, Museum Specialist in the Division of Musical Instruments, and authority on the American band movement. Through his exacting research and conscientious revivals of the nineteenth-century band tradition, he has been a key figure in the renewed interest in early American bands. Bob has always been ready and willing to discuss historical questions with insight and humor. He has uncovered many important sources, helped in the preparation and analysis of early band photographs, and prepared a detailed review of the book's first draft. His original ideas are reflected throughout this book.

Finally, we thank our editors, Daniel Goodwin, Ruth W. Spiegel, and Jeanie J. Kim, whose careful work on the manuscript greatly improved the text. We are also grateful to Janice Wheeler who designed the book and integrated the illustrative materials with creativity and style.

CHRONOLOGY OF AMERICAN BAND HISTORY

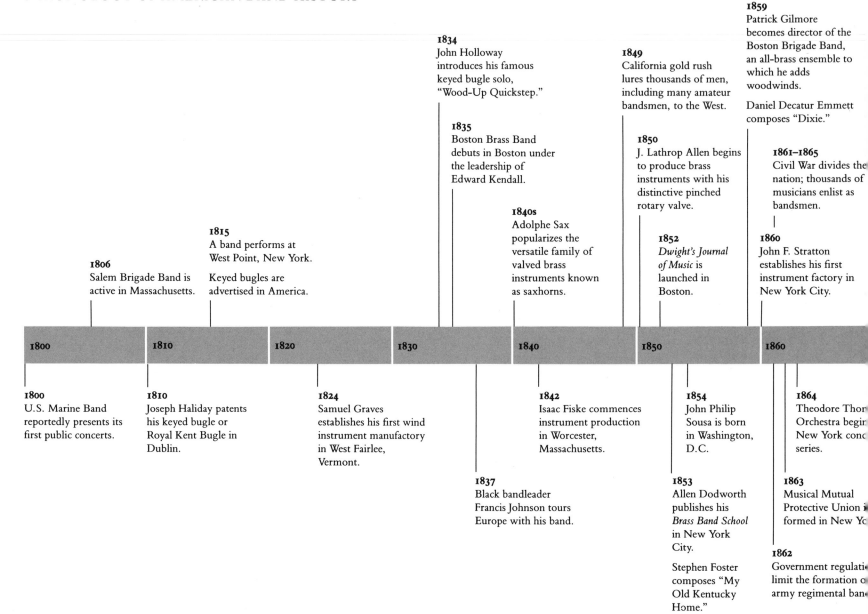

1834
John Holloway introduces his famous keyed bugle solo, "Wood-Up Quickstep."

1835
Boston Brass Band debuts in Boston under the leadership of Edward Kendall.

1859
Patrick Gilmore becomes director of the Boston Brigade Band, an all-brass ensemble to which he adds woodwinds.

Daniel Decatur Emmett composes "Dixie."

1849
California gold rush lures thousands of men, including many amateur bandsmen, to the West.

1850
J. Lathrop Allen begins to produce brass instruments with his distinctive pinched rotary valve.

1861–1865
Civil War divides the nation; thousands of musicians enlist as bandsmen.

1840s
Adolphe Sax popularizes the versatile family of valved brass instruments known as saxhorns.

1852
Dwight's Journal of Music is launched in Boston.

1815
A band performs at West Point, New York.

Keyed bugles are advertised in America.

1806
Salem Brigade Band is active in Massachusetts.

1860
John F. Stratton establishes his first instrument factory in New York City.

| 1800 | 1810 | 1820 | 1830 | 1840 | 1850 | 1860 |

1800
U.S. Marine Band reportedly presents its first public concerts.

1810
Joseph Haliday patents his keyed bugle or Royal Kent Bugle in Dublin.

1824
Samuel Graves establishes his first wind instrument manufactory in West Fairlee, Vermont.

1842
Isaac Fiske commences instrument production in Worcester, Massachusetts.

1854
John Philip Sousa is born in Washington, D.C.

1864
Theodore Thor[...] Orchestra begi[...] New York conc[...] series.

1837
Black bandleader Francis Johnson tours Europe with his band.

1853
Allen Dodworth publishes his *Brass Band School* in New York City.

Stephen Foster composes "My Old Kentucky Home."

1863
Musical Mutual Protective Union [...] formed in New Yo[...]

1862
Government regulati[...] limit the formation o[...] army regimental ban[...]

1877
Henry Distin, noted English musician and instrument maker, arrives in New York to start manufacturing brass.

Thomas Edison begins research leading to the invention of the phonograph.

1892
Patrick Gilmore dies.

John Philip Sousa forms his own band.

1917
America enters the First World War.

Kansas band law passes and provides funds for community bands.

2
rick Gilmore's rnational ce Jubilee ures 20,000 ers and rumentalists, ce as many as 1869 National ce Jubilee.

1880
John Philip Sousa becomes the fourteenth director of the U.S. Marine Band.

1896
Sousa composes "The Stars and Stripes Forever."

Musicians affiliate with the American Federation of Labor and soon form the American Federation of Musicians.

1918
Goldman Band begins its summer band concerts on the Green at Columbia University.

1873
Patrick Gilmore becomes leader of the Twenty-second Regiment Band of New York, soon known as Gilmore's Band.

1886
National League of Musicians is formed.

1899
Scott Joplin composes "Maple Leaf Rag."

1919
Prohibition Amendment is ratified.

1929
American Bandmasters' Association is formed.

| 1880 | 1890 | 1900 | 1910 | 1920 | 1930 |

1876
Centennial Exhibition in Philadelphia features daily band concerts.

C. G. Conn begins mass production of his patented rubber-rim cornet mouthpiece.

1889
An estimated ten thousand bands are active in the United States.

1903
Bands play for festivities at the first World Series.

1920
First permanent commercial radio is established.

Americans purchase eight million automobiles annually.

1932
John Philip Sousa dies in Reading, Pennsylvania.

1875
The Leader, a periodical for bandsmen, is first published in Boston.

G. F. Patton publishes his guide on band music and brass band formation.

1888
Sousa composes "Semper Fidelis."

1898
Spanish-American War is fought and won by the United States.

Helen May Butler organizes and conducts a professional women's band.

Frank Holton establishes his band instrument company in Chicago.

1915
Tom Brown's Dixieland Jazz Band plays in Chicago.

1887
Salvation Army sponsors a staff band in New York City.

Henry Distin establishes an instrument factory in Williamsport, Pennsylvania.

THE MUSIC MEN

The Fourth of July was a day for celebrating the nation's promising future as well as its distinguished past. Bands were featured throughout the day's festivities in towns across the United States.

I.

MUSIC FOR THE PEOPLE

All at once the idea of a *Brass Band* shot forth: and from this prolific germ sprang up a multitude of its kind in every part of the land. . . .

—John Sullivan Dwight

SCOPE OF THE BAND MOVEMENT

To William Allen White, who grew up in a small Kansas town in the 1870s, a concert by the local band was one of childhood's delights. "I can recall now . . . hearing the Eldorado silver cornet band playing down in Burdette's grove by the mill," the noted journalist wrote in his autobiography. "The strains wafted across our creek to our place. I remember even that I was sitting under the grape-vines preparing my little stomach for a gorgeous belly-ache, eating the half-green grapes and listening to what I felt was heavenly music. It was the first band I had ever heard."[1]

Like Mr. White, Americans in communities across the country were introduced to the pleasures of band music during the nineteenth century. Whether marching in pa-rades on the Fourth of July, welcoming visiting dignitaries and officials to town, or "discoursing sweet music," bands—either primarily or exclusively brass in instru-mentation—were unquestionably the most visible and audible musical organizations of the day. They could be found regaling graduates and guests at commencement ceremonies, inspiring the wayward at temperance meet-ings, and entertaining holiday makers on steamboat ex-cursions. Brass bands enlivened military units on the parade ground and accompanied civilian couples on the dance floor. When politicians launched their campaigns they hired bands to punctuate their promises. And when the circus came to town, it was the band that made the first announcement with ringing brass and at show time was on hand to accompany the daring acts with dramatic and spirited tunes.

As early as 1856, Boston music critic John Sullivan Dwight surveyed the situation around him and concluded

The epigraph at the head of this chapter is from *Dwight's Journal of Music* 3:2 (April 16, 1853), 9.

Bands were a prominent feature of the Civil War, with hundreds of regimental bands taking an active musical role. Mathew Brady photographed the Second Rhode Island Infantry Regiment during the winter of 1861.

Mr. and Mrs. Charles Scripture were serenaded by this band in Nelson, New Hampshire, at their golden wedding anniversary around 1890. Small-town bands provided music for every sort of social gathering.

that brass bands were virtually "everywhere." But, as astute an observer as Dwight was, he probably did not realize how pervasive band performances were in America at midcentury or how their popularity would increase in later decades. Just as Commodore Matthew C. Perry took several bands with him when he "opened" Japan to American trade in 1854, many U.S. Army regiments had brass bands with them as they opened up the American West. When the Civil War broke out, brass bands played at recruitment rallies, at troop farewells, and in almost every major campaign from Fort Sumter to Appomattox. Bands provided background music for roller skating and ice skating and, with the advent of the bicycling craze in the 1880s and 1890s, bands were hired to set the proper atmosphere for learning the art of wheeling. Embodying an almost perfect blend of entertainment and art, bands were also standard attractions at the many Chautauqua

assemblies held across the country in the late nineteenth and early twentieth centuries.

Band music was considered suitable for virtually any occasion. When the first white woman arrived in Columbia, California, in 1851, she was heartily welcomed by a brass band leading a parade of more than six thousand men.[2] Montana miners, seeking a meeting with management about a labor dispute, placed a brass band at the head of their delegation. Newlyweds were serenaded by the strains of brass bands and older couples celebrated their anniversaries in much the same way. Real estate, patent medicine, and ice cream are just a few of the many products advertised to the tune of band music. Even somber occasions such as funerals and military executions utilized bands to evoke suitably solemn emotions. Most rites required the services of small bands for the short walk to the cemetery or for brief graveside ceremonies,

2

but for robber-baron Jim Fisk's opulent funeral in 1872, the band of New York's Ninth Regiment (of which Fisk had been colonel) was augmented to a magnificent two hundred pieces in order to provide a "proper" farewell for the deceased.[3]

America's achievements in the realm of engineering and technology were particularly suited to commemoration by brassy, open-air bands. The grand opening of a suspension bridge between Minneapolis and St. Paul in 1853 was heralded by a brass band. So was the completion of the first electric plant in Athens, Illinois, four decades later. During the heyday of canal construction, bands were commonly recruited to celebrate their inauguration. The famous keyed bugle virtuoso Richard Willis composed "The Grand Canal March" especially for the opening of the Erie Canal, and Francis Johnson's renowned band from Philadelphia played from the decks of the steamship *William Penn* for the festivities to inaugurate the Chesapeake and Delaware Canal in 1829. Balloon ascensions, which became popular in the wake of Charles Durant's daring exploits in the 1830s and 1840s, were frequently accompanied by bands. Music not only attracted crowds but also highlighted the excitement of the launch.

The opening of the nation's many railroads would have been unthinkable without band music. In 1834, the Boston Brigade Band played a new piece by James Hooten to commemorate the advent of the railroad to the little town of Westborough, Massachusetts, and for the next fifty years brass was commonly used to celebrate steel. From the inauguration of small trunk lines to the joining of great transcontinental roads, bands were as regular a feature of the ceremonies as the spirited orators and the booming cannon. At ordinary railroad construction sites, too, bands might be heard. As bandsman Joseph Barton

Numerous bands performed for President William McKinley while he served in office—and for the funeral and memorial processions following his assassination in September 1901. Bands contributed to both festive and solemn public ceremonies. John Waldsmith Collection.

Bands were used to celebrate many technological achievements. According to the account in the Charleston Courier *of this train excursion in 1831, "Following the barrier car [which protected passengers in the event of a boiler explosion] came an open car, upon which was seated the well-known colored band of Charleston, who discoursed most excellent music in their performance of national airs, which added much to the hilarity and pleasure of the occasion."*

recorded in his journal, the brass band of Kaysville, Utah, followed a Union Pacific work party into Weber Canyon one day in 1869 and serenaded the work train as it laid the tracks. Much to Barton's surprise, the band was eventually invited to get on board. So it was that, in Barton's words, the band "had the honor, yes the sole honor, of riding into Salt Lake Valley on the first railway train and on the first rails that entered that Valley." Barton added proudly, "Band playing all the time."[4]

Given this well-established tradition of celebrating engineering feats with band music, it is hardly surprising that at the 1876 Centennial Exhibition in Philadelphia—where America's technological productions were displayed to the world—a large bandstand was erected and daily used in the central transept of the Main Building. For the grand celebration glorifying the opening of the Brooklyn

Bridge, unquestionably the engineering feat of the century, the band-loving organizing committee pulled out all the stops. Among the many events scheduled for opening day on May 24, 1883, were performances by both the Twenty-third Regiment Band from Brooklyn and the famous Seventh Regiment Band of New York. The renowned and dashing cornetist Jules Levy made a featured solo appearance. He began his performance with a special rendition of the "Star-Spangled Banner" and then played "Hail, Columbia" as an encore. He was, apparently, just warming up, but was hustled off the stage by schedule-conscious organizers. To the delight of the crowd, however, the irrepressible Levy continued to play—this time "Yankee Doodle" from the sidelines. And if this were not enough music for the day, bands played from the decks of several small boats in the East River during the evening's fireworks display.[5]

It would, in short, have been difficult to avoid band music in nineteenth-century America—and few Americans desired to do so. "There is nothing that rouses the universal enthusiasm of everybody as does a spirited band," claimed the Wurlitzer Instrument Company in what was an apt observation as well as an adroit business ploy.[6] Americans across the country contributed generously to the support of bands and congregated enthusiastically, often by the thousands, to hear the bands play. Even before the Civil War, many towns had some sort of brass band either connected with a local militia unit or organized on an independent basis. By the 1880s and 1890s the band movement expanded to such a degree that most towns of any size were actively supporting some sort of civic band. Many modest-sized communities could boast several such performing groups. There were, in addition, numerous professional concert bands such as those conducted by Patrick Sarsfield Gilmore and John

Hartington, Nebraska, in 1899 had a population of less than a thousand, yet it boasted a smartly uniformed band of twenty-four players. Towns of as few as two hundred residents supported bands in every state and territory.

Philip Sousa. Crisscrossing the States on extensive tours, these superb musical organizations almost always attracted loyal and approving audiences willing to pay money to hear a band play.

Among the musicians themselves, bands were no less a source of pride and enthusiasm. Talented professionals such as Edward Kendall, Allen Dodworth, Patrick Gilmore, Alessandro Liberati, Matthew Arbuckle, and Arthur Pryor devoted their lives to the performance of high-quality band music. Hundreds of other hopeful professional musicians saw in the band movement an opportunity for gainful employment in the field of music. For John Philip Sousa, probably the most famous bandleader of all time, the medium was so enticing that in 1880 he gave up a promising career in theatrical orchestras in order to conduct the U.S. Marine Band in Washington, D.C.

Amateur musicians were similarly attracted to band performance, for which they gave up many hours of leisure and often a considerable amount of their spare change. One of the more famous of these avocational musicians was still-life painter John Peto, who depicted band instruments in several of his best tromp l'oeil canvases and pursued a lifelong hobby as a cornetist. New York Mayor Fiorello La Guardia, President Warren G. Harding and popcorn king Orville Redenbacher are a few other distinguished Americans who enjoyed playing in amateur bands in their younger days.[7] Hundreds of thousands of lesser-known amateurs also joined bands in their communities or places of employment. Some improved their musical skills so markedly that they were ultimately able to become professional bandsmen.

The exertions of both the public and the players on behalf of bands—indeed the almost fanatical eagerness of the two groups to incorporate band music into a variety of settings—catapulted bands into the national consciousness. Far outstripping the classical symphony orchestra in prominence and popularity, bands were the most important source of instrumental entertainment heard outside the home. Bands became social as well as musical institutions, and the universality of their appeal rendered them conspicuous features on the American cultural landscape. Many intellectuals of the period acknowledged this fact in the context of their own artistic productions. William Sidney Mount, the well-known painter of American genre scenes, included a sketch of the Setauket Military Band among his many renditions of rural Americans at work and play, and Walt Whitman highlighted both military bands and "bugle calls in the ballroom" in his panoramic poem "Song of Myself." In later years Charles Ives, the son of a Danbury, Connecticut, bandmaster, immortalized the blaring sounds of the town bands in his

The Setauket Military Band was sketched by the noted American genre painter, William Sidney Mount, in about 1840. The group may have been performing at a militia parade on Long Island, New York. The Museums at Stony Brook.

orchestral composition the *Holidays Symphony*. It is also curious to note that in De Wolf Hopper's classic ode to America's favorite pastime, "the band is playing somewhere" while "mighty Casey" is striking out. But nowhere, perhaps, is America's wholehearted acceptance of bands more clearly illustrated than in the charming and widely circulated Wagner and McGuigan chromolithograph that depicts Henry's United Silver Cornet Band on the quintessential American site, Niagara Falls.

FUNCTION AND FORMAT: THE HISTORICAL OVERVIEW

The roots of the American band movement are buried deep in the musical traditions of western Europe. Recognizable forerunners of modern wind bands began to appear in Germany and France as early as the seventeenth century. By the middle of the eighteenth century, small ensembles of wind instruments were to be found in many European towns and cities where they were employed for concerts, street parades, and ceremonial displays by the local military organizations. These so-called Harmonien utilized a variety of instrumentations, the most common being pairs of oboes, clarinets, bassoons, and horns. When Frederick the Great reorganized the Prussian army in 1763, he is thought to have stipulated that the bands should conform to this instrumentation. Other European countries adopted similar patterns, although it was not unusual to find a flute, natural trumpet, or serpent added to the ensemble. Eventually, the "Turkish elements" such as triangle, drums, and cymbals were also incorporated into many European military bands.

Continental conventions regarding both the function and format of bands were readily, if haphazardly, introduced to the American colonies by musically inclined immigrants. The Moravians, who placed a high value on musical activities, demonstrated an early interest in wind bands. In the Moravian community at Salem, North Carolina, a band was offering secular music along with the customary religious selections by 1785 and in the sister settlement at Bethlehem, Pennsylvania, a fine wind band performed classical European Harmoniemusik in concert and as an accompaniment to the community's activities by the early nineteenth century.[8]

Of considerably more significance in terms of the overall development of American band music were the various military bands that appeared in the colonies in the eighteenth century. As early as 1756, one such band of musicians played for a volunteer regiment in Philadelphia. During the American Revolution a number of additional wind bands are known to have been formed for the pleasure and entertainment of the officers of the Continental Army.[9] Other scattered examples testify to a passable American interest in bands: Josiah Flagg amassed a band and singers for a large concert in Boston in 1773; the citizens of Temple, New Hampshire, organized a band in 1799 to play for a memorial service for George Washington on the President's birthday the following year; and in 1798 the U.S. Marine Corps formed a band that was busy giving concerts by 1800.

Although the Moravian-supported Salem Band was an all-brass unit consisting of four trumpets, four horns, and eight trombones, most of these early American bands reflected standard European instrumentation patterns. The Marine Band, which originally consisted solely of fifers and drummers, is believed to have presented its first concert on August 21, 1800, with two oboes, two clarinets, two horns, a bassoon, and a drum.[10] A few years later, in 1806, the Salem Brigade Band of Salem, Massachusetts, performed with a roster of five clarinets, two bassoons, one trumpet, triangle, and bass drum.[11] Eventually, a French horn, two trombones, and a serpent were introduced to fill out the ensemble. In other words, despite the occasional use of brass instruments, there was an overwhelming reliance on the woodwind instruments to furnish the melodies and most of the harmonies in band music.

That this convention worked well aesthetically is undeniable—Haydn, Mozart, Beethoven, and other classical composers wrote a number of charming compositions to prove it. But there was another, more practical reason for the prominence of woodwinds: they simply had greater tonal range and more versatility than most brass instruments available at the time. Early in the nineteenth century, however, European instrument makers were busy experimenting with innovations that would enable brass instruments to play chromatic and diatonic scales rather than the limited bugle-call notes of earlier brass. The ultimate success of these technical improvements was phenomenal. They not only allowed brass instruments to

be used in bands in greater numbers than formerly, but also served to transform the popular idea of a band from a woodwind group to a predominantly brass ensemble.

The keyed bugle (also called the Royal Kent Bugle) was one of the first of the new chromatic brass instruments to achieve popularity in America. Essentially a bugle equipped with a series of saxophonelike keys to effect pitch changes, the keyed bugle was patented in 1810 by the Irish maker Joseph Haliday and was introduced to the United States as early as 1815.[12] In the hands of a master musician such as Richard Willis, leader of the Military Academy Band at West Point, the instrument could play either loudly or softly and could render the most intricate melodic passages with grace and precision. It was not long, therefore, before a number of American players, including Francis (Frank) Johnson and Edward (Ned) Kendall, were using the novel little horn for band work and in virtuoso solo playing.

Although clearly the brightest star, the keyed bugle was not the only new instrument in the emerging constellation of chromatic brass. The ophicleide, larger relative of the keyed bugle, was soon available to furnish a bass line. In addition, a variety of valve mechanisms that greatly simplified the process of changing notes on a brass instrument were successfully introduced during the 1830s and 1840s. These devices, utilized effectively on instruments in every register, eventually brought about the evolution of the wind band from an elite ensemble for technically skilled performers to an ideal medium for amateur music making.

Although initially the new brass instruments were integrated into existing wind bands to enrich and strengthen the sound, their brightness of tone, tantalizing novelty, and proven effectiveness for ensemble playing made the creation of bands composed *exclusively* of brass instruments inevitable. Drawing on their long-standing preference for trumpet music, European cavalrymen had begun to experiment with all-brass instrumentations for their bands in the early decades of the nineteenth century. It was not long before American bands adopted this pattern for both military and civilian ensembles. Dodworth's Band of New York City is thought to have changed to an all-brass instrumentation in 1834 or 1835. The Salem (Massachusetts) Brigade Band in 1835 and the Boston Brigade Band in 1838 followed suit.

At about the same time many new all-brass bands came into existence. Probably the most famous of these were the Boston Brass Band organized by Edward Kendall in 1835 and the American Brass Band of Providence which gave its first concert in January 1838. Similar groups cropped up elsewhere in the country. As early as 1838 the New Orleans *Picayune* reported a "real mania in this city for horn and trumpet playing." The newspaper complained that it was impossible to turn a corner without running into a brass "blower." Some people, it was claimed, were so overwhelmed by brass that they found themselves ardently wishing for the "last trumpet."[13]

There was no way this wish could possibly come true. The brass band movement had only just begun. Eagerly discarding their outdated woodwinds, musicians would continue to form brass bands throughout the rest of the century. The trend was so decisive and so widespread that one distraught observer worried that within a few years wooden instruments would become virtually unknown in America.[14] This exigency never materialized. Yet even in those ensembles that adopted a mixed brass and woodwind instrumentation, the brass elements generally reigned supreme.

The number of American bandsmen who participated in this musical movement is impressive. It is possible that

The Boston Brass Band, better known in 1851 as Flagg's Brass Band after its leader, wore elegant uniforms with red pants, blue coats, and plumed hats. This group was widely acclaimed as one of the best American bands.

several tens of thousands of bandsmen participated in the Civil War, and the number of band performers increased dramatically in the ensuing decades. It has been estimated that there were approximately ten thousand bands in America in 1889.[15] If each group had only fifteen members, there were about one hundred fifty thousand bandsmen in America by the last decade of the century. By 1908, according to one observer, the number of bands had increased to eighteen thousand.[16] With a concomitant increase in the average size of bands, this was arguably the peak of the band movement.

America's contribution to the development of bands was not simply the large numbers of players. Several important and internationally recognized innovations in band performance were made by Americans. In the field

The band stationed at Fort Delaware near Wilmington, Delaware, in 1863 employed a matched set of over-shoulder instruments. This shape allowed the musicians, who customarily marched at the head of a column of troops, to play for the troops behind them. Fort Delaware Society.

The Fourth of July, 1865, was a day to celebrate the end of the Civil War, but it was only the beginning of America's golden age of bands. Library of Congress.

of instrument manufacture, American makers designed a unique and highly successful method of string linkage for the smooth operation of rotary valves. In composition, conductor-cornetist David Wallis Reeves has been credited with pioneering the use of a countermelody in marches. This in turn paved the way for the extraordinarily popular and well-crafted compositions of John Philip Sousa, justifiably celebrated throughout the world as the March King. And American brass bands played a pivotal role in the development of jazz. According to one researcher, the brass bands of New Orleans gave jazz its instrumentation, and also lent musical techniques and repertoire to this uniquely American musical idiom.[17] As a 1917 advertising poster succinctly put it, a jazz band was simply a "brass band gone crazy."[18] This "craziness" would spread throughout the world during the early twentieth century.

MUSIC FOR THE MASSES

How is this burst of musical activity to be explained? After all, the United States was not exactly a hotbed of musical activity in the early nineteenth century. When Charles Dickens made his famous tour of the country in 1842, he remarked upon the total absence of street bands in New York City. "But how quiet the streets are!" he exclaimed in his published notes of the visit. "Are there no itinerant bands; no wind or string instruments? No, not one."[19] De Tocqueville had managed to find some

9

The Manchester (New Hampshire) Brass Band of 1861 was typical of town bands that flourished in the years before the Civil War. Many of these amateur ensembles enlisted together to become regimental bands in their state's volunteer fighting units. Vermont Historical Society.

music during his visit to America a few years earlier, but this he dismissed as being "of an unbelievable barbarity."[20]

The lack of sophistication in musical matters was partly a result of the newness of the nation and partly a result of public attitudes. Some people objected to secular music on religious grounds. Others, like the character John Philip Sousa created in his novel, *The Fifth String,* took pleasure in the sounds of the dinner horn and the tea kettle and saw no need to pursue any kind of "artificial" music.[21] Still others held the view expressed by western explorer and governor of Colorado William Gilpin that America's proper destiny was, among other things,

> to subdue the continent, to rush over the vast field to the Pacific Ocean . . . to set the principle of self-government at work, to agitate these herculean masses, to establish a new order in human affairs, to set free the enslaved . . . to perfect science, to emblazon history with the conquest of peace, to shed a new resplendent glory upon mankind . . . and to shed blessings around the world.[22]

For these activists, the issue of music was simply irrelevant to America's more serious purposes.

Yet, somehow, bands and band music did catch on. Part of the explanation touches on the hospitable social scene in many cities and towns during the several decades before the Civil War. The twenty-year period between the financial panics of 1837 and 1857 was a particularly prosperous and dynamic time for most Americans. Population nearly doubled, national income increased more than twofold, and many citizens had more leisure than ever before. Moreover, while confident that they had created the best political system on the face of the earth, many Americans were sensitive about their shortcomings in the arts and were receptive to tutoring.

These conditions coincided neatly with the invention and perfection of new varieties of brass instruments perfectly suited to mass music making. With the invention of the keyed bugle and the subsequent introduction of diverse valved instruments, musicians suddenly had at their disposal groups of instruments that were not only able to carry the melody, but were also loud and durable—unequaled for outdoor performances. Although the keyed bugle and ophicleide required considerable technical expertise, the valved brass instruments that superseded them proved to be relatively easy to learn. When Adolphe Sax and others devised entire families of matched valved brass (often called saxhorns), it was even possible to teach an entire band how to play at one time. Dramatic improvements in methods of transportation meant that these impressive new instruments, along with skilled craftsmen who could make them and trained musicians who could teach them, were easily conveyed to American shores and across the continent.

If the time was right for the appearance of brass bands, then the music they offered was also right for the times. Patriotic airs such as "Yankee Doodle" and "Hail, Columbia" were in perfect tune with the feelings of nationalism that developed throughout the country in the years after the War of 1812. Despite sectional conflicts, patriotic feelings increased during the rest of the century. The fact that civilian bands played for military groups and that Regular Army bands gave concerts for the general public made it easy for bands to function as boosters of American spirit. Equally engaging were the bands' renditions of popular romantic ballads or dance tunes of the day. Sentimental favorites such as "Sweet Home" and light-hearted waltzes and quicksteps appealed to the emotions of a people struggling to create an ordered society on a vast and often forbidding continent. A band performance was an entertaining and enjoyable situation for most people. The uniforms were flashy, the soloists were impressive,

and the music had a rousing, measured beat. "Object—pleasure," claimed an 1875 advertisement for a band concert in Minnesota.[23] And pleasure was what the audience got.

But while fortuitous circumstances and appealing music may explain the existence of brass bands, these factors alone cannot account for the immense popularity and scope of the movement. Without additional benefits, too many people might have reacted to bands in the manner of one dour Detroit resident. When informed that a concert "for the amusement of the people" was in progress one summer evening in 1859, this baffled individual replied, "Ye don't say so; is that all it's for?"[24]

Amusement was *not* all that bands were for. According to newspaper editorials, instrument company literature, and band programs of the day, bands also had a higher utilitarian and moral purpose than mere diversion. Many brass band boosters, including the renowned instrument inventor Adolphe Sax, pointed out numerous health benefits that were to be derived from blowing musical instruments and from marching in bands. Good lungs, broad shoulders, strength, and vigor were all attributed to participation in this form of musical activity. Bands were justified and defended because they could attract crowds and help sell land, promote amusement parks, and publicize numerous other commodities. Bands were also employed to underscore the philosophies espoused by diverse religious, social, and political organizations. But by far the most influential argument in favor of bands was the idea of a band as a culturally elevating institution that fostered democracy.

The two parts of this claim were equally important. On the one hand, bands, like the mass-produced chromolithographic reproductions in the field of art, were seen to have a power to enrich and improve the common people.[25]

The Union Brass Band of Cape Elizabeth, Maine, achieved sufficient expertise to be in demand in Portland, Maine, for those occasions when the larger and more famous Chandler's Band was not available. Maine Historical Society.

This did not mean simply that bands would confer a higher level of musical taste on the listener, although that was certainly part of the theory. (It is not unlikely, as a matter of fact, that a higher percentage of the American population could identify a Rossini overture in 1887 than in 1987.) It also meant that a band was a measure of civilization itself. "We consider this band," wrote the *Minnesota Pioneer* about the Fort Snelling band in 1850, ". . . of infinite value to St. Paul. In fact, it is the most powerful element of influence amongst us, for our good, next to the pulpit and the press."[26] This same viewpoint was still being expressed in 1911. An editorial in support of the Chicago Band's concerts claimed that this music was "as great a blessing and almost as much a necessity to real civilization as fresh air or pure water."[27] Progress was almost unthinkable without bands, and to fail to support them, it was stated time and again, was to be "dumb, backward, [and] uncivilized."[28]

On the other hand, as band publicity always emphasized, bands were seen to bestow their benefits on communities as a whole. If anyone was going to be "elevated" at a band concert, *everyone* was going to be elevated at once. Just as baseball was to become the sport of the people, bands were understood to provide the music of the people. A concert review published in the *Minneapolis Tribune* in 1875 reflects the typical attitude: "These concerts are the contribution of art to the people, to be enjoyed by the occupant of the humblest cabin and by the master of a mansion, and harmonizing all classes in the democracy of music."[29] Echoing these sentiments, the Chicago Band chose as its motto "Free music for the masses." Even for the players there was a democratic appeal in belonging to a brass band. The instruments were fairly inexpensive and they were not too difficult to play. Most of the brass instruments could be played inter-

"Come Everybody, Forget Your Troubles" proclaimed the advertising banner for the Denver, Colorado, Eagles' Club dance. The Eagles Band drummed up business during the day and then played for the dance at night.

Bands played everywhere. A Union Army band scaled Lookout Mountain, Tennessee, in 1864 to pose for this dramatic view, which in many ways symbolizes the bold, brassy spirit of America's age of bands. State Historical Society of Wisconsin.

changeably with similar mouthpieces and identical fingerings, and could be shared among bandsmen according to the needs of the ensemble.

The predisposition of Americans for "the immediately useful and practical,"[30] the avid desire among people at all social levels for self-improvement, and the universal commitment to a democratic society meant that all of these arguments in favor of bands had validity for Americans, who willingly ascribed to the band a relevance beyond the purely musical. Ultimately, however, it may be the band's unparalleled adaptability that ensured its success. A band could provide music indoors or outdoors, in ensembles large or small. It could furnish light and cheery

quicksteps and polkas, and it could present transcriptions of music by the more serious composers of the day. One could stand and watch a band march by in a parade, or the band could stay put and the audience could promenade past the musicians. As far as instrumentation was concerned, a band was capable of almost infinite variety. Unlike the symphony orchestra, which changed the instrumentation to fit the music, bands typically altered the music to fit the instruments on hand.[31] Such a flexible attitude toward instrumentation meant that almost any group of wind instruments, with or without percussion could function as a band and be deserving of the name. A band could be a club for men, a conservatory of music, an advertisement for a town, or a celebration of the nation. If not all things to all people, a band certainly meant something to most people.

Music critic John Sullivan Dwight hardly knew how to approach such a phenomenon. In one review he conceded that bands had certain merit as a means of introducing music to the people. Any music, Dwight reasoned, was better than none at all. But in other columns Dwight was severely critical of ensembles that seemed to have so few standards and were so little concerned with the spiritual side of man. Other critics and proponents of "high art" values agreed. But for better or for worse, not many of the common people in the United States in the nine-teenth century saw music or the world the way Dwight did. Active rather than introspective, the majority of Americans were, as historian Howard Mumford Jones has stated, vitally concerned with the visible world.[32] To them, a brass band was a thoroughly appropriate mode of musical expression.

From the vantage point of the twentieth century, we can see that bands were more than that. Loud, boisterous, frequently in motion, they were, as Mark Twain said of baseball, "the very symbol, the outward and visible expression of the drive and push and rush and struggle of the raging, tearing, booming nineteenth century."[33]

2.
THE PROFESSIONALS

In the field of music, perhaps the most gratifying
development of my time has been the gradual evolution
of music as an American profession.

—John Philip Sousa

For most people, the story of band music in America means the story of John Philip Sousa. This is not at all surprising given the prominence and influence of the March King, but thousands of other professional bandsmen plied their trade across America. They worked hard and often endured hardship and disappointment. Their experiences are worth recalling.

LIFE OF A BANDSMAN

In the autumn of 1837 William Robyn, a twenty-three-year-old Prussian musician, emigrated to St. Louis, Missouri, where he planned to use his musical skills to earn a living. With a young family depending on him and an elderly mother in Germany hoping for financial assistance, Robyn immediately notified the public of his ability to furnish instruction on a variety of musical instruments. The results of this advertising campaign were not at all encouraging; Robyn failed to attract any students for the stipulated fifty-cent fee. He soon discovered that in all of St. Louis there were only four other active musicians, and each of these men had to pursue an additional trade—instrument making, instrument repairing, or barbering—in order to earn a livelihood. Even more disheartening to the young musician were the laughably unorthodox instrumentations of the existing musical ensembles in town. "Just imagine what I saw!" Robyn exclaimed in his autobiography:

> A member of the Odd Fellows who was brought to his last resting place and as customary was buried with music. And what [do] you think the band consisted of? An E-flat clarinet, a violin and bass drum. The funeral march they played was "Adeste fideles."[1]

The epigraph at the head of this chapter is from "Music Becomes an American Profession," in *Sousa and His Band,* souvenir program (1925), 5.

All in all, concluded Robyn, music in St. Louis was "in a most primitive state," and there seemed "very poor prospects" for making a living as a musician in the late 1830s.

Undaunted, the eager Robyn decided to pursue his chosen career and gradually he began to earn a little money from his talents. From sporadic work in a German dance band and in the two-piece "orchestra" of an Indian medicine show, he moved on to regular engagements with a visiting theater troupe orchestra in which he and the thirteen other musicians—the majority of whom were also of foreign birth—received twelve dollars a week for playing the symphonies of Mozart, Haydn, and Beethoven. Shortly after contracting for a season with this group, Robyn found a permanent position as a music professor at St. Louis University. He not only gave lessons on the piano, violin, cello, contrabass, flute, clarinet, trumpet, cornet, trombone, horn, post horn, and ophicleide, but also joined the other German military bandsmen on the faculty to launch the school's Philharmonic Band, a group that functioned both as an orchestra and a marching band.

In 1839 some new brass players arrived in town. The enterprising Robyn expanded his income and his duties further by forming the St. Louis Brass Band, which rehearsed every week and offered its services for parades, military gatherings, and funerals. In addition, the indefatigable Robyn, who was proficient on virtually every band and orchestra instrument then in existence, played every Sunday morning for Mass at a local church and performed several times a week in a six-piece serenading band. And in his "spare" time he composed and arranged music.

The schedule was grueling. "I generally gave lessons till seven o'clock and had to be at the theatre at half-past seven and seldom came home before twelve," recalled Robyn of those early years. "I continued to work in this manner, playing wind instruments from morning until night."[2] And yet, despite the hours of work, Robyn's earnings were inadequate for his family's needs. Work and worry eventually took their toll, and by the summer of 1841 Robyn's physician advised him to take a rest.

Since Robyn could not afford a vacation, he decided to do the next best thing. He headed south to New Orleans where he had been promised regular employment in a theater orchestra and could supplement his income by playing each Sunday (at 5 dollars an appearance) in a parading military band. Six months in the southern climate, away from his teaching responsibilities, restored Robyn's health. He was able to return to St. Louis and his family early in 1842.

His work was still demanding, but it now became a manageable routine of private teaching, band performance, and church work. Committed to the dissemination of good music, Robyn also donated his time and services to the Polyhymnia, an orchestral society founded in St. Louis in 1845. Under Robyn's direction the group presented a concert every month and was pivotal in bringing symphonic music to the city. By midcentury, Robyn, with his colleague Charles Balmer, had promoted an oratorio society and various chamber music groups.

Upon his arrival in 1837 Robyn had vowed to change the musical world of St. Louis. There is little doubt that he did.

MUSIC AS A PROFESSION

William Robyn was just one of many Americans who made a living as a musician during the nineteenth century. His experiences were unique, but his particular story also serves to highlight some fundamental truths about the world of professional bandsmen. Robyn's biography is a cogent reminder that foreign-born musicians were extremely important in the development of music in America. Outstanding European soloists such as Patrick Gilmore, Jules Levy, Matthew Arbuckle, Frederick Innes, and Giuseppe Creatore, as well as many less renowned musical immigrants, contributed substantially to the growth of orchestras and bands across the country. The reputation of European musicians was established early in the century and continued for decades. As late as 1870 the U.S. Census listed more foreign-born performing professionals than native American players. The situation had altered substantially by the 1880 census, but a reverence for European musicians persisted. John Philip Sousa even confessed to having grown a beard in order to *appear* foreign so that "Americans would take my music seriously."[3]

Robyn's career also underscores the remarkable versatility of many early professionals. They moved easily from instrument to instrument, and they bridged the gap between "popular" and "classical" performances with dignity and finesse. Like Robyn, many bandsmen of the nineteenth century played in theater orchestras and some even switched from wind instruments to string instruments in order to play in dance orchestras. By the end of the century bandsmen were less likely to be jacks-of-all-trades, but for many professionals band work represented only one aspect of their musical careers. Some famous examples are Scott Joplin, pianist and ragtime composer, who played cornet with the Queen City (Missouri) Concert Band; Carlo A. Cappa, who played trombone with the Theodore Thomas Orchestra between stints with the Seventh Regiment Band of New York; and operetta composer Victor Herbert, who traded in his position as cellist in the Metropolitan Opera orchestra and the New York

Success for most professional American musicians depended on flexibility. Saunders's "Band" provided music for diverse popular functions, switching from brass band to string orchestra as required.

Philharmonic to try his hand at conducting Gilmore's Band.[4]

Lest the Gilmore-Sousa mystique overwhelm us as it did audiences of their day, Robyn's story may stand as a reminder that for every bandsman who became a star, there were hundreds of ordinary musicians working steadily and unobtrusively at their craft to earn a modest living for themselves and their families. For these largely forgotten rank and file bandsmen, music making was hard work.

It was so hard that in the days before the Civil War few individuals made a full-time commitment to the profession. There were a few success stories. Francis Johnson of Philadelphia, the Dodworths of New York, Joseph C. Greene of Providence, and Eben B. Flagg of Boston garnered well-deserved reputations as soloists and bandlead-

17

ers and were able to capitalize on their fame to make a living. Patrick Gilmore, a skillful Irish cornetist who arrived in America in 1848, merged musical talent with managerial skills in 1859 to organize the thirty-two-man band that would become the standard by which all others were judged. As a result of his tireless efforts on behalf of bands, Gilmore became a widely recognized and celebrated personality.

Yet the number of individuals who could make their living in band work or in any other branch of music was small. By the middle of the nineteenth century there were, according to one estimate, about twenty-six hundred men and women able to live in New York City by their "musical labors," which included teaching and/or performance in churches, orchestras, and bands. This musical coterie, which represented about one of every two hundred citizens, was unusually large, probably owing to the large proportion of foreign-born residents in the city.[5] Only about one hundred and sixty such professionals (or one out of nineteen hundred citizens) lived in Boston at that time,[6] and in less populated cities the numbers were much smaller. As late as 1865, St. Paul, Minnesota, reportedly had only eight performing musicians and five music teachers in the entire city.[7]

Gradually, with the growth of urban areas and with society's increasing demand for leisure activities, the fraternity of professional musicians expanded. In 1870, out of a countrywide total population of about thirty-nine million people, 6,519 men and women told census takers that they were "professional musicians," and 9,491 individuals claimed to be music teachers. Just ten years later, when the population had increased by 30 percent to about fifty million, the total number of people reportedly active in these two fields jumped 90 percent to 30,477—more than three times the number of artists and about six times

the number of actors in America at the time.[8] One researcher has labeled the end of the nineteenth century a veritable heyday for professional musicians in the United States,[9] and bandsmen enjoyed increased employment possibilities along with the rest of their colleagues. To the standard jobs at patriotic celebrations, political gatherings, military parades, and funerals were added a host of new playing opportunities. Bandsmen found work at skating rinks, amusement parks, and seaside resorts, as well as at affairs held by fraternal lodges, Sunday schools, and firemen's associations.

Two musical masters dominated this vibrant period. "Of course everybody knows all about Gilmore," proclaimed a program for the 1888 tour of Gilmore's Band.[10] And by then, probably everybody did. Having acquired a reputation as a capable conductor in the Boston area before the Civil War, Patrick Gilmore demonstrated to an admiring public the marvelous things that military bands could do. He took over the Boston Brigade Band in 1859, reintroduced a complement of woodwinds to balance the brass, and turned the group into a first-rate performing ensemble. During the Civil War he directed the band of the Twenty-fourth Massachusetts Volunteer Regiment and received wide acclaim for his music making. Gilmore organized a huge choral and instrumental display in New Orleans in 1864 and then, just five years later, choreographed the mammoth National Peace Jubilee in which ten thousand singers and one thousand instrumentalists were united in Boston for several days of glorious music making. Upstaging himself in 1872, Gilmore successfully organized the World Peace Jubilee, an international extravaganza twice as large and impressive as its predecessor.

By this time Gilmore was ready to turn his talents to a smaller ensemble and in 1873 became leader of the Twenty-second Regiment Band of New York. Usually

*Gilmore's Band performed regularly in the Main Building of
the Philadelphia Centennial Exhibition. A spacious bandstand
at the central transept seated ensembles of up to one hundred
players while the audience stood to listen.*

referred to simply as "Gilmore's Band," this ensemble of
about sixty superlative players maintained a regular concert series in New York City and performed seasonally at
various summer resorts. The band was also featured at
special celebrations and exhibitions—including the Philadelphia Centennial Exhibition in 1876 and the dedication
of the Statue of Liberty in 1886—and toured extensively
throughout the United States. In 1878 Gilmore and his
men went to Europe to demonstrate their prowess to
foreign audiences. Gilmore's success in attracting some of
the best American musicians (including the famous
cornetists Arbuckle, Levy, and Liberati and renowned
saxophonist E. A. Lefebre) and his ability to present
programs that were popular and flawlessly executed
earned the maestro a reputation as the "unrivaled bandmaster of [America] if not of the world."[11]

Gilmore's Band is said to have reached its peak around
1890, about the time the energetic leader began to make
plans for his Columbian Tour.[12] This grand expedition,
which was to utilize as many as one hundred bandsmen,
was scheduled to begin in St. Louis in 1892 and climax at
the opening of the 1893 World's Fair in Chicago. The
proposed schedule of events was never realized, however,
because suddenly, on September 24, 1892, Gilmore died.
There were valiant efforts to keep the ensemble alive, first
under Gilmore's assistant conductor, Charles W. Freuden-
voll, and later under David Wallis Reeves and Victor
Herbert. But it became clear that Gilmore's Band was
unable to prosper without the man himself.

The band movement, on the other hand, had no difficulty finding a successor to the great Gilmore. His death
coincided almost exactly with the debut of the Sousa
Band, a superbly trained ensemble that in many ways
picked up where Gilmore had left off.

The Sousa Band visited Oak Grove, Illinois, during the tour of
1905. Though the bandsmen were all male, Sousa often featured
female violin, harp, or soprano soloists.

John Philip Sousa had received extensive musical training as a child, first at the Esputa Conservatory of Music
in Washington, D.C., and subsequently through the music apprenticeship program in the U.S. Marine Band.
He spent several years as a violinist and conductor in
theater orchestras in Philadelphia and elsewhere before he
was invited to return to Washington to become leader of
the Marine Band. Sousa accepted the offer in 1880 and
served in this capacity until 1892. During his tenure he
improved the performance level of the group and organized several national tours. Sousa also composed music,
and his marches, in particular, thrilled an enthusiastic
public wherever they were played.

It was at this point, with his band career well-established, that David Blakely, onetime manager of Gilmore's Band, suggested to Sousa that he might enjoy more flexibility and fame if he were at the head of his own band. Sousa agreed and in May 1892, the two men created "Sousa's New Marine Band." The first performance was presented by forty-nine well-drilled bandsmen in Plainfield, New Jersey, on September 26, 1892.[13] Almost immediately renamed the "The Sousa Band," the exemplary ensemble continued to dazzle the world with its precision and style for almost forty years. The band maintained a rigorous traveling schedule that included annual American tours as well as four European tours between 1900 and 1905. In 1910, just three years after President Theodore Roosevelt sent the American fleet around the world to demonstrate America's military power, Sousa took his band around the world to exhibit America's cultural strength. As a result of this wide exposure, the name of Sousa and the caliber of his stirring compositions became known to audiences throughout the world.

Hundreds of professional bandsmen lived and worked in the shadow of the two giants, Gilmore and Sousa. Some were lucky enough to have played with them. Many heard their bands, and some may have hoped to model their own careers on the Gilmore and Sousa patterns. Yet there were many different ways to make a living as a professional bandsman before World War I.

TYPES OF PROFESSIONAL BANDS

Military and Naval Bands

"Military parades without music are like love without kisses."[14] Such was the popular opinion of southern mili-

The U.S. Military Academy Band at West Point, established in 1815, contributed music to many events from parades and ceremonies to serenading and dances for the officers and cadets. This photograph was taken in 1870. West Point Museum.

tiamen in the 1880s and, indeed, the connection between bands and military organizations was so fundamental that all types of band equipment, from music to uniforms to instruments, were influenced by military practices. The term "military band" became the accepted designation for any mixed brass and reed band, regardless of the military status of its personnel. Under such circumstances many professional musicians readily found employment as military bandsmen.

American military units are known to have hired bandsmen to perform at ceremonial and social occasions well before 1800, and by the 1830s it is estimated that

In the first year of the Civil War there were more than one hundred and forty regimental bands in the Army of the Potomac. By 1863 the serious business of warfare had decreased the size and number of bands. Bands stationed at general headquarters, such as General Sherman's unit photographed at Beaufort, South Carolina, in 1864, were exempt from these cutbacks.

most U.S. Army regiments had bands of fifteen to twenty-two players.[15] Although the funding for such entertainment came initially from donations by the officers, the value of "bands of music" was soon so generally acknowledged that official arrangements to employ musicians were made. The *General Regulations* of 1834 allowed U.S. Army regiments to maintain bands of two chief musicians and ten regular musicians, a complement that gradually increased until about 1900, when the regulation army regimental band boasted twenty-eight players. In addition to these corps musicians, the U.S. Marine Corps

organized a band in 1798, and by 1815 the U.S. Military Academy at West Point also supported a band.

In the thirty years of peace between the War of 1812 and the Mexican War the Regular Army was small—only about ten thousand soldiers—and the number of full-time army musicians was correspondingly modest. Most able-bodied men had to serve in state militia units, however, and these part-time regiments were even more supportive of bands than federal troops. Many citizen-soldier units hired professional or town bands to play at seasonal musters and encampments, and in the early nineteenth century some state militias allowed qualified individuals to fulfill their military obligations by performing in the unit's band. Competition among regiments was keen, and some of the larger organizations sought the services of the outstanding bandmasters of the day. New York City was fortunate and attracted men like Harvey Dodworth (Thirteenth Regiment), C. S. Grafulla (Seventh Regiment), D. L. Downing (Ninth Regiment), and Patrick Gilmore (Twenty-second Regiment) to serve as regimental band leaders.

The Civil War dramatically increased employment opportunities for military bandsmen.[16] Within the first few months of the conflict several hundred Union volunteer regiments were called up. Each unit had about one thousand men, including as many as twenty company musicians (drummers, fifers, and buglers) and a band of up to two dozen men. It has been estimated that in the war's first years approximately one soldier in forty was a musician, a complement that places the total number of Civil War bandsmen in the tens of thousands.[17] Many regimental bands were simply amateur town bands that enlisted along with their area's unit. But, once enlisted, these bandsmen became professionals, paid about twenty dollars per month for their musical services. Bandmasters, most of whom were professional musicians in their pre-army days, were paid eighty-six dollars per month plus the help of a servant.

Band music served the war effort in a number of ways. Bands were often a prominent feature of recruitment rallies, where patriotic songs helped inspire young men to enlist. The untested troops were given an important morale boost through the efforts of the bands—and band music must have been everywhere. Union Private James Christie wrote his family from Corinth, Mississippi, in 1862:

> As I write the splendid brass band of the 15th Michigan is practicing about a quarter mile from here. The stirring notes of the "Red, White and Blue" swell triumphantly through the still night air, but such things are so common here that the beautiful tune is but little attended to. We have a perfect surfeit of music here.[18]

But the glamour of war that lured untrained troops by the thousands gave way to the horrible slaughter of both Union and Confederate forces. The luxury of volunteer regiment bands was soon curtailed. New regiments were not allowed this musical complement, and bands were permitted only at the brigade level. The duties of bandsmen were expanded to include the battlefield chores of stretcher bearing and assisting in amputations and other medical operations. By the end of the war many bandsmen came home as seasoned veterans who had borne their share of risks and seen their share of carnage. For many bandsmen the end of the war marked the end of music as their temporary profession.

State militia units persisted in the years after the Civil War and operated in much the same way as in pre-war years. In the 1880s and 1890s, the National Guard movement gradually replaced the state militia, and by 1898 the

Top: *Bandsmen were seldom involved directly in fighting during the Civil War, but if the tide of battle shifted suddenly then bandsmen—and their instruments—could be at risk.* Leslie's Weekly *published this dramatic woodcut of a Confederate regiment in retreat from Union gunboat shelling in November 1861.* Bottom: *State militia encampments, such as this one near Ogdensburg, New York, in 1870, were enlivened by the music of the unit's band. Militia bands were often composed of the members of a local town band who fulfilled their military obligations in this way.*

The Ninth U.S. Cavalry Regiment was one of four Black regiments in the army of the 1870s and 1880s. Stationed in Santa Fe, New Mexico, the unit joined the 1880 Decoration Day (May 30) parade through the territory's capital.

Guard was the major force backing up the Regular Army. In spite of a general antimilitarism in the United States in the decades before 1900, the National Guard was viewed as a fraternal society that "appealed to the manly virtues of physical fitness, duty, and discipline."[19] The National Guard bands enjoyed the same prestige and support as their predecessors in the state militia.

Throughout the second half of the nineteenth century fifers, drummers, and other field musicians who regulated daily camp life had a narrow sphere of activity. The bandsmen, on the other hand, played for a wide range of official and unofficial functions, some of which were not strictly associated with the military unit that employed them. In addition to parades, recruitment rallies, and funerals, military bands on both the federal and local levels furnished music for balls, ceremonial events, and serenades. It was also common for army bands to schedule

formal and informal concerts for the pleasure of the post and neighboring civilians. In an unusual event, the Eighteenth Infantry Band made its debut at Fort Hays, Kansas, at the local skating rink.[20]

To fulfill their many engagements, most units had to be trained in marching as well as in sedentary forms of music making. Some bands specialized. The Seventh Regiment Band of New York under the direction of Carlo A. Cappa was split into two subgroups consisting of a marching band and a concert band, each of which had its own instrumentation and repertoire. Cavalry bands needed special training; it was no mean feat to play a brass instrument while riding a horse in formation.

Though less numerous than infantry and cavalry bands, naval bands employed professional musicians, too. A band was authorized at the Naval Academy in 1852, but bands had been common on shipboard long before. The idea of carrying a band to sea was so irresistible to the crew of the USS *Boston* that they tried to kidnap a visiting Italian band during a shipboard concert held in Sicilian waters in 1802. As the story goes, the American ship sailed before the musicians had disembarked.[21] Such behavior was not acceptable to the United States government, of course, but eventually American seamen were allowed to have their own bands. By 1826 there was a bandmaster assigned to the USS *Constellation,* and in the ensuing years other naval vessels were similarly equipped. As of 1864 the official naval *Table of Allowances* permitted bands of six to twenty players, depending on the size of the vessel.[22]

The activities of the U.S. Navy's bands varied but included entertaining the officers, providing music for funerals, and playing for visiting dignitaries. Commodore Matthew C. Perry, who made his historic voyage to Japan in 1852–1854, recalled that during a ceremonial banquet

24

U.S. Army Cavalry bandsmen had to master the difficult art of playing while riding. At the 1909 inauguration of President William Howard Taft the bands had to contend with freezing Washington, D.C., temperatures as well.

The armored cruiser USS Montana *(ACR13) rated a fifteen-piece shipboard band in 1909. This professional group followed the practice of many small-town bands of the same period, adding a pair of clarinets to a predominantly brass instrumentation.*

held in honor of the Japanese on the *Powhatan,* two bands "added to the din."[23] It was not unusual for balls to be held on ships' decks when in port. Lieutenant John B. Dale recounts in his journal one incident that occurred on board the USS *Constitution* during her famous circum-navigation of the globe (1844–1846):

> We returned to . . . [find] another scene of enchantment, a ball room on the quarter-deck of the Frigate, with ladies siding out right and left with gentlemen in uniform doing the honors of the ship. . . . There was music and dancing above, while feasting and fun prevailed in the Wardroom below. . . . There were flags and flowers, music and waltzing, bright buttons and brighter eyes. All were happy and for a moment forgot that we had wives and sweethearts far away. . . .[24]

The ship's band provided the music for this enjoyable evening.

Owing to the length of voyages and the difficulties of shipboard life, naval band jobs were not easy. Seamen's journals mention the deaths of bandsmen at sea. Perhaps the inherent danger and discomfort helps explain why so many bandsmen serving in the U.S. Navy were of foreign birth.

Local Bands

The itinerant bandmaster was as common a figure in the early nineteenth century as the itinerant singing master. Traveling almost constantly, he shared his musical skills with anyone willing to pay. Mr. F. W. Jewett, a roving bandmaster from Connecticut, worked hard to keep his business going, as the following excerpt from a letter written in 1828 detailing his terms of employment reveals:

> I can attend upon a Band in Litchfield about one week in three during the coming winter. My terms are the same as I am now receiving for instructing the Band for the Governors' Guards at Glastonbury, which is ten Dollars per week of five nights together with my keeping and horse keeping while employed.[25]

Jewett apparently had a successful business for he advised his potential client to decide quickly, citing numerous other "applications." But surely he and other musicians who peddled their art in the early days would have been happy to center their businesses in single locales as soon as public interest warranted it. As towns grew and as citizens had more time and money, such arrangements became possible. Eventually, hundreds of professional musicians found employment as the local "music man."

The duties and rewards of such a position varied, but for many hometown harmonists their professional lives conformed to certain patterns. Most were considered valuable *artists* and were accorded the respect of their fellow citizens, particularly the newspaper editors who

never failed to publicize musical efforts and accomplishments. Frequently the honorary title of professor was
bestowed to accentuate their revered position. These local
maestros were extraordinarily versatile and enterprising.
They led the town band, organized string dance orchestras, and supervised the musical entertainment for grand
celebrations. Many also served as church musicians, functioning as choir director or organist or both. Almost
without exception these musicians were skilled on a number of instruments and supplemented their income by
giving private lessons. Isaac Fiske of Worcester, Massachusetts, branched out from his career in band performance to establish an instrument manufacturing business.
Professionals John F. Stratton of New York and George
W. Lyon of Chicago opened and operated their own music
stores. In short, if there was a musical job to be done, the
professor would take care of it.

Fred L. Grambs of Birmingham, Alabama, is a good
example of this kind of professional. Reportedly the first
professional musician to locate in Birmingham, Grambs
migrated from Scranton, Pennsylvania, in the late 1870s
or early 1880s. Just why he chose Birmingham as a home
is unclear, although it is known that several other Scran-
tonians, including the owner of the opera house, were
already ensconced in the city. Like most town-based music
men of the day, Grambs centered his activities around the
band, in this case a fifteen-piece group of brass instruments and two clarinets. He drilled and rehearsed the
bandsmen regularly, and soon they were performing for
outdoor concerts, picnics, serenades, lawn parties, and
horse races, and were hired regularly by one of the local
militia units to accompany the soldiers to encampments
and reunions. By the 1890s Professor Grambs's Military
Band was a regular act at nearby resorts and had, at least
locally, a reputation as the "best band in the state."[26]

*Cornetist and bandmaster Fred L. Grambs was a leading figure
in the musical life of Birmingham, Alabama. Grambs (standing,
front and center) posed with his band during a Sunday school
picnic at Blount Springs in 1884. Birmingham Public Library.*

"Ain't it grand and a glorious noise!" proclaimed Charles Ives in his song "The Circus Band." The band added a joyous highlight to the excitement of the "circus coming into town."

Grambs's activities were not restricted to band work. As the city newspaper was quick to point out, he was a "most thorough and artistic musician." He led the orchestra at O'Brien's Opera House and organized special services at a number of local churches and synagogues. He taught privately and performed publicly as a soloist on violin, E-flat cornet, trombone, and piano. Most notably, he organized his own dance orchestra—basically his band to which he added two violins and double bass— and in so doing became one of the "finest orchestra leaders in the South." When he was not performing or conducting, Grambs was busy running his music store and serving as president of Local Number 52 of the National League of Musicians.

There were enterprising musicians like Grambs all over the United States during the second half of the nineteenth century. Their success in establishing bands and other musical organizations had benefits for the local citizens, their public. In addition, their work benefited fellow musicians. As local bandleaders succeeded in building up first-rate bands and orchestras, they were increasingly able to hire more professional musicians to help them. Ultimately, in the larger towns at least, the music man was supplanted in his musical efforts by a whole cadre of music men.

Circus Bands

To the midwestern writer Hamlin Garland, the circus offered a variety of pleasures during his youth. "It brought to our ears the latest band pieces and taught us the popular songs. It furnished us with jokes. It relieved our dullness. It gave us something to talk about."[27]

Yet to hundreds of musicians of the nineteenth century, circuses were more than a diversion. By prominently featuring band music before, during, and after the show,

Traveling with a circus band could be a far from glamorous life for professional bandsmen. Constant travel, exhausting performances seven days a week, and the vagaries of foul weather and mediocre accommodations took their toll on small groups such as this unidentified American circus band ca. 1880.

traveling troupes afforded an unparalleled opportunity for bandsmen to learn and practice their profession. Edward Kendall, keyed bugler extraordinaire, frequently demonstrated his virtuosity to circus crowds during the 1840s and 1850s.[28] Thomas Coates, David Wallis Reeves, and John Dolan were also associated periodically with circus bands during their distinguished careers. Many accomplished players, including Henry Fillmore, Karl L. King, and Frederick Alton Jewell, spent large portions of their professional lives as "windjammers." Even John Philip Sousa tried to join a circus band once, but his father, who strongly disapproved, promptly turned the eager fourteen-year-old musician over to the Marine Corps band apprenticeship program.[29]

The advantages of working in a circus band were obvious. Such ensembles enabled musicians to travel to faraway places in the company of exotic performers, and also promised to pay steady—if low—weekly wages. To a seventeen-year-old trombonist named Nels Hokanson these prospects seemed too good to be true. Hokanson recalled his eagerness as he set off with Bosco's Circus in the summer of 1902:

> I had seen a circus parade but never a circus performance. Now I would not only see one but be a part of it. I would meet famous artists like animal trainers, acrobats, and bareback riders and would perform with professional musicians. At the same time I would be receiving more money than I had ever earned before. . . . I was the happiest boy in town. . . .[30]

As everyone who has traveled the sawdust trail knows, and as Hokanson himself soon found out, circus bandsmen worked hard—harder, perhaps, than any other group of professional musicians. Traveling in itself could be an arduous task. Thomas T. Bennett, a British-born musician who joined the Gale and Sand Circus in June 1837, left a record of a grueling tour in which the troupe averaged twenty miles of travel every day for almost five months as they "showed" throughout the remote regions of Illinois and Missouri.[31] Furthermore, circus bandsmen contended with bad weather, bad food, and bad accommodations, to say nothing of local ruffians who disrupted shows by bullying the performers or, in one instance encountered by Bennett, by throwing fireballs at the tent.

Such hardships were merely incidental to the exhausting demands of circus work itself. As Hokanson recalled, the bandsmen with Bosco's Circus were required to play for two shows every day except Sunday and participate in the

One of the more remarkable accomplishments of any band was balancing—not to mention playing—on the back of an elephant. The Great Patterson Shows circus band of twelve players achieved this feat early in the twentieth century. Robert Good Collection.

parades and evening concerts scheduled in each town to drum up business. This was a typical pattern and helps explain why Hokanson and other circus musicians carried antiseptic mouthwash or lip balm to soothe their abused lips. Before unions forced musicians to proscribe their range of activities, many circus bandsmen had to perform nonmusical duties such as setting up tents, positioning benches, and distributing publicity notices. In larger organizations such as the Ringling Brothers Circus, bandsmen did less custodial work but they had problems of their own. Under the able direction of Professor

George Granweiler, the Ringling bandsmen were required to perform on horseback for the 1897 season. As the bass drummer quickly discovered, falling off a horse—even in time to the music—was not much fun.

Circuses varied greatly in size and sophistication and so did their bands. It was possible to run a show with five or six brass instruments as Bosco and many other small troupes did. On the other hand, by the turn of the century, twenty-four-piece or thirty-piece bands of brass, wind, and percussion instruments had become the norm for larger organizations such as Sells Floto and Barnum and Bailey. In 1897 the Ringling Brothers Military Band boasted forty musicians. Within a few years this group's "popular concerts," held before each circus performance, consisted of a substanial program of crowd-pleasing songs alternated with classical selections by Verdi, Bizet, and Victor Herbert. To round out their musical offerings, many large circuses had, over and above their wind bands, extra bandsmen who doubled on violins, guitars, and calliope.

In addition to circus work, bandsmen occasionally found employment with other sorts of traveling troupes such as medicine shows and vaudeville acts. Minstrel shows, in particular, enjoyed great popularity, and by the turn of the century they featured brass band music along with or instead of the banjo and tambourine instrumentations typical of the pre–Civil War minstrel acts.

Concert Bands

Most professional bands presented formal concerts in addition to their appearances at dances, parades, military assemblies, and other affairs. But during the second half of the nineteenth century there arose a select group of touring concert bands whose sole function was to present polished band concerts. These elite ensembles provided the professional bandsman with a splendid opportunity to exercise his musicianship and demonstrate his technical skills.

The seeds for the success of the full-time concert band were planted by such outstanding pre–Civil War ensembles as the Dodworth Band of New York and Francis Johnson's Band of Philadelphia. Both groups traveled widely and concertized extensively during the 1830s and 1840s. In 1837 Frank Johnson toured Europe with his band, perhaps the first American group to do so. Nevertheless, these fine bands had to rely on regular engagements of functional music in order to survive.

Gilmore's Band was one of the first American ensembles to deviate from this pattern and specialize in concert performances. The overwhelming success of this endeavor paved the way for other concert groups, most notably the great Sousa Band, which rarely performed "on the march" in spite of the bandleader's reputation as the March King. Though less well known than Gilmore and Sousa, many other professional bandsmen carried their music to the people between 1890 and 1910, the golden age of the touring concert band.

Prominent among bandmasters eager to share the limelight with Gilmore and Sousa were Jules Levy and Alessandro Liberati, both of whom branched out from established careers as soloists to form their own concert bands. The exchanging of one's solo instrument for a baton became so commonplace that it seemed to constitute a necessary stage in career development. Thus, Frederick Innes, the talented trombone soloist with Gilmore's Band, formed the "Innes Festival Band" in 1893, only to have his widely acclaimed cornetist Bohumir Kryl leave within a few years to form *his* own band. Other notable concert bandleaders were Ellis Brooks, whose forty-piece touring band was available "for all great military or civic events in any part of the country,"[32] Helen May Butler, who organized an all-female touring band around the turn of the century (*see* Chapter 9), and Al Sweet, who booked his White Hussars into the large Chautauqua circuit and kept his concert band alive long after most others had failed.

For its leader, a touring concert band meant fame, personal satisfaction, and sometimes fortune. But directing a traveling troupe also brought organizational and financial worries, and even with an able business manager the problems of taking a large group of musicians on the road were considerable. For the players, too, a touring band was a mixed blessing. Like a circus band, it provided steady employment in settings that ranged from the novel to the exciting. But constant traveling, even under the best conditions, could be tiring and difficult. It is a matter of record that Sousa, whose tours could last as long as six months or more, often required his bandsmen to play two concerts a day, seven days a week.[33] Long runs at summer resorts such as Willow Grove Park in Philadelphia and Manhattan Beach, New York, cut down on the travel fatigue, but such engagements were demanding in their own ways. It is not surprising that many touring musicians seem to have been younger men and women.

For the public there was no ambivalence: a touring band was pure pleasure. From the moment a band arrived in town—and Patrick Gilmore, in characteristic fashion, frequently arranged to have his band's own cannon announce its arrival at the local depot—there was an aura of excitement and anticipation among the local populace. The touring bands provided a break in the routine, and offered an opportunity to hear and see some of the best musical ensembles of the day. Moreover, these bands were a welcome source of musical instruction. J. J. Montgomery, bandmaster of the Clarksville (Arkansas) Citizens

Among the most distinguished bands at the Twenty-third Triennial Conclave of the Knights Templar, held in St. Louis in September 1886, was the professional concert band conducted by Alessandro Liberati. Liberati's band joined many others in a massed band concert conducted by Patrick Gilmore that netted thousands of dollars for a widows' and orphans' home.

The Noss Family of New Brighton, Pennsylvania, was a multifaceted act, but brass instruments dominate their publicity photographs and business cards ca. 1890. The band distributed these cards as a form of advertisement during tours.

Band from 1901 to 1916, claims that his formal training on the B-flat cornet consisted of thirty minutes of instruction on a train platform from one of Sousa's assistant directors.[34] For countless other amateur bandsmen, the touring professionals gave them their first clear idea of what good band music should sound like.

Family Bands

It was common during the nineteenth century for musicians to teach artistic skills to their children. As a consequence, many bands included among their personnel individuals with close family ties. If a musician's family was unusually large and talented, it probably seemed natural to carry this one step further and establish an ensemble made up entirely of relatives—i.e., a family band. Such a notion occurred during the mid–1890s to William Henry Mitchell, a band teacher from Sauk County, Wisconsin. When his wife died, leaving him with six daughters between the ages of three and sixteen, Mitchell bought the girls band instruments and uniforms and launched the Mitchell Concert Band. They traveled for years throughout Wisconsin, Minnesota, Iowa, and Nebraska entertaining an appreciative public with their military music.

Dudley Jewell, father of the circus musician and composer Fred Jewell, inaugurated a similar ensemble in Worthington, Indiana, in the late 1880s. Taking advantage of the demise of a traveling minstrel show, Mr. Jewell purchased the company's band instruments and soon had his children—six sons and two daughters—functioning effectively as the Jewell Family Band. Fred Jewell's mastery of the euphonium developed out of this early experience.[35]

Other musical patriarchs created their own versions of the family band. Before the Civil War the seven-piece Mann Family Band of Platteville, Wisconsin, carried band music to their neighbors in small towns and villages. The peak of popularity of such groups occurred in the 1890s when numerous groups were active, especially in the Midwest.

Though multitalented, most family ensembles of this period highlighted their performances with band music. Since such groups were generally small, an all-brass instrumentation was common. In 1885, for example, the Strohl Family Band of Pottstown, Pennsylvania, consisted of three cornets, two alto horns, baritone, tuba, and snare and bass drum. Naturally, the variety of compositions rendered by such bands was limited, and duets and solo

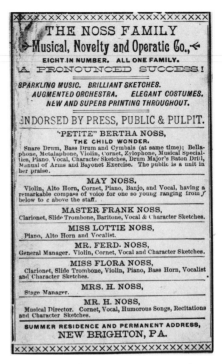

The impressive individual talents of the Noss Family are detailed on the reverse of their trade card ca. 1890.

pieces were frequently interspersed with selections requiring the entire ensemble.

While family bands clearly drew their inspiration from the traditional bands of their day, they developed in unorthodox ways. It was common for family bands to switch in midperformance to vocal selections or instrumental compositions performed on nonwind instruments such as banjos or violins. Family band shows also included nonmusical numbers such as elocutionary demonstrations or tableaux vivants. In terms of personnel there were obvious differences between family bands and other professional ensembles. Female musicians were featured prominently with the adult males of the group or, less commonly, composed an entire band themselves. Children—the

The Strohl Family Band of Pottstown, Pennsylvania, was one of the largest such ensembles, with ten participating family members. This talented group of the 1880s also performed on string instruments. Jon Korzun Collection.

younger the better—were given conspicuous roles, even if only to beat the drum. By adopting these quasivaudevillian patterns, family bands hoped to offer audiences alternatives to a formal band concert.

Many companies succeeded. Mr. Mitchell's girls were on the road off and on for eleven years. The Shepherd family enjoyed such public acclaim that they periodically had to update their photographic publicity "cabinet cards" to reflect the changing ages of the juvenile performers. Eventually, the inevitable maturation of a family forced the finale of many groups, but for some of the children who participated, experience in family bands introduced them to musical careers that would last a lifetime.

35

The Shepard Family Band, based in Massachusetts, enjoyed considerable success in the 1890s and issued new publicity photographs each year. The growth of the five Shepard children is chronicled in these images ca. 1893, ca. 1896, and 1898.

Band Hierarchy

Although useful in its way, a description of professional
bands may fail to give an accurate picture of the activities
of individual bandsmen. In the first place, few musicians
of the last century would have played exclusively in one
type of organization or setting. Most musicians moved
from band to band—and even from band to orchestra—
with the ultimate choice of employment based as much
on financial considerations as on artistic preference.
Moreover, with the exception of the local music professor
who operated on his own, each of these band jobs offered
a range of positions to be filled, and the life of a musician
was affected as much by his status within a band's hierarchy as by the sort of band he joined. The most common
position was that of corps musician. Even if these bandsmen were extraordinarily skillful performers, and in the
best bands they were, their function was to blend with
each other and contribute to the total band sound. One
step above these rank and file players were the soloists
who were usually both better trained and better paid. In
smaller groups the position of soloist was generally filled
by the first cornetist who carried the lyric solo passages,
performed standard "theme and variation" showpieces,
and may even have been the leader of the band. In larger
touring bands there was often a roster of virtuosi, whose
place it was to thrill the crowds with specially chosen solo
works. The best performers, such as Matthew Arbuckle,
Jules Levy, and Alice Raymond were free agents who
negotiated their own seasonal contracts with individual
bandmasters. Finally, towering above all these players,
much as a ship's captain stands above his crew, was the
bandmaster. This position was desirable because of both
its prestige and the increased salary it commanded and, as
a result, many bandsmen, including the prominent soloists, tried to form their own bands. In addition to audi-
tioning, training, and conducting their musicians, bandmasters had to choose the music to be presented. Many
became adept at arranging and composing their own
works.

BECOMING A PROFESSIONAL

Whatever the context of their performances, the best
professional bandsmen rarely failed to impress their public. Handsomely outfitted and meticulously trained, they
marched into the humdrum lives of ordinary people and
projected an image that was as exuberant as their music.
Ladies' bands may have been less flamboyant in their
appearance than the men, but they could produce an
equally appealing sight. The Springfield (Nevada) *Republican,* considered the "handsome ladies" of Helen May
Butler's band to be "one of the prettiest grouped pictures
that the mind's eye could picture." [36]

Top-notch professional players sounded as good as they
looked. When the Royal Prussian Band gave a concert in
Minneapolis in 1875, the local newspaper declared that it
was "impossible to write too extravagantly in praise of
their performance" because it was, quite simply, the "best
instrumental concert ever given in Minneapolis." [37] The
superior American bands stimulated similar reactions.
Cornetist Herbert L. Clarke recalled that he was "en-
thralled beyond words" by the magnificent playing of
Gilmore's Band when they gave a concert in Indianapolis.
"Oh, how tame our own town band sounded at our next
rehearsal!" exclaimed Clarke, for whom the polished
sounds of this professional ensemble were an artistic reve-
lation. "Right then and there I made up my mind that if I
became a good cornet player I would make every endeavor
to become a member of Gilmore's great band, which was
the best in the world." [38]

Clarke's reaction was not unusual. Many young Americans who saw and heard the professionals play yearned to become bandsmen. And many, including Clarke—who not only joined Gilmore's Band, but also became a featured soloist with the Sousa Band—succeeded. But establishing a career as a bandsman was not easy, and most aspiring musicians encountered formidable obstacles along the way.

The most serious problem was the most basic: how to obtain adequate musical training. Formal school programs were severely limited throughout the century. Although music conservatories were established in Oberlin (Ohio), Baltimore, Boston, Chicago, Cincinnati, and elsewhere during the 1860s, these academies offered little that was geared specifically to aspiring bandsmen. More useful were institutions such as the Dodworth family's band school in New York (which reputedly trained fifty bandmasters and five hundred federal military bandsmen during the Civil War)[39] and the various music apprentice programs run by military organizations. John Philip Sousa, for instance, was enrolled as an apprentice in the U.S. Marine Band at the age of fourteen. But these few institutions were hardly adequate, and as late as 1889 the prominent American bandsman Leon Mead deplored the "lack of proper schools and conservatories in the United States."[40]

Musicians were forced to rely on a pastiche of individualized instruction that typically included private lessons augmented by printed instruction manuals and hours of ensemble practice in small circus bands, theater orchestras, or, most effective of all, town bands. Town bands were deemed so important in educating professional musicians that Sousa credited these community organizations as being "perhaps the greatest factor in the production of fine bandsmen."[41] Would-be professionals from musical families were clearly at an advantage in negotiating the intricacies of this system of education. R. B. Hall, for instance, studied cornet with his father and then went on to become a successful bandleader and composer. Likewise, Arthur Pryor benefited from early associations with his family's band. There were those who had no such support but persevered and got results on their own. Frank Holton, Herbert Clarke, and Jules Levy are among the many bandsmen who claimed, with justification and pride, to have been virtually self-taught.

Not until the twentieth century did band instruction become more organized and, hence, more easily acquired. In 1911, at the suggestion of Arthur Clappé, Frank Damrosch (son of the more famous Leopold) established an army bandleader training program at the Institute of Musical Art in New York City. Five years later Frederick Innes set up a successful correspondence school of music in Denver. Similar institutions emerged during the 1920s. Innes's National School of Music (the successor to his Denver enterprise) was established in Chicago in 1923 primarily to train bandmasters, and the Conway Military Band School commenced operation in Ithaca, New York, in 1929. By this time, however, American colleges and universities were active in band education.

If learning musical skills posed difficulties for bandsmen, so did learning business skills, but anyone who wanted to make a living in the band world needed business acumen almost as much as musicianship. Unless a bandsman had steady, full-time employment with a touring band or a military organization, he had to attract and fulfill contracts with a variety of employers for a variety of jobs. John Prosperi of Washington, D.C., was one of many musicians who learned to do these things successfully during the last quarter of the nineteenth century. As his carefully kept account book reveals, he maintained a full schedule of regular theater and amusement park work supplemented by numerous special performances (including parades, balls, and funerals) for which he received the adequate income of about eight hundred dollars a year.[42] Other bandsmen were not so fortunate.

After moving from Salisbury, North Carolina, to Columbus, Ohio, in 1857, bandmaster William Neave found it difficult to establish himself as a musician. Although he had a regular job as a bandleader, his salary, paid in quarterly installments, was insufficient. "We do not go ahead as fast as I was led to suppose we would," he wrote to his brother Edward, also a bandsman.

> Nearly all our money (currency) is gone; our specie we cannot possibly touch: my quarter is only half out or not quite, and I get no money till the end of it—so I have not been able to get out my [advertising] circulars yet for scattering all over.

The unhappy Neave concluded his tale of woe by asking his brother to try to collect some of the money due from past jobs. "At no time [would] a hundred & fifty dollars or so be more appreciated by us than now!"[43]

It was not unusual for a musician to keep his problems in the family as Neave did. But there were ways in which professionals and their public were able to help needy musicians during financial and other crises. Letters among bandsmen reveal a considerable amount of networking around employment opportunities. In addition, benefit concerts were commonly organized to raise money for the local bandmaster or his family. Beyond these informal arrangements, there developed as early as the 1820s a number of musicians aid societies to collect and distribute money as needed. These organizations acquired more members and power until, with the establishment of the Musical Mutual Protective Union in New York in 1863, musicians had the clear forerunner of a union—complete

At least six different photographs of this one-armed musician are known. He was apparently a Civil War bandsman who lost his arm in battle. After the war he supported himself by playing his Stratton rotary valve trumpet and selling his photographs.

with fee scales and regulations. Cities like Baltimore and St. Louis soon established similar associations, and many of these united in 1886 to form the National League of Musicians. Besides working for better wages, this organization lobbied against the importation of foreign bands and, as they put it, the "competition of government bands with those composed of American citizens."[44] Regional band associations also appeared with increasing frequency in various states during the last quarter of the century. They supported band work in many ways, including the sponsoring of competitions and furthering communication among bandsmen. There was some resistance among musicians to identify too strongly with the larger labor movement, but in 1896 the American Federation of Musicians was founded with the first locals organized in Cincinnati, Chicago, and Indianapolis.

These professional organizations helped solve some of the basic employment problems, but they by no means eliminated worry. On the contrary, worry was almost an occupational hazard and, as the diaries and correspondence of bandsmen reveal, the hindrances to a successful career were legion. Traveling with a band could be a dreadful experience, especially if one joined a company, as Thomas Bennett did, that was "half-starving" its performers and musicians.[45] The position of bandmaster could be depressing in its own way. According to one seasoned musician, the incessant problems with insolent and egotistical professional players rendered the lives of many leaders a "sort of martyrdom."[46]

Professional bandsmen who led amateur bands had different problems as they tried to reconcile their desire for musical excellence with the far from excellent musical abilities of the players. William Neave was probably not alone in finding his unappreciative students in the Salisbury (North Carolina) Brass Band to be "conceited, igno-

rant, stingy, grasping, and in many cases dishonest wretches."[47] Northern men were often barred from jobs in the South, foreigners sometimes had trouble getting employment in rural areas, and almost everyone suffered from lean times during parts of the slow winter season. And, on top of all this, many professional bandsmen suffered at the hands of "high art" critics who lambasted them for catering excessively to popular taste. For serious bandsmen, this was perhaps the most painful indignity of all.

Not surprisingly, the rigors of maintaining a career as a professional bandsman forced some musicians into other lines of work. Thomas Bennett progressed from circus bands to army bands to several years of unemployment before he finally found a satisfactory position as a government agent. For those who stuck it out, however, adversity had at least one positive result: it stimulated loyalty and affection among bandsmen and helped to unify the profession. On a personal level this devotion to one's fellow bandsmen was revealed in the formation of elite associations for the alumni of certain bands (the American Bands' Veterans' Association was formed in 1887) and in the rigorous observance of special funeral rituals for deceased bandsmen.

Pride in the profession was expressed publicly, especially by the more famous and articulate bandmasters of the last part of the century. David Wallis Reeves, for instance, sought to silence denigrators of band music by playing Dix's "A Music Critic's Dream," an unusual programmatic piece in which a severe music critic is shown, through musical variations on a common street melody, that it was not the music that was important but how the music was played. Sousa, who frequently expounded on the virtues of bands, took a verbal approach. Time and again, in a calm but firm fashion, he explained to the public that military bands were not inferior to symphony orchestras—just different. Declared the March King, "There is no hierarchy in art. The artistic effect is the sole criterion of values." [48]

The flamboyant Gilmore would have none of this balanced rationality. In his opinion, there obviously was a hierarchy, and, as everyone well knew, bands were unquestionably at the top. "Somebody may bring the string orchestra to such a degree of perfection as to make it a very queen among its kind," proclaimed Gilmore in his now-famous homage to bands, "but my military band shall be king!" To make sure his conviction was well publicized, Gilmore occasionally printed this statement in his concert programs. [49]

Critics may not have sympathized with these band-boosting points of view, but the average citizen certainly did. Although the general public often failed to take musicians as seriously as they might have, affection for professional musicians and their work was genuine and strong. This reverence was demonstrated in ways beyond simply attending performances. Many towns awarded their local bandmasters with handsome and expensive presentation instruments. When an esteemed local bandsman died, it was not unusual for the entire town to turn out for the funeral and for the local press to publish a glowing obituary. Finally, and perhaps most important, amateur musicians by the thousands paid these professionals the supreme compliment of emulation. Having witnessed the glory of the bandsmen's uniforms and having heard the majesty of their music, citizens across the country showed their appreciation by forming marching and concert bands of their own.

Bandmaster Ira W. Wales was presented a beautifully engraved, sterling silver E-flat keyed bugle by the grateful citizens of Abingdon, Massachusetts, in 1853. The bugle [now in the authors' collection] was played by Wales for at least a decade in his job as bandmaster in Augusta, Maine, but he eventually succumbed to the trend of the times and switched to a piston cornet.

3.
THE BAND BOYS

Now we the undersigned members of said Band do
associate ourselves a body politic and corporate by the
name of the Saint Albans Brigade Band for the purpose of
mutual improvement and entertainment of Saint Albans
in Franklin County.

—St. Albans (Vermont) Brigade Band,
November 22, 1869

In contrast to professional musicians, who played in bands
in order to make a decent living, the amateur bandsmen
of the nineteenth century joined bands in order to make
living decent. "We the undersigned citizens of Princeton,"
wrote the members of Farr's Band in their constitution of
1892, "seeking relaxation from the cares and burdens of
life and deeming a social organization for the cultivation
and practice of music as leading to a higher and better
appreciation of the same, do hereby resolve to band ourselves together for this purpose."[1] These sentiments were
echoed by amateur bandsmen all over the country. Seeking congenial fellowship and an opportunity for self-
improvement, novice musicians by the hundreds of thousands turned to band performance for its enriching power.
The fact that, as one old bandsman put it, there were
"always some silly girls who would run after any fellow if
he wore a uniform" did not hurt either.[2]

This is not to say that amateur bandsmen were un-
touched by the desire to profit financially from their
musical performances. They frequently received cash
gratuities, over and above the customary donations of
food and drink. But, as William Rannells makes clear in
his evocative history of brass bands in Rochester, Indiana,
it was impossible to make much money by playing part-
time in an amateur band. Referring to his group's finances
for 1909 Rannells, who was the band's leader, reckoned
that although his men were paid fifty or seventy-five
cents for each summer concert, if one balanced this income against the group's expenses, "there would not be a
member but would come out in debt."[3] Some amateur
groups managed a little better, but the monetary rewards
were secondary to the less tangible benefits of band work.

41

The epigraph at the head of this chapter is from the constitution of the
St. Albans Brigade Band, St. Albans Brigade Band Record Book, 1869–
1899, Vermont Historical Society, Montpelier.

Astonishing numbers of bandsmen not only accepted this situation but embraced it. Amateur musicians in America's isolated Moravian communities had performed in wind ensembles of one sort or another as early as the late eighteenth and early nineteenth centuries. By the 1840s and 1850s, owing to the perfection and increased availability of keyed and valved brass instruments, enthusiastic musicians in communities throughout America were forming wind bands in their spare time. Sometimes these organizations were associated with the local militia, but often they were independent groups of private citizens who gathered together to learn music and play for the public.

A typical amateur ensemble was formed in Battle Creek, Michigan, in 1848 by three wagonmakers, a hardware store operator, and a pattern maker for threshing machines. Struck by the lack of band music at the local Independence Day celebration that year, these enterprising young men organized a brass ensemble. They acquired a keyed bugle and four saxhorns and, after some practice, were soon busy playing in public. By 1852 the popular quintet had expanded to become a thirteen-piece band in demand for social functions throughout the region. Still in existence when the Civil War broke out in 1861, the band reportedly played when soldiers departed from Battle Creek for the battlegrounds.

Many early amateur bands went to war themselves, becoming for a short while professional musicians. Town bands from Yarmouth, Maine, Manchester, New Hampshire, and Salem, North Carolina, for example, enlisted as musicians with the volunteer regiments in their areas during the early phases of the war. The Williamsport (Pennsylvania) Band—by the time of the Civil War known as the Repasz Band, in honor of its leader—served with three different Pennsylvania regiments, one of them

a cavalry unit. In addition to performing concerts and serenades in camp, some of these town musicians offered musical inspiration during the fighting itself.

Although some amateur groups disbanded during the war years, with the cessation of hostilities avocational bands flourished as never before. In the last quarter of the nineteenth century, as instruments became easier to obtain and less expensive, and as the average work week of factory employees dropped from about sixty-six to fifty-five hours per week, virtually every community had a performing ensemble. Factory workers, hospital inmates, and students at a variety of educational institutions also formed bands. Almost any social group that had a name could have a band. There were farmers' bands and dentists' bands, miners' bands and dock workers' bands. Democrats had bands, as did Republicans and other political groups. Cowboys formed bands and so did Indians. The American branch of the Salvation Army established a staff band of thirty men in New York City in 1887. From that beginning the Salvationist movement expanded, as it did in Britain, with amateur Salvationist bands eventually active in many cities.

The number of individuals involved in the band movement is as impressive as their diversity. By the turn of the century, when Saturday and Sunday afternoons were typically set aside for recreational activities, the number of bands, most of them amateur, was increasing at a greater rate than the population at large. The peak of amateur band activity occurred during the first decade of the twentieth century.

The rise of the amateur bands must be seen as part of a larger music movement in America. As early as 1810 a Philadelphia journalist confidently claimed that "almost every young lady and gentleman, from the children of the judge, the banker, and the general, down to those of the

Residents of Beaver Creek, Minnesota—population about three hundred in 1910—featured their school, hotel, railroad station, and Main Street in a composite postcard, but the town band enjoyed the central position. The town band was seen to epitomize the best of civic virtues: patriotism, public service, and artistic achievement.

and presented their newly acquired skills to the public. Prominent among these organizations were glee clubs, choral societies, and orchestras. Rare was the town that did not nurture some such association before the Civil War—and afterwards, with the active encouragement of musical instrument companies, the number of amateur musicians multiplied dramatically.

The amateur band was, thus, one type of amateur musical organization among many. Yet, it was also something more. Though avowedly musical in purpose, this fraternity was so prominent, so popular, and so persistently appealing that it may be seen as a sociological phenomenon. Valued as an avocation by men from all walks of life, bands became inextricably tied up with the popular conception of what was masculine, patriotic, and virile. Only the piano, which became identified with femininity, domesticity, and gentility, can be said to have transcended its musical identity in quite the same way.

COMMON TYPES OF AMATEUR BANDS

The Town Band

The town band was the most common type of amateur band in nineteenth-century America. Many communities such as Allentown, Pennsylvania, Camden, Maine, Clarksburg, Maryland, Staunton, Virginia, Lawrence, Kansas, Bloomington, Indiana, and Grafton, Vermont, had active bands before the Civil War. By the last decades of the century most towns not only supported bands, but considered it a civic duty to do so. For some towns, the establishment of a band was only slightly less important than the establishment of schools, churches, and newspapers. And in Virginia City, Nevada, as Mark Twain vividly recalls in *Roughing It,* a brass band existed long before any church was built.[5]

constable, the huckster, and the drummer [salesman], can make a noise upon some instrument or other, and charm their neighbors with something which courtesy calls music."[4] The trend continued. Throughout the thirties, forties, and fifties, Americans turned to the study of music in unprecedented numbers. Driven by the same desire for cultural betterment that gave rise to the Lyceum movement, these musical novices sought instruction on flute, violin, voice, accordion and guitar. Toward the middle of the century when pianos became widely available, the number of beginning keyboard students grew to such proportions that, for ladies at least, the ability to play piano became a social requirement. To supplement these private studies, budding musicians formed musical clubs

The twelve members of the Mineral City (Ohio) Cornet Band sported uniforms with three rows of buttons, reminiscent of the standard outfit of the Civil War soldier. This style persisted in many communities until the 1880s.

view, the contrast between towns with bands and towns without bands was striking:

> . . . when we see a town with flourishing public enterprises, such as news-papers, schools, libraries, picture galleries, literary and scientific societies, concert halls, theaters, *Brass Bands* etc., we need not be told that it is the dwelling place of intelligent and cultivated people, for in all these institutions supported by its inhabitants we recognize the unfailing indications of culture and refinement, and, on the other hand in a place where the news-papers are poor and badly patronized, where the churches and school-houses show broken window-panes, dilapidated fences, weather stained, paintless walls and gates off their hinges, where there is no theater, no literary societies, no *Band* and no musicians, in such a place the stranger can see at a glance that enterprise, public spirit and vital energy are wanting in the people.

Summing up the point with characteristic verve, Patton continued:

> . . . in this age the horn blowing organisations are recognized as essential elements in the great march of popular enlightenment, and a town that can not sound its own trumpet, but must send off and hire assistance from its neighbours on all public occasions, can not lay claim to having reached a very high standard of advancement.[8]

This was powerful propaganda, but it was in tune with the popular attitudes of the time. Townsmen did compare themselves with one another and they did seek to improve their images by supporting cultural organizations such as bands. Between a town and its band, consequently, there developed a close relationship, usually to the advantage of both parties. The band would be available to play for public celebrations and regular outdoor concerts. The town, in return, would support the band through financial contributions of interested citizens and even through general taxes, though the latter were rare before the twen-

Instrument companies capitalized on the value of civic pride by incorporating it into their sales pitches. Quoting from the Chicago *Daily Inter-Ocean,* the Lyon and Healy Band Instrument Company 1881 sales catalog states: "No town or village . . . can pretend to have attained much progress in social esthetics which is not blessed with a good brass band."[6] Decades later the J. W. Pepper and Son catalog advanced the same idea. "A brass band is as much a public institution as a private one," claimed the company. "It gives almost as much pleasure to the people who do not play in it as it does to those who do play."[7]

G. F. Patton, an experienced bandsman affiliated with the Stratton Company of New York, underscored the importance of a town band with particular vigor in the appendix to his book, *A Practical Guide to the Arrangement of Band Music,* published by Stratton in 1875. In Patton's

44

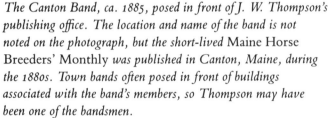

The Canton Band, ca. 1885, posed in front of J. W. Thompson's publishing office. The location and name of the band is not noted on the photograph, but the short-lived Maine Horse Breeders' Monthly *was published in Canton, Maine, during the 1880s. Town bands often posed in front of buildings associated with the band's members, so Thompson may have been one of the bandsmen.*

tieth century. The Marysville (Ohio) Union Brass Band, incorporated in 1863, spelled out its relationship with the town in a formal contract. According to the document, if the townsmen agreed to furnish twelve instruments plus a drum, the band would promise to practice and "to play as a Band for the citizens who Assist in procuring the instruments, at any time & on any occasion, when and wherever they may require Band Music, within one mile of the public Square . . . for the term of three years . . . Free of Charge."[9] In most towns the symbiotic relationship developed more casually, but it was conspicuous nonetheless.

Although each town band evolved in its own way, some generalizations can be made about these organizations.

Top: *Like so many other small-town bands, the twelve-piece Laurens (Iowa) Band had two percussionists and the rest of the musicians on brass instruments. The uniform code of the band ca. 1890 was rather haphazard. Helen Ducommun Collection.* Bottom: *The Milford (New York) Cornet band, ca. 1885, was an all-brass and percussion ensemble with the unusual complement of five valve trombones: three B-flat tenors (back row at left), two E-flat altos (front row).*

Owing to their prominence in the community, bands developed membership policies carefully. Some bands had a residence requirement and many, such as the Navarre (Ohio) Citizens Band, stipulated that prospective members must be of "good moral standing and character, and of temperate habits."[10] At the same time, the town bands emphasized their openness to anyone who met with the approval of a majority of the other members. These policies, which were simultaneously exclusive and inclusive, improved the chances of forming a band that worked well as a unit and also satisfied the demands of the town.

Band size was variable. While the experts recommended recruiting at least ten men to start with, the Navarre Citizens Band required a minimum of six and the American Cadet Band of Portland, Maine, got by in its early days in the 1880s with just four members. But some town bands, especially those that had official associations with Volunteer Militia or National Guard units, could swell to more than two dozen players. In 1872 the Allentown (Pennsylvania) Band consisted of twenty-five players, and during the 1880s the famed Alexander Band of Wilkes-Barre, Pennsylvania, boasted a membership of twenty-eight musicians. However, photographic and documentary evidence suggests that during the last quarter of the nineteenth century town band membership averaged from twelve to fifteen players. Later, as instrumentation changed, the average size of these groups increased.

Though open to membership in the community generally, many town bands were "family affairs" in that several families predominated. The Myersville (Maryland) Band is a good example of this trend. Of the fifteen bandsmen active in the 1880s, there were three named Bisser, three named Stottlemeyer, two named Flook, and four named Moser. A similar situation existed in Silverton, Oregon, where the twenty-two-member Silverton Marine Band

The Telluride (Colorado) Band posed in Yosemite Park with scenic Bridal Veil Falls in the background during an excursion to California in September 1886. Denver Public Library.

relied on one family, the Steelhammers, to make up almost one-third of its roster during the 1890s. If a band's leader had a musical family, it was common practice to fill the ranks with talented relatives. For years the Barrington (New Hampshire) Band, founded in the 1830s by James Wiggin, drew heavily on the talents of the Wiggin family, in which the finer points of instrumental performance and conducting were passed on from father to son for three generations.

Town bands were especially successful in attracting tradesmen and laborers, yet this was by no means the only pattern. One researcher has found that many California bands from the second half of the nineteenth century were composed of professional citizens such as bankers, attorneys, and storekeepers.[11] Nevertheless, it was more common to find amateur brass bands composed primarily of "hard-working mechanics," as the Manchester (New Hampshire) Band described itself. The Middletown (Connecticut) Municipal Band, organized in 1879, was composed almost exclusively of workers, especially clerks and livery stable employees. Most were boarders, not homeowners.[12] Likewise, Farr's Band, which was active in Princeton, New Jersey, in the 1890s, included an upholsterer, a carter, a carpenter, and a postman, while the leader, H. H. Farr, was a clerk.[13]

Even in the decades before the Civil War, this pattern was well established. During the years 1847–1850, the Brigade Cornet Band in Providence, Rhode Island, counted among its officers a tanner and machinist, a music professor, a painter, a house carpenter, a carriage painter, a blacksmith, and a jeweler.[14] Concomitant with this trend, there emerged the widely held belief that bands attracted men "from almost every station of life." That was how William L. Hubbard put it in his *History of American Music* of 1908, and that was how the bandsmen saw it themselves.[15] This democratic credo is still treasured by amateur bandsmen today.

It is difficult to generalize about the age of bandsmen. Contemporary newspaper accounts often referred to the "boys" or "young men" of the band, and in many communities the bands seemed to function as clubs for unmarried men in their late teens and twenties. The Browningsville (Maryland) Cornet Band, formed in January 1884 by a group of twenty men and boys ranging in age from eleven to twenty-nine, is not atypical. But older musicians played in bands with equal enthusiasm, and it was not unusual to find men in their sixties, seventies, and eighties still practicing regularly and still marching with their bands. In the opinion of the Rudolph Wurlitzer Company, there was no age limit. "Anyone, with few exceptions," claimed a company catalog, "can learn to

The Baraboo (Wisconsin) Band enjoyed a weekend of fellowship and music on a camping trip to Delton, Wisconsin, in 1887. State Historical Society of Wisconsin.

play if he will only study and practice."[16] This assertion reflects the reality accurately. Photographs of town bands of the nineteenth century reveal instrumentalists in every age bracket from about eight to eighty. In many cases young, middle-aged, and older bandsmen mingled together in these versatile musical ensembles that ignored generational barriers.

A town did not have to be particularly large to support a band. The villages of Many, Louisiana, Saxtons River,

Bands often incorporated three generations of players. Most of the players in the North Conway (New Hampshire) Band ca. 1880 had matching uniforms and relatively new piston valve instruments, but the youngest player (front row on right) did not have a uniform and had to learn to play on an older rotary valve cornet.

Vermont, and Vienna, South Dakota, all had populations of only about four hundred when they formed town bands. Most towns with bands were larger, but communities of one or two thousand inhabitants could easily support a band of fifteen pieces or more. It was quite a different matter to keep the band going, however. Despite the enthusiasm of musicians and townsfolk alike, the history of the typical town band is a story of years of musical performance punctuated by periods of disorganization and discontinuity. But no matter how long the lapses in band activity lasted, sooner or later someone usually struck up the band again.

Industrial Bands

In 1929 the National Bureau for the Advancement of Music published a monograph advocating the formation of musical ensembles by groups of industrial and commercial workers. According to author Kenneth S. Clark, bands, orchestras, and choruses improved worker attitudes and the relations between employees and management, and also enhanced a company's image. Having surveyed some six hundred and twenty-five firms with active music programs, Clark concluded unequivocally that "music in industry is no longer an experiment. Its efficacy has been practically demonstrated under varying conditions and in nearly every field of industrial activity."[17]

One reason why "music in industry" was no longer an experiment in 1929 was that the concept had undergone years of testing during the nineteenth century. Bands, in particular, were formed in association with factories as early as the middle of the century, as the example of the Wheeler and Wilson Sewing Machine Company demonstrates. When, in 1855, that company transferred its factory from Waterville, Connecticut, to Bridgeport, one of

Top: *The Charlevoix Cigar Company Band had one of the most ornate bandwagons of its time. Companies gained excellent publicity as well as worker loyalty through band sponsorship. Michigan State University Archives.* Bottom: *The Dodge City Cowboy Band was composed of working cowhands, shown here on a roundup in Indian Territory in the 1880s. Kansas State Historical Society.*

the major stockholders decided that the formation of a band might help minimize the unsettling effects of the move. Consequently, a band of sixteen employees was formed and a leader was hired. The burgeoning Wheeler and Wilson Band survived both the Civil War and a two-year disruption, and by 1885 it had become a nineteen-piece mixed wind ensemble with a considerable reputation. Always composed entirely of company men, the band enjoyed the encouragement of management throughout its existence.

Other industries sponsored bands in similar fashion. In 1881, the Illinois Watch Company of Springfield established a band for its employees. Directed for more than forty years by Professor Louis Lehman, the band attracted many outstanding musicians with the combined offer of factory work and recreational music. Wearing caps adorned with watch emblems and toting a bass drum emblazoned with a clockface, these bandsmen traveled throughout the Midwest entertaining the public and publicizing the factory. Farther west, in Butte, Montana, Sam H. Treloar organized a company band among the miners of the Boston and Montana Copper Mining Company. Although the group commenced in 1887 with only six musicians, the Boston and Montana Band was soon thriving. By 1889 it had twenty-three members and was rehearsing three nights a week. Incorporated in 1892, the miners' band toured extensively during the 1890s and won regional band competitions in 1902, 1906, and 1909.

As might be expected, instrument manufacturers were attracted to the idea of the company band. In 1881 the Lyon and Healy Company launched what they believed to be the first such "music house" band. The group's existence was originally justified by its usefulness for testing and tuning a full set of instruments, but soon, under the able direction of such men as George Lyon and D. S.

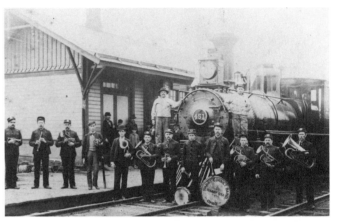

Granite Mountain, Montana, was a boom town that ran out of silver ore by 1894. The well-dressed "Granit Mountain Coronet Band" was formed from the ranks of local miners. Richard Dundas Collection.

Railroads sponsored local depot bands as well as "route" bands that gave concerts at towns along a specific line. The Summit Cornet Band of Summit Station, Ohio, appears to be a depot type. Johnny Maddox Collection.

McCosh, the Lyon and Healy Band became a highly valued vehicle for advertising the company's band supplies.

The examples could go on. There were typewriter factory bands, cigar manufactory bands, and textile makers bands. By the early decades of the twentieth century, steel companies, oil refineries, automobile manufacturers, and cereal makers were also developing bands. Railroads were particularly energetic in sponsoring bands for their workers, and by 1927, the Union Pacific System alone boasted seventeen active bands along its lines.[18] Probably the most famous American industrial band of all was the critically acclaimed ARMCO Concert Band, launched in the 1920s at the American Rolling Mill Company in Middletown, Ohio. Directed by the widely admired cornetist Frank Simon, this band reputedly rivaled the great professional organizations of the day.[19]

The methods of operation of these company bands varied considerably. The Isthmian Canal Commission Band, composed of employees of the Canal Zone Commission and the Panama Railroad, enjoyed a monthly salary from the company in return for performing a specified number of concerts along the canal. Other bands received uniforms, practice space, and time off from work in exchange for performances. Companies usually helped arrange for the hiring of a capable director, and occasionally, as in the case of the Elgin Watch Band, the company expended considerable money to hire an expert bandmaster (in this instance, Arthur Clappé) to teach the men the art of band performance.

A Union Pacific survey of fifty railroad bands active in the early 1920s reveals interesting trends among those company bands. Railroad bands tended to be initiated by the men, who usually supplied their own instruments. At the same time, they were generously supported by the company, which typically bought uniforms, gave employment preference to bandsmen, and paid the men their hourly wage for performances presented during working hours. Band size ranged from twenty to sixty-five players, with an average of thirty-seven in the mid–1920s. Rehearsals were held one or two times a week, often during working hours.

Whatever the specific arrangements, most observers agreed that both the company and the bandsmen benefited from the operation of company bands.

Institutional Bands

Writers of the nineteenth century frequently acknowledged the power of music to drive away weariness and depression. More than that, these writers sometimes ascribed a regenerative influence to the musical arts in general and to the performance of band music in particular. Hence, in 1830, members of the Society for the Suppression of Intemperance felt justified in circulating a petition advocating the presentation of band music on the Boston Common during general elections to "promote order and suppress an inclination to riot and intemperance."[20] It was not long before this philosophy, refined and embellished, prompted the routine inclusion of recreational bands in prisons and reform schools. One such enterprise was undertaken by an industrial school in San Francisco during the 1880s. Under the direction of a German music teacher, about twenty of the school's boys were organized into a brass band. These children reportedly detested their abc's and were uncontrollable by parents and guardians, but the taming influence of band music had the desired reforming effect. The boys played well and several improved so much that they were discharged from the school with a new profession under

Prisons formed bands as a rehabilitative activity. At some prisons incarcerated bandsmen actually wore striped uniforms, but other than the name on the drum there was little to distinguish the Wisconsin State Prison Band of Waupun, Wisconsin, from small-town ensembles.

their belts.[21] Adult penitentiaries tried similar experiments, often with satisfactory results.

Band music was introduced to individuals with health problems as well. According to the theory prevalent at the time, the performance of band music had physical and psychological benefits. For these reasons, Henry Berger, the capable Prussian director of the Royal Hawaiian Band in Honolulu, founded and supervised a band at the leper settlement at Kalaupapa, Molokai.[22] Early in the 1870s a band was formed for the employees and patients at the Jacksonville (Illinois) State Hospital. Music was of such importance to the therapy program at this mental health facility that eventually three bandstands were built on institution grounds.[23] Other hospitals, sanitariums, and homes for disabled veterans are known to have maintained active bands for their patients during the nineteenth century.

Lodge Bands

In Sinclair Lewis's novel *Main Street,* Carol Kennicott and her husband visit a neighboring town where a street fair is in progress. They note a handsome delegation in exotic Zouave costumes. It is the United and Fraternal Order of Beavers with their band, explains their host. "They're a good bunch. Good strong lodge. See that fellow there that's playing the snare drum? He's the smartest wholesale grocer in Duluth, they say. Guess it would be worth joining."[24]

As Lewis obviously knew, the relationship between bands and fraternal organizations was a close one. It is said that at any given time, from one-third to one-half the members of Sousa's band were Masons.[25] More to the point, most lodges regularly scheduled band music to accompany their many activities. When members participated in lodge-sponsored parties, picnics, and parades they could expect to be treated to band music. Deceased members of fraternal clubs and lodges were almost always honored with band music at their funerals. It is perhaps no coincidence that the peak in popular interest in lodges corresponds closely to the peak of the band movement.

The sources for lodge-sponsored band music varied. Some organizations hired their local town band, which may have used the lodge meeting hall for their practice sessions. Many lodges formed amateur bands among members. A survey of extant programs and photographs reveals a plethora of bands manned by Masons, Odd Fellows, Redmen, Elks, Eagles, and other groups between 1880 and 1915. Ever watchful of market trends, the C. G. Conn Company noted in the first decade of this century that many complete sets of band instruments were being sold to Masonic lodges. The company confidently predicted even greater interest in the years to come. In reality, lodge bands, like many other types of bands, lost support after the Great War, though fraternal bands can still be found in many American communities today.

Ethnic and National Bands

Amateur bands frequently organized according to the ethnic origins of the musicians. Bands like the Polish Band of Albion, New York, and the Portuguese Band of Watsonville, California, took their names from the nationalities of the players and, to a certain extent, incorporated their musical heritage into their performances. There were German bands, Italian bands, Swiss bands, Norwegian bands, and Chinese bands. In central California in the years after the 1849 gold rush, there was a veritable multitude of such bands. Reflecting the diversity of the miners, these rustic organizations included Mexican bands, Cornish bands, Black bands, and German bands. With the surge of immigration that occurred at the end of the nineteenth century, there appeared a new crop of bands formed by recently arrived Bohemians, Slovakians, eastern European Jews, and others. In some parts of the United States, Hibernian bands were found, although the number of these ensembles is smaller than might be expected given the prominence of Irish bandsmen like Richard Willis and Patrick Gilmore. Sometimes the ethnic character of amateur bands was based on a conscious desire to segregate individuals according to their background. Or sometimes, as in the case of the remote Eskimo bands of Alaska and northeastern Canada, the exclusiveness was inescapable. Mostly, though, bandsmen joined fellow countrymen as a matter of convenience, compatibility, and pride.

The most common of these ethnic bands in the nineteenth century was the German band. In 1863, upon hearing a volunteer military band in Williamsport, Pennsylvania, the famous American pianist and composer Louis Moreau Gottschalk wrote in his journal, "Is it necessary for me to say that it is composed of Germans (all the musicians in the United States are Germans)?"[26] The remark was an exaggeration, but it was true that German bands and bandsmen were prominent throughout the United States. German musicians formed wind bands to perform both religious and secular music in the various Moravian settlements of Pennsylvania and North Carolina as early as the end of the eighteenth century. Not long thereafter German musicians began to introduce their band traditions to other American communities, and by the 1870s Germania bands could be heard in towns from New England to Texas to Oregon. On occasion, these bands provoked the animosity of their neighbors as, for example, when they played too boisterously on Sundays or seemed excessively clannish. During World War I, when anti-German feelings ran high, many German bands ceased operation, never to resume. But in their heyday during the nineteenth century, German bands were considered a positive musical force. Aside from furnishing an enormous number of capable music "professors," these organizations profoundly affected the instrumentation and repertoire of bands throughout America.

Although far less prevalent than German bands, Italian bands were formed in many communities across the United States. As early as 1839, one group offered the citizens of Portsmouth, New Hampshire, a substantial and thoroughly appropriate program of American patriotic airs interspersed with Italian opera transcriptions. While it is quite likely that this ensemble and the other early Italian bands were largely professional groups, there is no doubt that the hundreds of Italian bands formed at

Black marching bands were formed in many American cities. This band marched for a patriotic holiday in Auburn, New York, ca. 1900. Copyright © by Schuler 1983.

the end of the century were primarily amateur organizations. Manned by music-loving immigrants who arrived in America by the hundreds of thousands between 1880 and 1914, these bands not only provided diversion for the Italian sections of various communities, but also are credited with helping to establish goodwill between the immigrants and their American neighbors. The incredible popularity of such professional Italian bandmasters as Giuseppe Creatore and Marco Vessella stimulated the establishment of amateur Italian bands on a local level.

Black bands, too, were common in many parts of America. Like the early Italian bands, many early Black groups such as Francis Johnson's Band of Philadelphia and

53

Peter Guss's Band from Boston were professional organizations. In time, particularly after the Civil War, amateur
Black musicians began to form brass bands. It has been
argued that the availability of Confederate band supplies
discarded after the Civil War greatly facilitated the organization of brass bands by Blacks, but this notion lacks
credibility. Many Black bands were well established prior
to the war. Furthermore, as jazz musician Charles Love
recalls, his father's Black band in the 1880s "put so much
money up" and "sent" away for instruments;[27] surely
other groups did the same thing. Taking advantage of the
inexpensive sets of instruments offered by instrument
companies, Blacks in many localities successfully formed
bands to enhance everything from holidays to funerals.
New Orleans was a center of such activity with numerous
Black marching bands reportedly taking part in a parade
on the occasion of President Garfield's visit to the city
in 1881.

In looking back on the early days of Black bands, Louis
Keppard, who eventually became the tuba player with
the E. Gibson Brass Band in New Orleans, recalled the
shortage of teachers for Black bandsmen. "We just had to
pick it up from the man above," he said in an interview.
"God Almighty give a gift."[28] In a way, this lack of instruction was an advantage because it allowed some Black
bandsmen to incorporate their musical heritage and
rhythmic vitality into the conventional brass band idiom.
The resulting music was quite different from that offered
by the white bands and the traditional Black bands of the
time. Recognizing the distinctive characteristics of many
Black bands at the turn of the century, the famous Black
poet Paul Laurence Dunbar wrote the following verses as
part of a larger poem that highlighted the spirit of Black
ensembles.

You kin hyeah a fine perfo'mance w'en de white ban's
    serenade,
An' dey play dey high-toned music mighty sweet,
But hit's Sousa played in ragtime, an' hit's Rastus on Parade,
W'en de colo'ed ban' comes ma'chin' down de street.

Oh, de white ban' play hits music, an' hit's mighty good to
    hyeah,
An' it sometimes leaves a ticklin' in yo' feet;
But de hea't goes into bus'ness fu' to he'p erlong de eah,
W'en de colo'ed ban' goes ma'chin' down de street.[29]

It was only a matter of time before this Black version of
band music evolved into the uniquely American mode of
musical expression—jazz.

In addition to the many bands formed by immigrants,
it was not uncommon, particularly toward the turn of the
century, to find avocational bands formed by Native
Americans. Such ensembles were prevalent at govern-
ment-sponsored Indian schools. The United States Indian
School Band in Phoenix, Arizona, was one of the first
school bands in the state. It participated in school ceremonies, patriotic celebrations, and even football parades
from the 1890s through the 1910s. At the Carlisle Indian
School in Pennsylvania, too, there was an active band as
early as the 1880s. The Indian bands ranged in size from
less than ten, as in the Tucson Indian School Band of
1910, to more than fifty musicians in the Carlisle Indian
Band in 1905.

That these bands existed at all is probably due more to
the schools' desire to Americanize the Indians than to a
genuine interest in the band movement on the part of
Native Americans. Indeed, Mrs. Annie Bidwell, one of
the sponsors of the Rancho Chico (California) Indian
Band, claimed that their brass band contributed a great
deal to diminishing the white people's prejudice against

Top: *Native American bands were organized at Indian schools and on reservations across the nation. Hoag's Indian Band of Salamanca, New York, performed at several railroad stops in New York and Pennsylvania.* Bottom: *Eskimo bands were found in Alaska and the northeast provinces of Canada. The message on the back of this ca. 1910 postcard reads: "Eskimo band of Hebron, Labrador, under direction of Geo. Harp Moravian Mission. As our ship entered the harbor at five in the morning they surrounded us in their own native boat playing O God our help in ages past and old hymns of the Moravian faith."*

the Indians in that part of California.[30] Nevertheless, there must have been some enthusiasm among Amerindians for band music. How else can one explain the fact that John Philip Sousa received honorary chieftainships from three different Indian tribes and that, in the process, he was dubbed Great Music Chief, Chasing Hawk, and Chief Singer?[31]

Women's Bands

Although Americans often categorized music as a feminine activity, this was hardly the case with brass bands. Military in origin and powerful in instrumentation, bands were unabashedly masculine organizations. Consequently, amateur band handbooks, instrument company catalogs, and uniform sales brochures catered exclusively to men for most of the nineteenth century. Even in the highly musical Moravian community of Bethlehem, Pennsylvania, girls were taught voice and piano, but not the wind instruments.

There was no logical reason why women could not play in brass bands. Writing on music in 1881, James M. Trotter declared emphatically that it was a mistake to restrict female musicians to the piano. "There are other instruments, for performance upon which many of them have talents," Trotter claimed.[32] "Nor need such performance detract from a graceful, ladylike appearance." But customs change slowly. Although professional women cornetists such as Louise Shaffer performed in public during the last two decades of the nineteenth century, and although women formed an integral part of touring family bands, it was not until the turn of the century that amateur ladies' bands began to appear with any regularity.

One group was organized in Ashland, Oregon, around 1898. Composed of seven young ladies, this Ladies' Cor-

Although playing in a brass band was generally considered to be a masculine activity, women also learned brass and percussion instruments. By the end of the nineteenth century, musical instrument companies were promoting sales to women as an important part of their marketing schemes.

The Utopian Ladies Band of Belleville, Wisconsin, posed for this group portrait on the Fourth of July, 1907. Several turn-of-the-century women's bands were located in Wisconsin or Michigan.

net Band regaled local citizens with music arranged for two cornets, two alto horns, tenor, bass, and E-flat tuba. A larger female band was formed in Watsonville, California, about 1908. Dubbed the Lady Hussars, this group of twenty musicians wore dapper uniforms of plumed hats, long capes, calf-length skirts, and boots. The women played in local parades and in concert. As was the case with almost all women's bands, the Lady Hussars were directed by a man.

Over the years, women in other communities formed similar groups. Musical instrument companies, quick to identify the trend, tried to capitalize on it. The C. G. Conn Company's journal, *Musical Truth,* carried articles

detailing health benefits to be enjoyed by women who played brass instruments. Some companies, such as H. N. White of Cleveland, Ohio, even developed a special line of small-bore, lightweight instruments that were claimed to be especially appropriate for female musicians. But despite such enticements and the prominence of a few professional ladies' bands, women's bands were never plentiful. Of the more than twelve hundred pre–1920 band photographs amassed at the Smithsonian Institution, only about twenty different women's bands are represented. As late as 1932, the H. N. White Company, maker of King instruments, referred to the Butler Girls' Band of Butler, Indiana, as "one of the very few bands composed of the fair sex."[33]

56

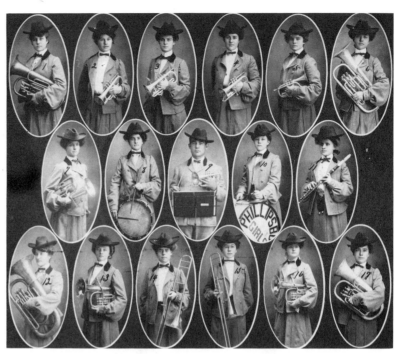

Bands with both men and women were rare in nineteenth-century America. The few mixed groups identified from photographs appear to have been from very small towns, like Wakefield, Kansas (population about three hundred in July 1899). A full complement of male musicians may not have been available in these small communities. Kansas State Historical Society.

Most women's bands, like the Phillipsburg (Kansas) Girls Band, were directed by a man. In spite of the fact that woodwind instruments such as flute were often associated with female musicians, women's bands almost invariably had the same predominantly brass instrumentation as contemporary amateur male groups. A women's band of twelve to sixteen players, therefore, might have had one or two woodwinds in 1890. Kansas State Historical Society.

Limited as they were in number, women's bands must have seemed abundant in comparison with mixed adult bands. If photographs are any indication, this type of band was truly rare. Even toward the end of the century, when men and women began to participate in more recreational activities together, there remained a reluctance to form a mixed band if the thing one was mixing was the sexes. The reasons for this hesitation ranged from habit to prejudice. One bandswoman, for many years the only female in her Iowa town band, recalled a visiting director who objected to her presence. "I wouldn't have any damn girl in the band," he exploded. "You can't talk like you want to!"[34] When on occasion men and women did play in bands together before World War I, it was often in remote areas where the number of musicians was limited, or in reform movement bands like the Salvationist groups in which men and women were working together. This situation did not change until well into the twentieth century when school band programs finally put wind instruments into the hands of more young women.

57

Children's Bands

When contemporary newspaper articles referred, as they commonly did, to the "boys in the band," they generally meant the adult players. Nevertheless, young boys, and to lesser extent girls, were sometimes associated with bands.

The appeal of brass bands to children is obvious. Thomas Wentworth Higginson, the famous abolitionist and author, recalled in his autobiography that a parading militia company evoked in his mind a veritable "ecstasy of childish love for costume and rhythm and glory."[35] Add to this the rousing music of a brass ensemble and most children were simply enchanted. "We were nine years old," recalled a Michigan bandsman, "and thought it was a wonderful thing to play in a band like the boys we saw blowing away and making such fine music."[36]

Most children had to be content to follow the band. If they were particularly clever and imaginative they might, as William Allen White did, carve trumpets out of green pumpkin stems and play at being bandsmen. Or, if they were persistent, they might become a drummer's helper or a band mascot. But a few lucky children were actually able to join bands. In Moravian communities, where musical ability was highly valued, separate boys' bands were formed with little difficulty. As early as the 1860s the Aurora (Oregon) Colony's adult Pioneer Band was augmented by the services of a younger band, the so-called Pie and Beer band. Likewise, in 1879 the Salem, North Carolina, community sponsored the formation of a band specifically for boys between the ages of thirteen and sixteen. In both cases these junior bands served as feeders for the adult bands already established in those communities.

By the end of the nineteenth century, the idea of children's bands gained wider popularity. Valued both for their educational benefits and for their novelty, juvenile

58 Top: *Children not lucky enough to play in a juvenile band could at least pretend. This photograph is entitled "Gilmore's Band."* Bottom: *This smartly uniformed juvenile band must have been one of the youngest in the country ca. 1880 when it posed in Bainbridge, New York. The four-member percussion section included a triangle, an instrument seldom observed in nineteenth-century American band images.*

bands were founded in such locations as Whitehall, New York (Juvenile Cornet Band, organized circa 1880), Elkhorn, Wisconsin (Boys' Band, organized in the early 1900s), Abilene, Kansas (Boys' Band, organized 1895), and Tucson, Arizona (Mariner's Juvenile Band, organized in 1897). Breeding's Band, which flourished in San Francisco around 1910, featured young boys as performers and also boasted a twelve-year-old cornetist as the leader.

Two types of children's bands—those sponsored by newspapers and those by orphanages—were widely publicized and deserve special note. Newsboy bands were formed by many large newspaper companies, particularly in the Midwest. Impressive bands of as many as forty boys were supported by the *Milwaukee Sentinel,* the *Co-*

lumbus Dispatch, the *Grand Rapids Evening Press,* the *Indianapolis News,* among others.

Several orphanages also sponsored fine bands to aid in fund-raising activities and to enrich the children's education. Of particular note was Tressler's Orphans Home Band (of Loysville, Pennsylvania), which was immortalized in thousands of picture postcards sold by the band to support the Home. Similar musical and commercial efforts were made by the Children's Industrial Home Band of Des Moines, Washington, which toured the country in its quest for donations, and the Hebrew Orphan Asylum bands of New York and Brooklyn, both of which provided testimonials for the Carl Fischer Instrument Company. Although most of these organizations were for boys

Sponsorship of newsboy bands provided newspapers with dual benefits: advertising for their publications and loyalty among the legions of paper carriers. The Milwaukee Sentinel *Newsboy Band was among the largest such groups ca. 1910.*

The Alabama Orphans School Band of Huntsville, Alabama, had to make the best of modest uniforms and instruments. This Black children's ensemble presents a sharp contrast to the large touring and fund-raising brass and reed bands of several northern orphanages such as the Loysville (Pennsylvania) Orphans Home and the Children's Industrial Home, Des Moines, Washington.

only, girls' bands and even mixed groups were not un-known.

Most communities were pleased with the efforts of their musical children. After only two months of training in Ann Arbor, Michigan, a group of eight "little fellows" between the ages of seven and fourteen were, according to the local newspaper, "better than some bands that have been practicing for many years."[37] Nonetheless, by the 1920s nonscholastic boys' bands were on the wane and, with the introduction of instrumental music in the public schools, they virtually disappeared.

ORGANIZING AN AMATEUR BAND

The Auburn Cadet Band of Auburn, Maine, was founded on July 4, 1876, when a group of six musicians casually joined forces to celebrate the Centennial in a local parade. A few weeks after that impromptu performance, the musicians met again with several additional players and formally established the band as a permanent organiza-tion. George H. Glover soon became its leader and in a few years he gave the organization his name and led the ensemble to several championships in regional band con-tests. The band was reportedly known throughout New England, and a number of its members went on to be-come professional musicians.

In contrast to this fortunate ensemble, most amateur bandsmen had to work very hard just to get their bands started. To acquire instruments and music, to maintain regular practice sessions, and to arrange for public per-formances, many interested individuals, both within the band and outside, had to join forces and work together.

For amateur musicians determined to form a band there was a wealth of published information on how to go about it. Allen Dodworth's *Brass Band School*, published in New York in 1853, included tips on everything from how to select an instrument to how to run a rehearsal.[38] Two decades later, G. F. Patton supplemented his text-book on the arrangement of band music with a twenty-two-page appendix containing practical hints "in relation to the organisation of bands, the management of rehears-als, parades, concerts, serenades" and a sample constitu-tion "suitable for brass bands."[39] Band instrument compa-nies typically offered useful information in their catalogs. Lyon and Healy incorporated an entire amateur band handbook, written by their company bandleader, D. S. McCosh, in sales catalogs of the 1880s and 1890s.[40]

In addition, various periodicals contained band notes. One of the most useful for the amateur musician (not to mention the band historian) was *The Leader,* first pub-lished in Boston in 1875. This monthly journal, issued in newspaper format, contained announcements about new bands and their personnel, notifications of upcoming band contests, including lists of prizes to be awarded, illustrated advertisements for band equipment and music, and classified listings of band-related job openings. Other publications such as *Musical Truth, The Metronome, The American Musician and Art Journal,* and *Dominant* carried features on how to improve your band and related topics.

According to the experts, the first step in forming a band was to find, in Patton's words, "some enthusiastic fellow who will take it upon himself to work the thing up."[41] All the good intentions in the world could not replace the skills of an able manager when it came to rearranging a random assortment of men into a band. With strong leadership, however, the organization could be launched. In some of the most successful bands, such as the Allentown (Pennsylvania) Band and the Royal Hawaiian Band, a single individual maintained several decades of uninterrupted leadership.

Although McCosh did not originally recommend it, many organizers found it useful to draft a formal constitution and a set of bylaws for their bands at the outset. These documents served to outline everything from the duties of the officers to the financial obligations of the members. They also stipulated acceptable behavior for the bandsmen and delineated the penalties, sometimes severe, for deviation from the code. If, as in the Belvidere (New Jersey) Cornet Band, there were to be fines for insulting the director (ten cents) or for unnecessary noise outside the band room (twenty-five cents), the charges could be clearly spelled out in the bylaws. Prohibitions, such as the Eckford (Michigan) Cornet Band's solemn strictures against dancing, wrestling, and "scuffling" in the band room could also be made clear. And it was in the constitution that the supreme authority of the leader could be established once and for all. These "Rules for Band Practice" were even printed in broadside form and affixed to the practice room walls in some communities.

In most cases, any man who agreed to these rules was welcomed to membership in an amateur band. But because it was in the best interests of a band to acquire good players, amateur band recruitment developed into a fine art. In an effort to attract capable musicians with the promise of steady work, town and company bands often advertised local employment opportunities along with their band openings. "Wanted," read one such listing in an 1888 issue of *The Leader,* "one or two good Job Printers, one Baker, one Carpenter, and one Painter, who are good musicians, to play in Port Henry (New York) Military Band."[42] Years later, periodicals such as *The Metronome* and *Musical Truth* were still promoting bands in the same way:

Musicians Wanted:
Clarinet or Cornet players who are blacksmith, baker or

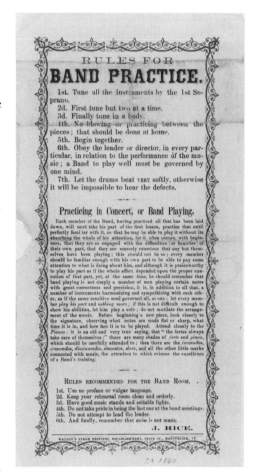

"Rules for Band Practice" were copied exactly from Allen Dodworth's Brass Band School, *published in New York in 1853, and were printed in broadside form in Montpelier, Vermont, for use in local band rooms. Donated by Ken Leach.*

TO THOSE WANTING POSITIONS

Hereafter, all parties sending in notices for positions wanted, must qualify by a short synopsis of their experience and ability. Otherwise, ads. will not be published.

It has been found that a number of very mediocre players often times advertise themselves as capable bandmasters; whereas, they are not capable on their own instrument, and in order to protect the worthy director and the worthy performer, the C. G. Conn, Ltd., feels that it has a duty to perform by the way of publishing nothing in the Want column other than that which is legitimate as far as it is possible for the C. G. Conn, Ltd., to ascertain.

Therefore, please bear in mind if you want your ad. in Musical Truth, you must qualify as to claims which you make in your Ad. to be published.

POSITIONS WANTED

Wanted—Position as Tuba player with some band. Victor Carlson, Julesburg, Col.
Wanted—Position as leader of band. Address, Joseph Vegetti, Box 520 Hurley, Wis.
Position wanted by a young man playing Eb Bass and Violin. E. G. Arnold, St. Paris, Ohio.
At liberty. Experienced band leader, Address, Musical director, care Oblong Concert band, Oblong, Ill.
Position as band director by cigar maker. Address Frank V. Parcells, 913 W. Superior street, Kokomo, Ind.
At Liberty—First class Cornetist. Experienced. Address, Fred G. Wagner, 185 E. Univ. ave., St. Paul, Minn.
Park B. Prentiss, bandmaster at liberty for first class engagement. Address 248 E. Fifth street, Los Angeles, Cal.
First class BBb Bass player desires position with good concert band. Address, R. L. Burroughs, Fort Grant, Ariz.
Experienced Cornetist, and band leader, desires position. Address, W. Sanders, 811 Wolfe street, Little Rock Ark.
At liberty. A-1 Bass-String and Tuba player, sight reader (barber). Address, D. B. Arkley, Box 543, Greentown, Ind.
Position Wanted—By painter and paper hanger. Plays B Clarinet or brass. Own Clarinets Address T. H. Clay, Tamaroa, Ill.
Bandmaster of twenty years experience wants location. Studied in Europe. Address, Jos. Vezzetti, Box 520, Hurley, Wis.
Wanted—Position for leader and director of band; who is also teacher and Trombone player. Prof. E. Orsoni, Thurber, Texas.
A good Slide Trombone player, also Cornet (or Baritone) desires position. Address, R. J. Schoonmaker, Box 98, Hensonville, N. Y.
Position as watchmaker and jeweler. First class Cornetist and also play Violin. Alvin Lorig, 1291 Rollamont avenue, St. Louis, Mo.
Play Bassoon, Slide Trombone and Baritone, also Violin for dance work, and want location. Address, Musician, 316 Bowen avenue, Chicago, Ill.
Wanted—Position by a teacher of wind instruments, harmony, bands, etc., who is a fine tuner. W. R. Douglas, care Orchestra Chautauqua, N. Y.
Experienced Violinist wishes to join reliable orchestra or locate in live town as teacher or with some music school. Miss E. Nichola, Box 316, Knightstown, Indiana.
Position Wanted—Play Clarinet, handle standard music, capable of teaching young bands. Experienced bookkeeper or clerk. Address, J. F. Anger, Wapella, Ill.
Bandmaster, 15 years experience desires a change of location. Cornet and Violin. Teach all string, brass and reed instruments. Have fine orchestral library. Address Bandmaster, P. O. Box 785, Swift Current, Sask, Canada.
At Liberty—Trap Drummer. Want to locate in picture house. Am dry cleaner, presser and repairer. Would clerk in clothing store and do cleaning etc., in conjunction. Play Flute and Piccolo. D. A. Fullerton, Weldon, Ill.

TO THOSE WANTING MUSICIANS

It will be necessary for you to qualify as to your claims in your ads. There have been so many misrepresentations made by parties desiring musicians and unsuspecting musicians who have traveled many miles to learn they have been beautifully "buncoed." This sort of thing must cease as far as the C. G. Conn, Ltd., is concerned. Therefore, do not fail to qualify by sending references; and we will soon place the Want Column of Musical Truth on a very high plane and one which will be of unquestioned value to those desiring musicians and those wishing engagements.

The circulation of the Conn Musical Truth is many many thousands and according to the best information obtained, is larger than that of all other similar musical papers in this country.

So help us to maintain its integrity.

MUSICIANS WANTED

Wanted—Cornet man, cigar maker by trade. F. L. Bliss, Merrill, Wis.
Cornetist who is barber. Address, W. W. Harrison, Box 747, Gulfport, Miss.
Musicians who are machinists. Address, C. G. McGahey, Covington, Va.
Wanted—A blacksmith who is a musician. Address, William Schott, Harrison, Ohio.
Wanted—A good cornet player to open a tailor shop. Address, W. I. Greene, Castle, N. Y.
Clarinet, Cornet and Trombone players wanted. K. of P. band (White), Clearwater, Fla.
Cornet and Clarinet players for Manistique band. C. H. Deerdahl, secy., Manistique, Mich.
We want a good band leader who is a barber and Cornetist. Address, H. M. Dayton, Alma, Nebr.
Cigar maker who is Cornetist. Must donate services to band. Address, F. L. Bliss, Merrill, Wis.
Wanted—Musicians of all trades, who are willing to work. Address, F. O. Box No. 244, Wolcott, Ind.
Good location open for competent band director. For particulars, address, Kable Bros. Co., Mt. Morris, Ill.
Wanted—Harness maker who is musician: Cornet, Piano or both. Woods, Thaler Mercantile Co., Seibert, Col.
Wanted—Band leader, who is barber, to locate here and buy shop. Address, P. O. Box, No. 172, Francesville, Ind.
Wanted—A good band leader who can instruct band. State your trade. Address, Box No. 1379, Sanford, Florida.
Three or four fairly good musicians who are machinists. Address, Clarence Edmund, Director Moose Band, Rock Falls, Ill.
We want a good bandman to buy and run bakery and play in band. Address, Clarksville, Citizens band, Clarksville, Ark.
Wanted—At once, machinists who are bandsmen. Write, Citizen's Concert band, Covington, Va., F. P. Obenchain, Secretary.
Machinists, pattern makers, floor hands, moulders, etc., who are band men. Address, Leader, Grove City band, Grove City, Pa.
Wanted—Blacksmith to rent or buy shop with full equipment. Tuba or Cornet player. Address Alfred Klein, Cut Bank, Mon.
Wanted—Clarinet player, must be good man who is pants and vest maker. State trades etc. Address, K. of C. Band, Carlo, Ill.
Wanted—A first class dentist. One that is capable of instructing and directing a beginners' band. Address, W. E. Bruce, Collinsville, Tex.
Wanted—Band conductor cornetist preferred, qualified to teach and act as principal in the High school, Cambridge Commercial club, Cambridge, Ill.
Wanted—First class Cornetist, that can read at least grade 3 through at sight, and position as barber. Sober and reliable. Address, W. H. Lamont, Dir. Prophetstown, Ill.
Wanted—A-1 musicians, clean cut habits and appearance—wanting steady positions—trades or clerical work—opportunities for business investors, etc. Tympani, Harp, Trap, Cornet, Basses, Horns. Large Concert Band. Address J. B, 209 N. Second street, Elkhart, Ind.

"Musicians Wanted" advertisements appeared in American band periodicals from the 1870s through the 1910s. Bandsmen were sought for positions in every state and territory in the country, thus suggesting a fair degree of mobility amongst the nation's bandsmen. Though most of these band "jobs" were not for professional musicians, the ability to play an instrument well significantly improved a worker's ability to get a good job.

newspaper men. No baker within 20 miles. Must be sober. Address, A. W. Guidrey, Church Point, La.[43]

Other inducements were used to attract bandsmen to a particular locality. Railroads often offered their bandsmen annual passes for free travel on their lines. In one of the more unusual arrangements, the mining bandsmen of the Copper Queen Band, located in the mining community of Bisbee, Arizona, were reportedly given the safest drifts in the mine.[44]

With rules established and players in hand, a band could turn its attention to equipment. Of primary importance were the instruments. While cornet players usually owned their instruments, most bands had to supply the larger brass and the drums, and many organizations had to furnish musicians with the entire set. In addition, a band needed music, blank band books, and a place to rehearse. Some sort of musical instruction was indispensable, be it in the form of printed tutors, a correspondence course offered through instrument companies, a hired professional teacher, or, ideally, a trained full-time director. Although it was often argued that dark suits were perfectly appropriate concert attire, many bandsmen considered an elegant uniform to be an essential piece of equipment. In some groups both summer and winter outfits were deemed desirable, though generally not at the outset.

In keeping with the customs of the mid-nineteenth century, many bands also sought the services of a "band boy" to perform the many custodial tasks associated with the band. Polishing brass on the instruments and uniforms, shining shoes, cleaning uniforms, sweeping the practice room, and other chores might be assigned to this nonmusician, who was often the only Black associated with the band. Finally, if a band were really going to do it right, at least according to Patton's standards, it needed the following: a couple of large swinging lamps, a table, a few benches, racks for the music, a storage drawer, a ready supply of drinking water (to discourage the use of "private bottles"), pliers, a screwdriver, and a quantity of rags.[45]

With the exception of the last item, these supplies could cost a great deal of money. To their credit, amateur bandsmen devised numerous creative methods of financing their ventures. Rehearsal space was often acquired free of charge in the workshops, homes, or even barns of band members. If such arrangements could not be made, the town, sponsoring company, or institution could usually be induced to offer a large hall or other suitable space at little or no cost to the band. To pay for the instruments and other accessories, bands collected money from a variety of sources, including membership dues and fines, supporter donations, and special fund-raising events. The enterprising members of the Manchester (New Hampshire) Cornet Band raised revenue by selling shares in their organization for thirty-two dollars, a sum which went a long way toward helping the band's finances in 1855. The Bloomington (Indiana) Band saved money by having its drum made by several of the town's craftsmen, and except for the fact that the original inscription was misspelled "E Pluribus Onion," it was a great success.

Many instrument companies eased the financial burden for new bands by offering inexpensive and used instruments. They also made their better lines available at attractive prices and allowed purchase through installment payments. In 1881 Lyon and Healy offered to outfit an entire ten-piece band for only one hundred and fifty dollars; by 1891 the price had dropped to one hundred twenty-five. With such incentives, there was, according to the J. W. Pepper Company, "no excuse for any community, no matter how small, to be without its own Brass

Cobb's Band in 1887 relied on the band boy to keep uniforms clean and instruments polished. The uniformed youngster may also have had to carry the bass drum on his back during parades.

Band."[46] Indeed, in most cases the requisite band instruments and supplies were readily acquired. Then it was time to learn to play music.

Since musical ability was rarely a requirement for amateur band membership, a band's musical director had his work cut out for him. As one observer saw the job, "the country band instructor has to explain and expound and demonstrate. The least part of his work is the time beating. He has to finger passages, show how to blow, how to attack a note, how long to hold it, when to stop it, and

63

try to get the untrained player to know what a musical tone is, and how it is to be produced."[47] For the musicians, the venture also entailed commitment. They were expected to accept the instrument assigned to them, to pay careful attention during rehearsals, and to refrain from "promiscuous blowing in the band room." More important, they were expected to practice faithfully, a responsibility that the Olathe (Kansas) Cornet Band took so seriously that its 1888 bylaws required bandsmen to sign an unusual pledge to that effect.

Of necessity, the teaching process began simply. Bernard Pfohl recalled his first day with the boys band in Salem, North Carolina:

> Each [boy] was supplied with a brass horn of varying type and condition. Kerosene oil and rotten stone with "elbow grease" soon made a change in the appearance of the instruments. The scale for each horn, written on a small piece of paper, was handed to each boy to memorize the notes and the fingering; then the noise began in different parts of the town.[48]

Judging from the number of contemporary jokes about the inelegant sounds of a beginning band, these first "noises" could not have been easy on the neighbors. One of the many popular gags, published in *The Leader* in 1885, defined a "band of mercy" as "a brass band that didn't practise evenings." Another often repeated one-liner proclaimed that the evil that men do lives after them because "when an amateur cornet-player dies, he leaves the fatal instrument behind."[49] Even that great promoter of brass bands, D. S. McCosh, had to confess that a brass band "in its commencement may be termed a noisy organization."[50]

The first noises could not have been easy on the teacher either. He had to impart the rudiments of music to a group of novices or, worse, to partially trained amateurs with ingrained habits of dubious artistic merit. This vignette of an amateur band rehearsal conveys some sense of the atmosphere and the difficulties of an early practice session. The story was created by "An Old Band Teacher" and was printed in *The American Musician and Art Journal* in 1913:

> But now let me tell you of an old time band practice, and you can compare it with the present up to date rehearsals. The teacher was seldom a resident of the town and generally arrived early enough in the day to copy or arrange a piece of music for the lesson. There was no printed music then, and teachers were expected to give new music with each lesson. The band room was invariably the workshop of an active member, an old barn or a hall or schoolroom, where there were always a number of influential citizens who had "dropped in to see how the band was getting along."
>
> "Here! you alto there—what in thunder are you working your valves for? There is no fingering in the strain—the notes are all open," shouted the teacher to an alto player who was playing the wrong tones.
>
> "Oh! Yes," said the alto man, "I thought they was F."
>
> "Say, you with the baritone—is that tuning slide of your instrument pulled out where I told you to keep it?"
>
> "No, Mister, I done forgot about it; let's try to tune it again," replied the forgetful baritone player.
>
> "All right," answered the teacher. "Now everybody get in tune. First we'll try the cornets."
>
> That being done the teacher called on the bass to tune his instrument. Holy smoke! What a time. It sounded like the snarling of a buzz saw, except there was not quite so much music in it.
>
> "Something the matter with your lip tonight, Ed?" queried the teacher.
>
> "Naw, it's me durned front teeth; they's been droppin' out for the last week or two. Just try it again."
>
> Finally the bass player gets an intelligible tone, his instrument was tuned, and then the others were brought into pardonable reach of the right pitch, except one wheezy clari-

net, which was incorrigible. Then the practice was continued.

"Now, boys," said the teacher, "I want you to pay a little attention to the forte and pianissimo marks. Notice that the first strain is in the forte, and that the second is pianissimo."

"Say, teacher," exclaimed the bass drummer, "I ain't got no forte in that second strain. Don't I come in there?"

"No; you'll need all your muscle for the finale, Jim," replied the polite teacher. "Now altogether; I'll count a bar and then you play."[51]

The saga of the band practice session concludes with Ed's discovery of his lost tooth which is at last extracted from within his instrument, much to the satisfaction of everyone.

Yet even such ridiculous difficulties as those described in this story could be overcome in time. Although it took an estimated seven years to become a first-class band instrumentalist,[52] amateur bands settled for lower standards of musicianship in order to get quicker results. The Lyon and Healy catalog of 1881 claimed that a band could expect to reach a basic level of proficiency within sixty days. This was apparently not an unreasonable estimate for the Fitchburg Military Band, organized in Fitchburg, Massachusetts, on March 26, 1868, reportedly played in public for the first time on May 27, 1868. Similarly, the Mankato (Minnesota) Saxhorn Band, founded in February of 1862, was actively serenading by April and, in the opinion of the local newspaper, was playing remarkably well "considering the brief practice of the members."[53] One early military band in Salem, North Carolina, was out marching on the streets less than a month after the group's creation.

Other bands took longer, and still other bands should have taken longer. Yet, with practice at home, with one or two band rehearsals per week, and with the appropriate shuffling of personnel so that the most capable musicians were put on first E-flat cornet, first B-flat cornet, and baritone, an amateur band could, in time, move on to simple melodies and, eventually, marches and quicksteps.

Many groups did just that, to the delight of their supporters. The following extract, taken from the record book of the New Bedford (Massachusetts) Brass Band, conveys some sense of the satisfaction in store for amateur bandsmen once they were able to offer their services to the public. The entry is in the band secretary's description of an excursion taken by the band on July 4, 1848.

The Band having made an engagement to play for the Engine Companies No. 7 & No. 9 on an excursion to be made to Nantucket on the fourth of July, assembled at Engine House No. 9 at 5 o'clock A.M. The Company was soon formed and proceeded to the House of No. 7 Company where they were received, and the two Companies accompanied by the Band repaired immediately on board the Steamer *Massachusetts*. It was a beautiful morning and the noble steamer was literally crowded with passengers. We left the wharf at 6 o'clock, and after landing at Fairhaven, Woodville and Holmes Hole, arrived at the Island of Nantucket at 10 o'clock. The Nantucket Firemen, a noble sett of fellows, were formed for our reception, accompanied by the Cattarac Band from Fall River. After proceeding through the principal streets, some of them a number of times, were conducted to the Congregational Church where an oration was delivered by Charles Bunker, Esq. The procession was again formed and marched to a large tent erected about one mile from Town, and the whole company was sat down to a sumptious calution, at which at that late hour, 4½ o'clock P.M., every one did ample justice and proved himself worthy of the cause in which he was engaged. When the cloth was removed, numerous patriotic toasts were offered and drunk in pure cold water. The Company dispersed to meet again in Town at 8 o'clock. At that hour a procession formed, and, presented by the Whale Fire Department of the Island and their guests with

Torches, marched out to view the Fireworks and returned about 10 o'clock, and such as chose, attended a Splendid Ball at the Town Hall. On the 5th, at 3 o'clock P.M. left the Island and arrived home about 8 o'clock in a heavy storm. Notwithstanding which the Companies were met on landing by a delegation from the other Fire Companies and escorted to their quarters, all highly gratified with their excursion. The Band was liberally and promptly paid for their services, receiving $200. and received assurances from the Firemen of having given them entire satisfaction.[54]

BAND RIVALRY

The players gave a band its identity and structure, but it was competition with other bands that gave it dynamism and the will to improve. Widespread even in the earliest days of the movement, good-natured rivalry stimulated amateur bands to play more often, to dress more attractively, and to practice more diligently. Rivalry among towns and companies can even be said to have led to the formation of many bands in the first place.

Amateur bands tried to outdo each other at every level. As their testimonial letters reveal, bandsmen in every state were eager to acquire the "finest" uniforms and the "best" instruments for themselves and their bands. These aspiring musicians spent enormous sums of money on plumed shakos, silken sashes, and the gold and silver replating and elaborate engraving of their instruments, just to create a more pleasing display than that of a rival band. There was fierce competition for good musical arrangements as well, and not a few bands "borrowed" liberally from their fellows without permission. In one incident, long remembered by residents of Battle Creek, Michigan, the Germania Band upstaged a neighboring band from Bay City by playing one of Bay City's original pieces, but in a far better arrangement, during the very

same concert at which the Bay City band premiered their work.[55]

Even more than fancy uniforms and pleasing music, a band required talented musicians and the resulting rivalry for skilled personnel often resulted in extreme measures. One foolproof method of snagging a good player before the opposition did was utilized with great success in Rochester, Indiana. Bandmaster William Rannells recalled the novel system as follows:

> If a new man came to town and he was a musician we would follow him all night. I remember when Walter Chapman came from Pennsylvania. George Adams discovered that he was a cornet player and passed the word. Two or three of the band boys were "put next" and stayed with him until one o'clock in the morning, then others talked to him until they had him solid for the band.[56]

Ultimately, however, the only meaningful way to establish one band's superiority over another was to fight it out in concert. Such "windy wars," as a New Orleans newspaper called them, were common occurrences in the nineteenth century.[57] On city street corners, in the middle of parades, and even on the decks of passing steamboats, rival bands tried to outshine the competition with the quality, not to mention the volume, of their playing. Similar musical battles, waged by Confederate and Union bands during the Civil War, have become legendary.

These spontaneous play-offs evolved into a highly organized forum for band competition known as band contests or tournaments. Sponsored variously by instrument companies, regional band associations, and chambers of commerce, band contests catered to the competitive nature of bandsmen while offering more tangible rewards. As *Trumpet News* pointed out in 1877, a band could learn more from one "well-regulated band contest than [from] months [of] the ordinary routine of band practice."[58] In addition to this educational function, band tournaments offered participants an opportunity to win fantastic prizes of cash or instruments. In one contest, held in Fremont, Ohio, in 1884, the grand prize was a wagon worth two thousand dollars *plus* five hundred dollars in gold.[59] Needless to say, winning competitions was another way a band could raise money!

Band contests became very popular, especially during the 1870s and 1880s. Some of the large ones, such as the three- and four-day tournaments held annually at Lake Maranacook, Maine, and Evansville, Indiana, attracted both amateur and professional bands along with thousands of spectators. Other competitions were small-scale affairs, featuring a few local bands and perhaps a few dollars in prize money for the winning bandsmen. No matter how the contests were administered, the opportunities they provided for bandsmen to hear each other and play together went a long way toward fueling the dynamism of the American amateur band movement.

AMATEURS AND THE PROFESSIONALS

There is a danger in making too fine a distinction between amateur and professional bandsmen. There were many professional players who had to take work in fields other than music in order to support themselves. On the other hand, there were numerous amateurs who were accomplished enough and who played often enough for money that they were professionals in fact if not in attitude. Amateur bands often had professional musicians as leaders. Occasionally, as in the case of the American Band of Providence, Rhode Island, and the Ringgold Band of Reading, Pennsylvania, a capable director could train his amateurs so well that the group eventually evolved into a professional organization. Both amateurs and professionals were well aware of each other's activities. Amateur bandsmen looked upon the professional groups as role models, whereas professional bandsmen regarded the amateur bands as fertile training grounds for their personnel.

Nevertheless, the emphasis upon amateur bandsmen as a separate group of musicians is perfectly appropriate. Too often music historians have concentrated so heavily on the most visible and accomplished of the professional bands that they have lost sight of these major contributors to the band movement in nineteenth-century America. Without the bandsmen who took up their brass instruments for their own enjoyment and for the pleasure of their neighbors, the country would have been a quieter, duller, and less joyful place.

68   *Belle Fourche in western South Dakota had a population of several hundred in 1906 at the time of this stock meet parade. A sizable percentage of the town's residents were apparently observers at this annual event.*

4.
MUSIC FOR EVERY OCCASION

There are hardly any gatherings, large or small, in human
society, where good music, appropriate to the occasion,
would not be acceptable and confer increased happiness
upon the hearer.

—*Universal Self-Instructor,* 1883

"There were brass bands all over the place," exclaimed
pitcher Cy Young on the opening day of the first World
Series in 1903. Although he was alluding specifically to
the crowded ball park, he might just as well have been
referring to America as a whole. Brass bands were prominent in all parts of the country in the early twentieth
century just as they had been for decades. Employed to
celebrate notable occasions, to sell products, to accompany dancers, and simply to entertain the public with
concerts, bands could be found in a myriad of settings,
many carefully designed to show off the performers and
their music. The set designers for the Broadway musical
The Music Man may have equaled but hardly outdid the
original bandsmen themselves in devising pleasing envi-
ronments in which their bands could play.

PARADES

Parades were among the most visible, audible, and cherished of the many settings for band performance in the
nineteenth century. Combining pageantry with a purpose,
parades were the perfect forum for showing off a band's
musical ability, resplendent uniforms, and shiny horns.

We "marched through some of the streets at the north
part of the City," wrote the secretary of the New Bedford
(Massachusetts) Brass Band after a parade in 1852. From
there

> we marched to the South End past ex-mayor Howland's to a
> vacant lot where a game of Foot Ball was put in motion. . . .
> We then took up our line of march over Sundry Stone Walls,
> through mud puddles to 2d street, then through Water to
> William and several streets too numerous to mention at the
> north end and back again to the Hall where we were dis-
> missed.[1]

The epigraph at the head of this chapter is from *The Universal Self-
Instructor and Manual of General Reference* (New York: Winter House,
1970, facsimile of 1883 edition), 293.

Bands in the mining towns of the Rocky Mountains had to contend with awkward topography while marching. Here, the band of the Redmen fraternal order of Bisbee, Arizona, is parading in Brewery Gulch, ca. 1901. Arizona Historical Society.

Firemen's conventions often featured a parade with several bands. This 1909 convention in Jersey Shore, Pennsylvania, near the musical instrument factories of Williamsport, must have boasted several fine ensembles.

Such were the highlights of a firemen's parade in New England at midcentury. Despite similar obstacles, other bands marched on other streets for countless other occasions.

70   There were military parades galore. On one Sunday in 1833 ten different companies were scheduled to parade through the streets of New Orleans. While this city was unusually fond of military display, militia units also paraded in thousands of American communities several times a year. Civilian organizations quickly adopted the format and character of these military processions, and bands were seen leading marching representatives of reform organizations, Sunday schools, and political candi-

dates. Professional musicians employed by traveling theatrical troupes and circuses usually paraded through town prior to the shows. And the more somber funeral procession—also a "parade"—was a standard element of America's mourning ritual throughout the century. Public holidays were particularly suitable for parades. In addition to Independence Day processions, which had been common since the early nineteenth century, parades were held to celebrate Emancipation Day (January 1), Washington's Birthday (February 22), Battle of New Orleans Day (January 8), and, on the local level, Founder's Day and Old Pioneer's Day. Decoration Day (May 30), first proclaimed a holiday in 1868 by General John A. Logan (commander in chief of the Grand Army of the Republic), became the classic occasion to decorate the town with flags and hold a patriotic procession. At the head of these parades was the smartly uniformed band, imparting order to the marchers' steps and spirit to the spectators' hearts.

It was only natural that Americans, those aficionados of movement who gave the world rocking chairs, should relish music on the march. But for the musicians, there was nothing natural about walking along a street, blowing into an instrument, and making music—*all at the same time*. It was an acquired art that both professional and amateur bandsmen worked hard to master.

The standard marching formation consisted of several rows of four to ten musicians standing side by side. Every effort was made to render the band as compact as the street width would allow so that the players could hear each other. Drums and cymbals, typically placed at the

Bands in parade formation were often employed to lead formal processions, such as this commencement exercise at Hampton Institute, Virginia.

Instruction manuals for brass bands invariably included instructions for marching formations. D. S. McCosh advised that over-shoulder instruments should precede bell-front instruments to enhance the ensemble.

rear to maintain a steady and audible pulse, were usually preceded by the high brass—the E-flat and B-flat cornets. Then in advance of the cornets came the altos and tenors who could mesh their playing easily with the cornets. Finally, in the front rows were the remainder of the tenors, plus the baritones and tubas. Less commonly a hollow square was formed with the drum in the middle. In this configuration, too, the high-pitched brass were placed to the rear of the lower instruments.

Ideally, this compact block of musicians would be led by a drum major, a very important individual in marching units. Not only did he lead the band and keep the musicians in formation, but his magnificent presence added dignity and drama to any procession. It was also claimed,

71

"The Mighty Drum Major" presented a grand sight to
spectators at a parade. The striking effect created by his uniform
and plumed shako was heightened by the manipulation of his
tasseled baton, which signaled the band in its playing and
marching maneuvers.

partly in jest, that he attracted people's attention away
from the awful faces made by the cornet players.[2] The
position of drum major was invariably filled by an imposing man who was rendered even more imposing by a
stunning uniform. In 1889 the Grafton (Vermont) Cornet
Band presented their drum major Baxter M. Walker with
a magnificent outfit that included a tall bearskin shako, a
tasseled sash, and a jacket bedecked with epaulets, braid,
and a swirl of brass buttons. The lucky Mr. Walker was
also supplied with the mandatory wooden baton decorated with a bright metal orb and gaily colored ribbons.
These accoutrements cost the Grafton bandsmen and their
supporters the princely sum of seventy-five dollars, but
they evidently thought the costume was worth the ex-
penditure.[3]

Under the tutelage of the drum major and the leader,
new bandsmen began learning how to march. As soon as
the individual bandsmen were comfortable playing their
instruments while walking, prospective marching bands
had to drill as a unit. Those organizations lucky enough
to have a large practice hall at their disposal could practice
marching and playing indoors, but most bands had to
find a quiet street or field for rehearsals. Lining up in
order, the band would march round and round, with and
without music, until they could maintain orderly ranks
with a simple drumbeat as well as with the music. And it
was important to learn to move "a little proudly," as one
teacher put it, so that the unit would present a polished
image.[4]

Bands also had to practice starting and stopping together. The leader's verbal command, combined with the
beat of the small drum, usually signaled the start of
march. Then a predetermined drum signal and perhaps a
cornet fanfare clued the musicians when to start the music. Bands by custom would stop frequently during pa-

Many bands adopted a circular formation for stationary outside performance. The locality of this turn-of-the-century celebration is not known, but similar scenes would have occurred in small towns across the nation.

Playing on horseback required special skills that few amateur bands acquired. This band, appearing in an Elks Parade in Portland, Oregon, is executing a difficult right turn while playing.

rades to play special little concerts at grandstands, at targeted businesses, and for special citizens. For these interludes the band often adopted special formations—such as the circular serenading formation—and the transition to and from these concert poses had to be practiced until the band could move smoothly. It was not uncommon for a band to go indoors during a parade. This required the fancy reworking of the ranks to fit through narrow doorways.

The manipulation of sheet music could pose problems for marching bands. Even though most instruments were outfitted with lyres to hold the printed music in place, many bands found it useful to have a young boy to help distribute and collect the parts during a parade. Many

groups memorized standard pieces to avoid the problem of wind-blown or lost pages.

Bands on horseback encountered difficulties of their own. Although many mounted bands were recruited from professionally trained military men, some—like the Fisherville (New Hampshire) Cornet Band—were amateurs. Totally inexperienced horsemen, these fearless musicians agreed to play for the Governor's Horse Guards in a review held in 1860. As one observer recalled of their heroic efforts, "The bucking broncos of the Wild West Show furnished no more sport, while it lasted, than did the gallant equestrians of the Fisherville Band while trying to train their horses to march and wheel by fours."[5] And yet the problems of the Fisherville Cornet Band were

*The St. Johns (Michigan) Bicycle Band in 1886 combined two
of America's favorite pastimes in what was a very unusual, if
not unique, ensemble. Photographs of at least seven band
members survive in the collections of the Michigan State
Archives.*

probably minimal compared to those encountered by the
St. Johns (Michigan) Band which paraded while mounted
on penny-farthing bicycles. How they kept formation is
a matter of speculation, but it has been suggested that the
chief supporters of this type of mounted band were not
the musicians but the instrument repairmen of America.

In spite of such problems, hundreds of musicians acquired the necessary parading skills and proudly demonstrated their accomplishments to the public. Band record
books and bandsmen's journals tell the story of their
successes:

> Arrived at Providence about 12 o'clock. Dined at the Earl
> Home and marched through some of the principal
> streets. . . . All seemed heartily to enjoy themselves. [New

Bedford (Massachusetts) Brass Band, 1848[6]]

[Our] little band of eleven led many parades at Indianapolis.
At the General Grant boom we led the parade, both day and
night. I could relate an account of a fight we had for it but
space is limited. [Rochester (Indiana) Band, 1870s[7]]

. . . We marched up to Fourth Street, then south through
Frenchtown around the Convent of the Sacred Heart, then up
to Seventh, from there back to the college where we had a
good dinner with music by the band. [William Robyn's St.
Louis Band, July 4, 1842[8]]

Songwriter Ted Koehler was clearly inspired by such a
rich heritage when he wrote the famous song, "I Love a
Parade," in 1931. Drawing on the same rich heritage,
most of us know exactly why he felt that way.

SERENADES

The serenade, essentially a cross between a concert and a
parade, was a very popular mode of musical expression in
the romantic nineteenth century. Usually performed outdoors and at night, these short, complimentary concerts
were frequently put on to honor local citizens or welcome
distinguished visitors to town. As depicted on the opera
stage, a vocalist or any small group of instrumentalists
could successfully perform a serenade, but in real life such
musical entertainment was customarily rendered by the
booming beat of a brass band. "If this does not go directly
to the heart," conceded Frédéric L. Ritter in his classic
nineteenth-century study of music in America, "it, at any
rate, can be heard for miles around."[9]

A pattern for the proper performance of serenades
quickly developed. Most bands hoped to take the honored
person by surprise, so the musicians tended to gather
quickly, usually under the cover of darkness. Forming a
circle near the targeted residence, the bandsmen would

launch into a rousing popular song to be followed, in quick succession, by one or two more selections. After this, if things had gone well, some acknowledgment of the musical efforts would customarily be made. If things had gone really well, the entire band would be invited indoors for refreshments and socializing.

Such a reward was just what the band from Climax, Michigan, had in mind one cold winter night in the 1880s. Eager to help a local couple celebrate their golden wedding anniversary and even more eager to share the food and drink at the party, the bandsmen set off for the appropriate farmhouse. One of the musicians recorded the details of their memorable serenade:

> The first note sounded fairly good, and some of the players were getting along according to the notes and signs by the way. Then something happened a little further along. The repeat sign was strictly observed by the good players. The others kept right on and lost their way after a few measures. Then it was decided it was best to go back to the beginning. After several wild signals the leader managed to induce a portion of the players to quit.
>
> The other players misunderstood the signals of distress from the leader and kept right on with the music until they reached the end. Then it was found that two players had been tooting what notes they could produce with all three piston-valves frozen solid. Several were all balled up about when to repeat and when to keep on going.[10]

Despite these problems, the serenade had a happy outcome. After attempting to play a few more notes the boys were invited in for the banquet where they "had a fine time at the table and went home late in fine spirits." But some of the problems these novices encountered could have been avoided altogether had they followed the sage advice of the guru of band etiquette, G. F. Patton. "If in a young Band there is any man who is known to be given

Dodworth's Band in New York formed the favored circle formation prior to serenading visitors at the Metropolitan Hotel in March 1860. Library of Congress.

to making mistakes, such as playing naturals for flats, losing the place etc. etc.," counseled Patton, "it will be best to let him 'play mute,' or carry a torch on all serenading expeditions, as the slightest discord comes out very distinctly in the still air of night." Patton continued, "It is well, in fact, to caution all men beforehand about their repeat signs, changes of Keys, and other points that might give [rise] to discords by being disregarded."

Other helpful hints on the art of serenading offered by Patton include:

The bells [of the instruments] should not be directed full against the windows.

Many musicians press into service a little boy or some other idle spectator to act as a music holder.

A serenading party . . . should always be careful to avoid injuring private premises, or trampling down flower beds and

Bands of Union and Confederate forces often serenaded officers, distinguished visitors, or each other during lulls in the fighting. Here a band entertains at the headquarters of General G. L. Hartstaff. Library of Congress.

shrubbery, and particularly to guard against smoking the walls or pillars of a gentleman's house or setting fire to it with their torches.[11]

Patton's detailed comments on the mechanics of brass band serenading were justified by the public's enthusiasm for the art form. Long before the Civil War, famous visitors such as dancer Fanny Elssler had enjoyed the private attentions of brass bands. And during the war regimental bands frequently serenaded officers, enlisted men, and even the enemy. By 1875, when Patton's guidebook for amateur bandsmen was published, serenading had become a common means for expressing goodwill toward newspaper editors, businessmen, political candidates, and other revered citizens. For professional bands, serenades provided an easy way to earn extra money with a modicum of effort. For amateur bands, which tended to be small and to have a limited repertoire, serenades were an ideal format for easing into the rigors of public performance.

It is a matter of record that not everyone so honored appreciated these musical gestures. The prominent citizens of Sacramento were so repelled by the discordant "soul distracting" serenades rendered by the local Chinese brass band that every time a performance was threatened, it became customary to pay the inept musicians fifty dollars *not* to play.[12] More commonly, the serenadees were enchanted by the attention. The following review, which describes a serenade presented in Garnavillo, Iowa, in March 1860, gives an idea of the popularity of this now all but forgotten concert setting.

The "German Brass Band" of this place were "out" on Thursday evening last. It was a clear moonlight night and all the peaceful inhabitants of Garnavillo were wrapped in the arms of Morpheus, for the time when ghosts are said to walk abroad had arrived, when suddenly a sound, as if from the trumpets of celestials, struck our ear so melodiously, so heavenly, that sleep was beyond expectation. We arose and looked out into the beautiful night, from our chamber window, and we heard that sound more distinctly. It apparently grew louder and louder. It reminded me of the stirring times of the revolution of Hungary of 1849, when at times, the victorious armies were returning and the anxious mothers and wives were tossing restlessly on their couch, and the sweet strains of music suddenly fell on their ear, telling them that their sons, their husbands, were returning. Oh how happy were they. . . .

We gazed and gazed; now at the dim and twinkling stars, then at the pale moon as she lit up the landscape before us, when we presently discovered that the music proceeded from the vicinity of Captain Reed's residence. And indeed, when we listened further, we were certain that the Germania Band was serenading the aged pioneer. The music must have awakened a pride in his heart, when he thought of the former condition of Prairie on which Garnavillo is located, and compared it to the lively and thrifty village of today.

Long may each member of the Band live to serenade such worthy citizens as Captain Reed, we muttered to ourself, as we sought the pillow and so undoubtedly spoke all that heard the delightful music.[13]

OUTDOOR CONCERTS

During the summer of 1907 a young girl from a small Illinois town visited the famous Bethesda Spring in Waukesha, Wisconsin. She bought a postcard depicting the spa's magnificent domed bandstand and sent the following message home: "We are sitting by the springs. This is a nice place. Band getting ready to play." Before mailing the card, her mother added a short note. "Will spend the day. It's swell here."

Without knowing it, these women captured the very essence of the period's outdoor band concerts: enjoyable music in an enjoyable setting. Although outdoor concerts could be held almost anywhere—on hotel balconies, railway platforms, or busy street corners—the more parklike and tranquil settings were clearly preferred. And the preferred setting within the park was the bandstand.

Bandstands came in many shapes and sizes, but the tendency in most localities was to start with simple structures. Some towns were so basic in their approach that they favored the use of temporary platforms ("one-night stands," architectural critic Horace Peaslee called them) that could be removed from public view when not in use. As late as the 1910s the Minneapolis Park System maintained a portable bandstand for its summer band concerts. Stored in a municipal building, the simple wooden plat-

Bandstands were found in every state of the Union in a wide variety of architectural styles. These three views illustrate a range from a simple open platform in West Wilton, New Hampshire, to an elaborate Victorian structure near Columbus, Ohio. Victorian bandstand photograph from the John Waldsmith Collection.

form was erected (at a cost of about fifteen dollars per setup) whenever and wherever the band needed it.

Less common, but more efficient, were temporary bandstands built on wheels. The Browningsville (Maryland) Cornet Band successfully used its bandwagon—a flatbed truck—as a portable bandstand. The bandsmen could drive the vehicle to any scenic spot, stop, and give a concert. In Lamoni, Iowa, a similar rolling bandstand was in regular use well into the twentieth century. Unlike the Browningsville truck, however, Lamoni's vehicle was a true bandstand that happened to be on wheels. Consisting of an eight-foot-square platform, it had a roof, handsomely turned pillars, and a wooden fence all around. At about five o'clock on the night of concerts, the bandstand was pulled by horses to the middle of the town square. One member of the band recalled that the musicians had to sit carefully on the bandstand during concerts or it would tip, but otherwise it functioned as well as the stationary pavilions.

Adequate as such arrangements were, a permanent bandstand had certain advantages, the most obvious being that it facilitated the presentation of concerts on a regular basis. More than that, a bandstand stood as a tangible symbol of a town's commitment to culture, and many municipalities were willing, even eager, to allocate land and money for the erection of these "temples of music."[14]

Such a structure did not have to cost much. The townspeople of Grafton, Vermont, spent a mere $8.13 to construct a sturdy, unroofed wooden platform in the middle of their town in 1902.[15] Then again, by spending a little more for a roof, some tasteful decoration, and perhaps the services of an architect, a town could create a showpiece. In the decades after the Civil War hundreds of American towns did just that, and the resulting pavilions

served as charming and useful summerhouses for the people.

In design these bandstands ranged from the austerely classical to the fancifully romantic. They were constructed of various combinations of wood, stone, cement, and iron. Consistent with their function of carrying music to the people, bandstands were open on all sides. Most commonly, they were built as round, octagonal, or square structures. But the gazebo erected on the grounds of the Jacksonville (Illinois) State Hospital in 1878–1879 was designed as an elongated rectangle to direct more of the music toward the long wings of the hospital building where the patients, who made up the audience, were located. Roofing, too, came in a delightful variety of configurations—from simple, flat tops to domes, gables, and cones. Atop these roofs were ornaments as varied as flagpoles, eagles, globes, cupolas, weathervanes, and an assortment of decorative finials. Most bandstands were raised above the ground to afford the spectators a better view, and many were raised high enough to have storage space (and, in later years, rest facilities) built underneath. Some pavilions had magnificent steps leading to the platform, some had elegant fencing, and some had ornate columns crowned by elaborate motifs. While most were designed to shelter a band of no more than about twenty players, the proportions were as variable as any other feature.[16]

Like the architectural style of these ornamental structures, the geographic placement of bandstands was a matter of choice, with the final decision resting on practical as well as aesthetic considerations. In many small towns, the bandstand was built near the intersection of several main thoroughfares. This position was favored because it was convenient for the citizens as well as conspicuous to visitors. Besides, before the days of heavy traffic, the distractions during concerts were minimal. Alternatively, for towns with large municipal squares, these centrally located expanses of open land were another logical place to build a bandstand. In many midwestern towns, the founders automatically laid out a square in the hope that their village would become the county seat. Since not every town could be so honored, the land that was saved for the courthouse was often turned over to the bandstand and other monuments.

As the park movement gained momentum toward the end of the nineteenth century, bandstands were increasingly nestled in the greenery of landscaped public gardens. "Music pavilions and concert courts should be considered as indispensable to all large parks," wrote landscape architect George Burnap in 1916,[17] and those who agreed with him created glorious little bandstands amidst decorative paths and vegetation. Water was especially attractive to bandstand builders, who regularly placed gazebos at the edges of lakes or above the sea at ocean resorts. The famous bandstand at Belle Isle Park in Detroit was ingeniously constructed on a bridge over the water so that the audience could either sprawl along the grassy banks or float languidly alongside the band in boats. Other bandstands were constructed to resemble islands in the water. Most such pavilions were connected to the shore by narrow bridges, but at Belle Isle Park in Oklahoma City the water-ringed bandstand was accessible only by boat. Some bands occasionally dispensed with the bandstand altogether and just played from a boat.

In addition to being scenic, a body of water near a bandstand helped carry the music to a larger audience. Most bandstands of the nineteenth century, however, were built with minimal consideration to acoustics, and

Bandstands near the water provided the dual advantage of reaching a larger audience (because of the great distance sound travels over water) while entertaining boaters. Many bandstands such as the one at East Lake Park, Los Angeles, California (top), were built on the shore. A few structures, including the famous island bandstand at Onondaga Park in Syracuse, New York, were in the middle of the lake and accessible only by boat.

The "band in a boat" must have been a fairly common event in nineteenth-century America, judging from the number of extant photographs. This view of a band on Echo Lake, Franconia Notch, New Hampshire, was taken by the famous Kilburn Brothers, stereoscopists of Littleton, ca. 1865.

Band shells presented a more formal and imposing setting for band concerts than the gazebo. The Mitchell Park bandstand in Milwaukee, with its manicured garden and Ionic columns, was particularly impressive.

this was a matter of concern to serious musicians. Contending that inferior bandstands affected both the repertoire and the performance quality of serious concert bands, professionals urged the adoption of such new designs as the semicircular bandstand, which directed the sound in one direction, and the niche or shell-type bandstand, which projected sound even more successfully.

To build a band shell was a major undertaking for a community. Generally standing twenty-five to thirty feet tall and containing as much as five to six hundred square feet of stage area, these stands were much bigger than the gazeboes. They were also more costly, with San Francisco's magnificent structure of the early twentieth century costing about one hundred thousand dollars. And if the architects made a mistake in erecting a band shell, as happened in Chicago, it was a major catastrophe. It cost the windy city eight thousand dollars to pick up the newly completed marble structure and turn it around when it was discovered that the sun shone in the musicians' eyes and the audience was blinded by the reflection of sunlight off the brass instruments.[18]

Despite these problems, band shells offered larger bands a chance to play effectively outdoors and thus they eventually became the favored structures for serious bandmasters. Although Americans were slower than Europeans to adopt this design, by 1915 shells were in use in such localities as Minneapolis, Minnesota, Williamsport, Pennsylvania, Los Angeles, California, St. Petersburg, Florida, and Salina, Kansas. At about the same time, many older, open pavilions were being removed from small towns because they had become easy, if inadvertent, targets for the fast-moving automobiles then taking to the roads. Thus, by the end of World War I, there was a shift in the style of building used for outdoor band concerts.

It was more than just an architectural trend. The newer, larger, and one-directional band shells curtailed that easy communication between audience and band that had long characterized American town band concerts. Setting the band so far above and apart from the audience, band shells symbolized the transformation of many bands in the early twentieth century from predominantly social organizations to more serious musical ensembles.

INDOOR CONCERTS

The indoor concert hall was one of the last places for many bands, particularly amateur ones, to perform. As a newspaper writer noted in 1857, "An indiscriminate crackling and tearing of bugles, trombones, and ophicleides, etc., may sound very well in the street, or off upon the water of a summer's night, but it requires great skill and control over the instruments to make them pleasant in a confined room."[19] It usually took considerable time and practice before a band was willing to make the attempt.

Once a band did decide to play indoors, there were any number of public halls that could house their performances. Churches, courthouses, town halls, and lyceum rooms were often used by bands before the Civil War. Later on, "opera houses"—those ubiquitous municipal theaters that cropped up in communities in the 1860s and 1870s—provided excellent accommodations. When various fraternal lodges erected their own meeting halls, these rooms too were utilized by performing groups including bands. Railroad depots, with their abundance of hard surfaces, were generally not suitable for band concerts, as Patrick Gilmore discovered when he tried to play in Chicago's newly built train station in June 1873. The three-hundred-piece band and the thousand singers assembled on this occasion produced, in one historian's words, nothing but "cracking, echoing discords" as the music bounced about inside the cavernous structure.[20]

Special celebrations sometimes required the construction of entirely new concert halls. Such was the case with the mammoth festival concerts choreographed by Patrick Gilmore in 1869 and 1872. For the first event, held to commemorate the coming of peace after the Civil War, a huge coliseum measuring five hundred by three hundred feet was constructed in Boston's St. James Park. With such dimensions, however, it is debatable whether this building qualifies as an indoor setting.[21]

The logistics of hiring concert halls were sometimes complicated. Professional bands usually employed experienced managers to make the proper arrangements, but amateur bands generally had to handle things on their own. In a typical agreement, the Belfast (Maine) Band contracted with the local opera house in 1900 to give six concerts one and a half hours each in return for which the managers of the hall would provide advertising, tickets, and a clean, heated, and well-lighted theater. Profits would be divided equally between the bandsmen and the opera house management, all of whom pledged to do their utmost to sell tickets. Other bands were occasionally required to pay a flat fee to rent the hall, and they had to hope they would make enough in ticket sales to cover this expense. Certainly the intricacies of these arrangements were one reason why inexperienced bands were slow to take their acts to the indoor concert stage. Yet many groups did so, especially during the winter months when the usual outdoor band activities were curtailed.

ACCOMPANIMENTS

That brass bands could easily capture and hold the undivided attention of the public was proven time and again

The Grand Ball of November 1863 at the New York Academy of Music featured both string orchestra and brass band. These ensembles would alternate selections, providing continuous music throughout a long evening's festivities. Library of Congress.

during the nineteenth century. But these versatile musical ensembles could also provide muted background music for people engaged in a variety of diversions. How delicately a band played was a matter of experience, but the accompaniment role was a common one for most bands. Ice skating and roller skating, for instance, frequently were enhanced by brass bands. In addition, the use of band music for dancing not only was widespread, but was the conventional method of employing bands during the winter months when open-air performances were sporadic. Bands played while people ate dinner, engaged in athletic competitions, and received diplomas. Bands also accompanied such dramatic presentations as tableaux vivants, panoramas, and fencing matches. The promenade concert was nothing more than a band playing while people walked about and talked.

In order to play on these varied occasions the bandsmen went wherever the action was taking place. If given a choice, the favored destination would probably have been an "excursion party." Frequently sponsored by railroad companies and steamship lines, these popular outings featured music, refreshments, and good fellowship along with a journey to a scenic spot. "A delightful sail through the most picturesque portion of Lake Champlain," claimed an advertising poster for a combined railroad and steamer voyage in 1895. Only slightly less prominently featured on the poster was the notice, "Band concert will be given, and refreshments served on the [steamer] both on the going and returning trip."[22]

Bandsmen understandably enjoyed providing the music for such expeditions. Even if the trip entailed nothing more than a local club's outing to a neighboring town, the bandsmen were, in a sense, being paid to have fun. The St. Albans (Vermont) Brigade Band, like many other instrumental ensembles of the day, frequently accepted

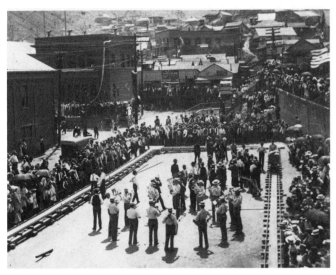

On the Fourth of July, ca. 1895, the Copper Queen Band of Bisbee, Arizona, played for an ore car loading competition in the middle of town. The musician just to the right of center on the far side of the circle is playing a double-bell euphonium, an instrument first introduced in America in about 1890. Arizona Historical Society.

invitations to participate in such excursions, as the band's record book for 1891 reveals:

> June 23: Band went to Farnham with Montcalm Club.
> July 2: Band went to Missisquoi Park with Sunday Schools.
> July 4: Band went to Rutland with Burlington Firemen.
> July 17: Band excursion to Providence Island.
> August 19: At Bennington with Knights Templar.

Up to this point the St. Albans records are nothing more than a dry and factual recounting of the band's activities. But their excursion with the Knights was apparently so

WORCESTER SKATING RINK.

Wednesday Eve'g, Feb. 6, 1884.

First Grand Excursion of the Season

FROM PROVIDENCE,

Accompanied by WHITE'S MILITARY BAND, who will give a GRAND CONCERT on the Skating Surface at 8.30 o'clock, assisted by

Signora BARRATTA MORGAN, Soprano.

PROGRAMME.

1. MARCH,	- -	"De Molay,"	- - - *Cappa.*
2. OVERTURE,	-	"Semiramide,"	- - *Rossini.*
3. VOCAL SELECTIONS,	-	- - - - - -
	Signora Barratta Morgan.		
4. SELECTIONS,	"Remembrance of Myerbeer,"		*Godfrey.*
5. CLARIONET SOLO,	"8th Air Varié,"	-	*Bresseant.*
	Mr. Ed. S. Onione.		
6. WALTZ,	-	"Dreams of Childhood,"	- *Waldtefelt.*

Doors open at 7. Skating at 7.30. Concert at 8.30.
After which general Skating until 11 o'clock.

CONTINUOUS MUSIC FOR SKATING.
NO CHANGE IN PRICES.

February 9, Afternoon and Evening,
Profs. ROURKE and ALLISON.
February 22, OLD FOLKS' PARTY.

83

The Worcester Brass Band, the Worcester Cadet Band, and White's Military Band all played for roller skating at the Worcester Skating Rink during the season of 1884. Band concerts on the skating surface were interspersed with the skating sessions.

enjoyable that the normally reticent band secretary felt compelled to add, "Had a good time."[23]

ILLUMINATION

Band performances in any of these settings were impressive, but if held at night, in the glow of artificial illumination, the effect was often breathtaking. Nighttime political parades or torchlight processions, in which the marchers and the crowd milled together in dramatic lights and shadows, had particular appeal. As an avid student of Maine's musical development recalls, such parades featured:

> . . . numberless lighted transparences [sic], revealing the sentiments of opposing political factions. [The signs] were borne aloft, and as the band, in passing, played inspiritingly and the local drum corps drummed thrillingly, they were greeted with unrepressed cheering from those gathered on the doorsteps and balconies of houses, the windows of which were illuminated with scores of flickering candles, while red fire burned at irregular intervals on the curbstones of the sidewalks along the line of march and brilliantly tinted sputtering stars shot fitfully into the air from numberless roman candles.[24]

Band concerts were also frequently held outdoors after dark, and serenades were by definition evening affairs.

The lighting for indoor concerts conformed to typical patterns of lighting of the day, but a wide range of devices were necessary to furnish adequate light for these nocturnal performances held outdoors. Huge quantities of candles, often in combination with coal oil or gas lamps, were placed around the bands as they played on the local village greens. For parades, bands recruited assistants to carry portable lamps hung on long, swinging handles beside the musicians as they marched along. Pitch torches,

though considered a nuisance by some bandsmen, were also employed for evening performances. At a huge torchlight procession held in Atlanta, Georgia, in honor of President Grover Cleveland, there were reportedly ten thousand torches used to light the way as two bands and members of militia units marched through the city's streets.[25]

To supplement these lighting arrangements, the musicians often carried their own individual band lamps. Available during the last quarter of the nineteenth century for about forty cents each, these lamps could be attached to the men's caps in place of the pompom or plume. When filled with kerosene or a mixture of kerosene and lard oil, the lamps furnished a bright light for up to four hours.

For serenading parties, in which the element of surprise was usually paramount, G. F. Patton recommended yet another method of illumination—the fireball. Created by soaking fist-sized wads of cotton in coal oil, these devices were designed to be carried unlighted in a wire basket to the proper house. Then, when the band was in position and ready to play, the fireballs were ignited; in an instant, a blaze of bright light would envelope the band.[26]

Near the end of the nineteenth century advances in the field of electric lighting affected the band world. An arc lamp, the simplest electric lighting device, was used to light the bandstand at Cape May in 1882, just five years after the first public exhibition of arc lighting in the United States and just two years after Madison Square Garden used the mechanism for the first time. About the same time, Thomas Edison was busy working on incandescent lamps. Because of their relatively small cost and simplicity, these devices superseded arc lamps on bandstands as well as in concert halls all over the country. As early as February 1883, the Haverhill (Massachusetts)

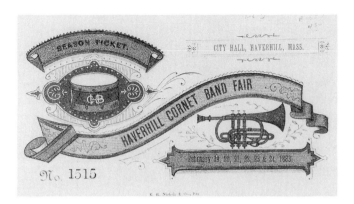

Technology and bands went hand in hand in nineteenth-century America. Celebrations of new buildings, bridges, railroads, and electric lighting required the music of the band.

Cornet Band played a series of concerts in a hall that was, as the tickets proudly proclaimed, "brilliantly illuminated with the electric light for the first time." Citizens of Rochester, Indiana, were so enthusiastic about such lighting that when they built their new bandstand in 1911, they covered the roof with strings of light bulbs that glimmered brightly against the night sky.

By 1895, many instrument companies were offering bandsmen battery-operated band lamps that were vast improvements on the earlier fuel-burning models. "Something neat! Something new! Something novel!" was how the C. G. Conn Company introduced their product.[27] The Conn lamp was easily attached to the cap while the battery pack could be comfortably slung over the shoulder. Best of all, it would last for ten hours without new batteries and was "perfectly safe under all circumstances."

Such progress was commendable but, in a curious way, dangerous. As newspaper editors were constantly pointing out, too much light would ruin the mood for the audience. On the other hand, too little light could make it difficult for the musicians to play. The sudden loss of electricity was a problem that plagued the Sousa Band often enough that, according to Frank Simon, the men memorized "El Capitan" and "The Stars and Stripes Forever" and played these pieces automatically whenever darkness threatened to end a concert.[28] It was a question of balance, and local communities worked long and hard to devise nighttime band settings that had the proper blend of romanticism and practicality.

BANDWAGONS

Bandwagons, desirable pieces of equipment for any active local band, provided an ever-popular setting for band music. In addition to transporting bandsmen, these carriages served the no less important purpose of adding drama and excitement to band performances. As a bandsman from Salem, North Carolina, recalled, it was a thrill when the bandwagon "with high springs and gaily painted body . . .[and] with the band riding high and playing its best on Washington's birthday, passed up and down the street."[29] In Salem, as in other towns, youngsters could always be found running happily after this marvelous vehicle.

Salem's bandwagon was constructed from the remains of a Yankee army wagon that had been abandoned after the Civil War. Rebuilt, repainted, and hitched to six horses, it made a striking appearance in local parades. Even more impressive were the fancy wagons designed and constructed especially for the use of bandsmen. In 1856, just two years after its founding, the Tallmadge (Ohio) Cornet Band commissioned the manufacture of a "suitable" carriage by the Oviatt and Sperry Carriage

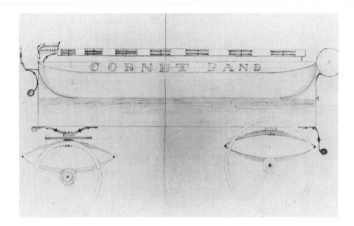

The Tallmadge (Ohio) Cornet Band paid two hundred and fifty dollars for an elegant new bandwagon in 1856. The money was raised by subscription from among the coal mining town's two thousand residents. When the Tallmadge Band was discontinued in 1866, the bandwagon was sold to the nearby town of Solon. Tallmadge Historical Society.

Works. Long, sleek, and beautifully balanced, this vehicle conveyed the Tallmadge musicians in comfort and luxury until they disbanded in 1866. The Hereford (Pennsylvania) Cornet Band, too, had a splendid bandwagon. Their vehicle, like many commercial wagons at the turn of the century, boasted a roof, a step for easy access, and sunshades that could be lowered as needed. The name of the band was painted in handsome letters on the side of the wagon, as well as on the bass drum which was displayed conspicuously at the vehicle's rear.

Circus bandwagons were essential for generating public interest in the shows and were among the most magnificent bandwagons of all. Brightly painted and often sculpted with scrolls and curlicues, these wagons were

Top: *A team of four plumed horses pulled the Plymouth (Michigan) bandwagon in 1868. The ten-member brass band played over-shoulder instruments, typical of town bands that doubled as state militia units of the time. Michigan State Archives.* Bottom: *This women's band decorated a simple wagon for use as the bandwagon on a patriotic holiday. The location of this event, illustrated on a ca. 1910 postcard, is not known.*

typically decorated with a gallimaufry of cupids, wild animals, and mythical beasts. American author William Dean Howells recalled in his autobiography that when a circus visited his hometown of Hamilton, Ohio, he saw two resplendent chariots. One carried the band and was pulled by eighteen piebald horses. The other wagon, which held some of the juvenile performers, was shaped like a giant seashell and was led by a team of Shetland ponies. "I do not really know how boys live through the wonder and the glory of such a sight," exclaimed Howells who remembered the circus wagons long years after they had left town.[30]

For bands that could not afford luxurious vehicles, there were alternatives. Simple wooden wagons could be constructed at minimal expense. Or, as many towns discovered, ordinary farm wagons, hay racks, or lumber carts could be readily adapted for use by bands. In 1906 the Grafton (Vermont) Cornet Band acquired a used wagon for thirty-five dollars, and it served the band for many years. Leased wagons, especially if decorated with bunting, flags, and a sign with the band's name, could also serve a band just as well as a wagon purchased out-right.

Most towns had one band and, if they were lucky, one bandwagon. Things were different in Rochester, Indiana, in the late 1860s. Owing to the divergent political views of the local bandsmen, there evolved two bands—the Union Band and the Democratic Band. As bandmaster William Rannells recalls in his history of the town's brass bands, there were also two glorious bandwagons and much excitement.

According to Rannells, the Union Band conceived the idea of a bandwagon first. Believing that such a vehicle would eliminate the necessity of marching in knee-deep mud on Main Street or on the noisy plank sidewalks,

The Maineville (Ohio) Sax Horn Band, ca. 1860, was beautifully outfitted with the latest in upright and bell-front instruments, fancy hats, and a gaily painted bandwagon. The percussion section, as usual, was prominently situated at the rear of the vehicle. Cincinnati Historical Society.

these bandsmen hired some carpenters to build a suitable wagon. "If it was not grand it certainly was a wonderful creation," writes Rannells. He continues the description:

It was so high they used a ladder to get in and out of it. As the band used over-shoulder horns, lead horns and all down to the bass horn, which was six feet long, they would extend considerably above the top of the wagon, and when all the boys were in it would resemble a great pipe-organ of a new pattern, but did not imitate one in sound.[31]

Not to be outdone, the Democratic Band decided they also needed a bandwagon. Luckily, they were able to buy a used circus wagon which was, in Rannells's view, a "gorgeous affair." It was

built very low in the center and high at front and back ends, an imitation of large golden dragons or serpents, with heads and tails up, mouths wide open, large teeth and fiery tongues protruding. The driver's seat was between the heads of the dragons, the body coiling up and down formed seats for the players, the tails turned up, with canopy top, for the drummers.[32]

Merely owning these wonderful wagons was not enough for the Rochester music men. They had to show off for the local populace, who were undoubtedly astonished at what took place next.

It was difficult to determine which wagon caused the greatest sensation. . . . They hitched from four to six horses (according to mud) to the band wagon and drove up and down town, Main street being about the only street passible when wet and it none too good. I think "Jap" True drove the Union wagon and I know "Bill" Hollman was driver on the dragon. "Jap" was a good driver but owing to the height of the wagon, could not drive very fast on account of upsetting. "Bill" Hol[l]man owned a livery barn from which he would

take six horses, hitch up to the dragons, take a couple of drinks or more, and drive up and down Main street as fast as the horses could go, turning on the run. That was the time for the musicians to get nervous. He could not upset, for the wagon was low down and heavy. I think he paid three fines in succession for fast driving. The marshal would march him up to the "Squire's" office, he would pay the fine, get on the wagon and start off on the run and they would "yank" him up again before the "Squire." The second time, he said he would pay another, for he was not done driving yet. I do not remember if the boys played while driving or not, but think some did. Al Pugh says he went in the wagon with the band to play at Peru, and after getting back was glad to take his meals standing up. No springs on the wagon and he had to carry a six-foot tuba horn.[33]

As Rannells's lively memoir points out, bandwagons sometimes caused problems, not the least of which were the injuries inflicted on bandsmen's spines, backsides, and—if they played while in motion—lips. More serious injuries resulted from occasional accidents as when the Myersville (Maryland) Band's wagon overturned on the way home from a Sunday school picnic. Fortunately, only a few of the men were hurt and the instruments, which suffered much more damage, were soon repaired by the local tinsmith. The horses that were required to pull the wagons could be somewhat of a nuisance too. It cost the bands some of their hard-earned money to hire and care for their teams, and at least one town band ultimately requested "horse keeping" as part of their standard fee for playing out-of-town celebrations.[34]

In spite of such problems, bandwagons continued to be a favored setting for bands. For small bands, the bandwagon fostered unity among bandsmen and became, in a sense, an extension of the band uniform. When motorcars came into vogue during the second decade of the twen-

The musicians of the Marinette (Wisconsin) Band employed an open truck at their Fourth of July appearance, ca. 1915. Note the photographer perched on the front of the vehicle.

tieth century, many bands began to use automobiles and trucks for transport. These vehicles, too, were decorated and became a source of pride to the musicians. The popular expression "get on the bandwagon" is an appropriate reminder of the esteem accorded these historic conveyances.

CODA

Like curios on the shelves of an antique store, bandwagons, old bandstands, and the images of bygone parades and concerts have an innate appeal. Yet their importance to the study of the history of the American band movement goes far beyond antiquarian interest. Taken together, the manifold settings of band concerts serve to underscore the important fact that the band movement was not just a musical phenomenon. Consider that the various settings for band performances were usually chosen more for their atmosphere than for any musical reason. To us, bandstands may seem charming, serenades romantic, and Independence Day parades inspiring—and this is exactly how they seemed to our forebears. The settings were devised for the enjoyment not just of the music but of the entire scene. Consider, too, that these settings affected the very instrumentation and repertoire of the bands. If, as bandsmen of the nineteenth century claimed, bands had a profound cultural influence on society, it is equally true that society had a profound effect on bands. Nowhere is this influence more forcefully demonstrated than in band performance settings, creations clearly molded according to the tastes of the people.

5.
TOOLS OF THE TRADE

What triumph of Art, seems more wonderful than this?—
that fifteen men with instruments of music as different as
their own faces, can produce such perfect harmony of
sweet sounds, that each seems part of all?

—*Minnesota Pioneer*, January 30, 1850

What is a band? We have avoided offering a precise definition because the concept of a band has varied widely and changed over time. We use the terms brass band, military band, wind band, band of music, and band all in all, according to the custom of the nineteenth century. The meaning of "band" at any given time and place depended primarily on the type and number of instruments. What were the instruments and instrumentation patterns used in these versatile musical ensembles of the street corner and concert hall?

The composition of America's bands requires close examination because of two interrelated circumstances. First, numerous and intriguing brass and woodwind instruments were invented and improved during the nineteenth century. Equally important, bandleaders—both by choice and by necessity—experimented widely with these inventions and willingly utilized them in new and unusual combinations as they organized performing ensembles and arranged the music for these groups to play.

Bands were called upon to celebrate many things in America, but their very existence was, in a sense, a celebration of progress in instrument-building technologies.

TYPES OF BAND INSTRUMENTS

The Brass

The most striking changes in instrument technology between 1800 and 1900—indeed, the changes that opened up the band world to amateur players—took place within the brass family.[1] To understand the evolution of brass instruments, it is necessary to understand how different pitches are produced. The pitch sounded by a brasswind is determined both by the length of the tube and by the tension of the player's lips. For a tube of fixed length, such as a Boy Scout bugle, the familiar harmonic series typical of bugle-call notes may be produced. If the intermediate pitches are desired, then a method must be devised for changing the length of the tube while it is played.

Photographs of keyed bugle players are relatively uncommon because the instrument was losing favor to valved brass in the 1850s, approximately the time when early photographic methods were first widely used in America. This 1863 ferrotype shows an unidentified American musician with a fine eleven-key instrument.

Three distinctive types of mechanisms—the slide, the side hole, and the valve—were developed to accomplish this task.

The simple slide, as incorporated in the slide trombone, is perhaps the oldest method of producing a chromatic brass instrument, that is, an instrument that can play all the half steps of the chromatic scale. Slides were applied to both soprano and bass brass prior to 1800, but for a number of technical reasons slides were neither well suited to nor widely used in trumpets and other small, high-pitched brass. An important limitation of slide brass was that a significant portion of the instrument had to have a straight, cylindrical bore; the gradually tapering, conical bores of French horns and saxhorns were not compatible with slide technology.

A second method for changing the effective length of brass instruments is the opening and closing of holes along the instrument's length. This principle, applied to woodwinds for centuries, was not widely introduced to the brass family until the early nineteenth century when the keyed bugle and its larger relative, the ophicleide, were first introduced. These novel members of the brass family revolutionized wind band music because a loud brass instrument could, for the first time, carry any melody.

At about the same time as the keyed brass were gaining general acceptance, significant metallurgical developments in the construction of airtight valves were ensuring their demise. A remarkable variety of valved windways were developed throughout the middle of the nineteenth century, and by 1860 both piston valves (especially in France and England) and rotary valves (in Central Europe and the United States) were in widespread use. The keyed brass suffered because they were awkward to play, uneven

A small street band, ca. 1850, retained keyed brass—a keyed bugle and an ophicleide—along with a clarinet, valved tenor horn, and trombone. Though warmly dressed, the group posed indoors in a stereoscopist's studio for this photograph.

Prior to the Civil War, most bands had adopted all-valved brass instruments in preference to keyed bugles and ophicleides. The nine brass players in this unidentified American ensemble, ca. 1860, played an interesting assortment of bell-up, bell-front, circular, and over-shoulder rotary valve instruments.

in tone, and easily rendered unplayable by minor mishaps such as a slightly bent key. Valved brass overcame all these deficiencies: they were simple to finger, more even-toned from the bottom to the top of the range, and durable under the stressful conditions of outdoor parades and performances. Pre–1860 photographic images of bands and bandsmen reveal that the keyed bugle and ophicleide were almost completely supplanted by valved brass prior to the Civil War.

The nomenclature of valved brass instruments is confusing. The principal variables include the total length of tubing, the shape of the wound tubing, the direction of the bell, the valve or key or slide system employed, and

the taper of the bore. Brass band instruments used in America prior to 1900 came in five common lengths, and the main designation of any brass instrument usually depended on this length. The shortest instruments, pitched in E-flat, were only about forty inches long and were called sopranos. The alto instruments (also referred to as sopranos after the Civil War) were constructed from fifty-five-inch-long tubes and were pitched in B-flat, just as are most modern band trumpets and cornets. The E-flat altos or tenors filled the middle registers of the band, with tubing about seven feet in length. Like modern trombones and baritone horns, the tenor and baritone members of the brass family were pitched in B-flat with a

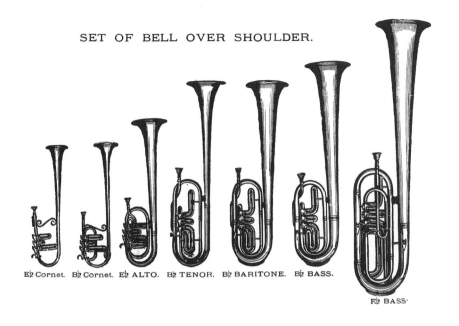

SET OF BELL OVER SHOULDER.

E♭ Cornet. B♭ Cornet. E♭ ALTO. B♭ TENOR. B♭ BARITONE. B♭ BASS.

E♭ BASS·

SET OF BELL UP.
Celebrated French Piston Valves, with Improved Light Action.

B♭ CORNET. E♭ CORNET.

E♭ ALTO. B♭ TENOR. B♭ BARITONE. B♭ BASS. E♭ BASS.

Valved brass instruments were sold in sets of seven basic sizes, from the E-flat soprano to the E-flat bass. The B-flat tenor, baritone, and bass instruments were all constructed from about nine feet of tubing, but they differed in the diameter of tubing and flare of the bell. These illustrations from the 1881 Lyon and Healy catalog show the rotary valve over-shoulder instruments that were popular during the Civil War and the piston valve bell-front and bell-up designs that became the norm by the late 1880s.

length close to nine feet, while the thirteen-foot E-flat bass or tuba, exactly four times as long as the E-flat soprano, was the lowest of brasses in most nineteenth-century ensembles.

Among the significant changes in band instrumentation that occurred in the first decades of the twentieth century was the abandonment of the E-flat soprano brass in favor of the B-flat soprano instruments. At about the same time the E-flat tuba was being replaced by the larger, eighteen-foot long BB-flat (bass B-flat) tuba in many bands. To be sure, brass instruments were not restricted to the E-flat/B-flat lengths common in American bands. Many instruments, especially cornets, were produced in C, or church pitch, so that instrumentalists could read piano or vocal music without the need to transpose notes. Instruments in other keys were also manufactured for special purposes, but the vast majority of brass instruments in bands conformed to the simple E-flat/B-flat pattern.

After the length, the characteristics of the bore (or taper) are next most important in defining the type of brass instrument. Trombones and pre–1920 trumpets are, for the most part, cylindrical-bore brass with most of the instrument's length composed of straight pipe. The resulting tone is often described as brilliant or penetrating. In contrast, the flugelhorn or bugle and to some extent the French horn are conical-bore brass, with a much more mellow, soft tone. The tuba and euphonium are common modern terms for the bass and baritone members, respectively, of this conical-bore group. Intermediate in bore characteristics are the cornets (*not* "coronets"), which incorporate both cylindrical and conical tubing. All gradations exist between straight and conical-bore instruments, and it is difficult to assign a definitive name (e.g., flugelhorn *versus* cornet *versus* trumpet) to every instrument. Adding to this confusion was the indiscriminate

The McGibeny Family Band of Philadelphia employed three "helicon" or circular-form instruments (an E-flat alto, B-flat tenor, and B-flat bass) in their act. Helicons found special favor with horse-mounted bands and with small children because they were easier to carry than conventional upright-bell models.

use of the name "cornet" for virtually any high-pitched, valved brass instrument.

A bewildering variety of shape names, trade names, and other descriptive terms in English, French, German, and Italian adds intensity to this already complex system of nomenclature. Instruments could be wound so that the bell faced forward, backward, straight up, or at an angle; thus, typical instrument names include the bell-front or solo alto, the over-shoulder tuba, the upright tenor horn, and the circular cornet. Alto horns wound in circular form were called concert horns or mellophones and served as a simplified French horn substitute. Tubas in circular

In 1915 the tuba section of the Sousa Band, shown here in front of a C. G. Conn Company sales office, used both conventional upright-bell tubas and an original form of the sousaphone with upright bell (affectionately called "raincatchers" by instrument sellers and performers alike).

form were referred to as helicons, raincatchers, or sousaphones depending on how the tubing was coiled.

Nomenclature also depended on mechanisms employed. The ophicleide, trombone, and baritone are all names for the B-flat baritone instrument, but with keys, a slide, or valves, respectively. Enterprising musical instrument makers introduced sets of matched brass and gave them personalized names. For example, Adolphe Sax, the famed Belgian instrument maker who eventually settled in Paris, produced a fine group of upright, conical-bore, valved brass instruments he called Saxhorns, in accord with nomenclature introduced by several other European

Louis Schreiber of New York was one of many instrument makers who devised his own distinctive brass design. Schreiber horns, with their characteristic tear-drop shape, never attained widespread popularity and relatively few instruments were sold before Schreiber turned primarily to sales of imported Besson instruments. This ferrotype of an unknown bandsman was taken ca. 1870.

instrument makers and dealers. The designation gained widespread use and "saxhorn brass bands" were common in the decades prior to the Civil War. Other matched families of brass instruments, including Antoniophones and Schreiber horns, made brief and less successful appearances.

As brass instrument makers honed their technical skills, a number of remarkable hybrid instruments were introduced to take advantage of characteristics of two contrasting bores or lengths. The double-bell euphonium, for example, combined a cylindrical-bore valve trombone with a conical-bore baritone. The musician could use this odd-looking beast as either valve trombone or baritone by the simple press of a valve. A number of complex solo pieces were written to take advantage of the striking effects produced when the two bells were employed in rapid succession. A similar technology was employed in the echo bell cornet, which had one normal bell and one specially designed bell that produced a distant echo effect. This instrument was, for a brief time at the turn of the century, a popular solo instrument as well. Of more lasting significance was the combination of two different lengths of tubing into one instrument, thus providing a wider range of low notes or greater security for high notes. The modern double French horn incorporates this practical feature, which had previously been applied to the baritone and bass range of saxhorns.

The Woodwinds

In contrast to the brass, with their rapid succession of radical technological innovations, the woodwinds underwent little fundamental change in the nineteenth century. Wind instrument makers focused on two problems: the improvement of key and fingering systems, and the de-

velopment of complete families of tonally matching soprano to bass woodwinds.[2]

Flutes. Transverse flutes—including the flute, piccolo, and fife—were employed in American bands throughout the nineteenth and twentieth centuries. Each of these instruments is sounded by directing a stream of air across a hole in the side of the tube. The pitch is varied by opening or closing finger holes along the tube's length, as well as by increasing or decreasing the velocity of the air stream. Most flutes have a slightly tapered bore about ¾ inch in diameter and a length of about 26½ inches. Piccolos are usually half this length with a somewhat conical bore. The fife is a small cylindrical flute, commonly pitched a tone one-third or one-fourth lower than the piccolo.

Throughout much of the nineteenth century the key and fingering systems of these instruments were not standardized. Early in the century the common one-key style was gradually supplanted by more sophisticated systems of from four to eight keys. Perhaps the greatest revolution in flute and piccolo design was the introduction of the novel key system of Théobald Boehm, an accomplished Munich flute player and skilled craftsman. In the early 1830s Boehm applied and improved a mechanism of horizontal axle rods that guide a sequence of key covers and key rings. This device resulted in the simple and versatile Boehm system of fingering still in use today.

In spite of Boehm's revolutionary improvements, earlier patterns of flutes and piccolos persisted for many decades, especially in amateur musical groups. As late as 1895 major band instrument dealers offered flutes of one, four, and five keys, while six- and eight-key "old-style" instruments persisted well into the twentieth century. Numerous different flute models resulted from the combination of the varied key systems with a plethora of construction materials, including boxwood, rosewood, cocuswood, ivory, silver, and gold. In 1900, for example, J. W. Pepper of Philadelphia was typical of large instrument companies in offering ninety-six models of flutes ranging in price from sixty-seven cents to one hundred fifty-three dollars.[3]

Fifes were less varied than flutes or piccolos, and a single pattern served most musicians throughout the brass band era. The typical military fife was a cylindrical wooden tube pitched in B-flat or A-flat with six open holes and protective metal ferrules at either end. Most instruments were constructed without any keys. Several fifes were often combined in fife and drum corps, but a single fife was occasionally used in combination with brass and winds in the band to provide a bright tone color in the upper register.

Clarinets. The clarinet is a single-reed, cylindrical-bore instrument with a flared bell. The simplest type, which was frequently employed in American bands during the first half of the nineteenth century, was constructed in several boxwood sections with ivory or bone protective rings and five brass keys. Early photographs indicate that five-key or six-key instruments were favored by American amateur clarinetists at least until the 1850s, even though more expensive models with as many as thirteen keys in a variety of fingering systems were available by the 1830s. Eventually, the great technical advantages of these more elaborate clarinets were generally accepted. Of special significance was the thirteen-key system devised by Ivan Müller of Paris. The Müller system, though modified and refined by Eugène Albert of Brussels and other instrument makers, was the basic pattern employed by most American bandsmen throughout the second half of the nine-

The shipboard band of the battleship USS Delaware *(BB28) included four B-flat clarinets and one E-flat clarinet, along with brass and percussion. This photographic postcard was taken shortly after the vessel's commissioning on February 6, 1909.*

teenth century. In fact, the thirteen-key Albert system instrument remained the favored band clarinet until well into the twentieth century, even though the more modern Boehm fingering system had become widely adopted among symphonic musicians.

Most nineteenth-century bands that included clarinets incorporated soprano instruments pitched in B-flat or E–flat. As the average size of American bands expanded towards the end of the century, an effort was made to include entire families of matching wind instruments; thus, the alto and bass clarinet occasionally found a place in the band.

Saxophones. Saxophones are conical-bore, single-reed instruments constructed out of metal and furnished with keys to effect pitch changes. Unlike most other woodwinds, saxophones were designed almost from their inception as a matched family of instruments available in seven sizes from the sopranino in high E-flat or F, to the contrabass (fully eight times as long) in E-flat or F. American saxophones for band use were almost always pitched in the E-flat and B-flat sequence of the brasswinds, though some F and C instruments also exist.

Saxophones were employed in French military bands shortly after the production in the 1840s of the first Parisian instruments by Adolphe Sax. It was half a century later before they began to appear with any regularity in the larger American ensembles. Patrick Gilmore did include a quartet of saxophones in his band of the 1870s, and Sousa's preferred Marine Band instrumentation of the 1880s did the same, but these large professional bands were the exception rather than the rule. Saxophones were not even illustrated in some American musical instrument catalogs of the 1880s, and when they did appear they were given minimal space in sections separate from the

ILLUSTRATIONS
OF
SAXOPHONES AND BASSOON.

FOR DESCRIPTIONS AND PRICES SEE OPPOSITE PAGE.

No. 10.   No. 12.

No. 16.   No. 14.   BASSOON. No. 1.

Lyon and Healy, who offered soprano, alto, tenor, and baritone saxophones in 1881, was one of the first American companies to illustrate this woodwind family in sales catalogs. Both the saxophones and the bassoons were imported from France.

featured brass band instruments. The scores of commercially available band music, in conjunction with contemporary photographic evidence, indicate that it was not until the first decade of the twentieth century that the distinctive tonal qualities of saxophones in alto E-flat and tenor B-flat—and less commonly in soprano B-flat or baritone E-flat—were widely accepted in American bands. By the early 1920s, however, the saxophone had come into its own. With the advent of jazz and other changes in popular music, the saxophone generated an enthusiasm that bordered on the hysterical. In consequence, saxophones outsold every other type of instrument between 1921 and 1924.

Double Reeds. Double-reed instruments, including the oboe, the bassoon, and the sarrusophone family, experienced sporadic usage in American bands. Before the development of keyed brass, oboes and bassoons were the loudest of the chromatic wind instruments. Thus, in spite of considerable difficulties in mastering these temperamental double-reed instruments, bassoons were commonplace and oboes not uncommon in wind bands at the beginning of the nineteenth century. With the invention of new technologies for brass, however, these woodwinds were gradually supplanted by the more forceful and durable keyed and valved members of the brass family.

With the exception of the largest professional bands, double reeds did not reappear in American bands until the late nineteenth century. At that time the traditional band instruments, oboe and bassoon, were challenged by a relatively new family of conical-bore, metal-body, double reeds—the sarrusophone family. Sarrusophones, like saxophones, were conceived as a matched set of woodwinds with uniform tone color from the sopranino in E-flat to the contrabass in BB-flat. Originally envisioned by

a French bandmaster named Sarrus, the first instruments were constructed in the 1850s by the Parisian maker P. L. Gautrot as substitutes for other double reeds in bands.

Sarrusophones begin to appear in larger American bands at about the same time that oboes and bassoons returned. Rather than employ the complete sarrusophone family, however, American practice was to include oboe and bassoon as the soprano and tenor double reeds, while using one contrabass E-flat sarrusophone to fill out the lower register. This practice was formalized in 1918, when the instrumentation of a "regulation" U.S. Army regimental band included two oboes, two bassoons, and a contrabass sarrusophone.[4]

The Percussion

Percussion instruments underwent only minor changes in design and technology throughout the nineteenth and early twentieth centuries. Three basic instruments—the small drum, bass drum, and cymbals—provided virtually all the necessary percussion for bands.[5]

The snare drum or side drum was a fixture of bands. A wooden or metal cylinder formed the body of the instrument. During the third quarter of the nineteenth century most side drums were about a foot deep and sixteen inches in diameter. Later, smaller drums of an approximate eight- to ten-inch depth were used with greater frequency, and some concert bands even adopted the lighter, crisper sound of the orchestral snare drum, which was only six inches deep. Calfskin or sheepskin heads were stretched across the body's two open ends and were held in place by wooden or metal hoops. The assembly of two hoops, two heads, and body was firmly held together by a lacework of ropes or by metal rods. Tension on the drumheads could be adjusted by leather braces or ears on the rope lacing, or by screws on the metal rods. The bottom

The percussion section of a small amateur band, including snare drum, cymbals, and bass drum, is featured in this ca. 1880 ferrotype. The image is believed to have been taken at a Decoration Day ceremony in Maryland. William T. Hassett, Jr., Collection.

100

or snare head of the drum was fitted with several strands of catgut, rawhide, or metal. These strands were kept taut against the snare head and thus produced the characteristic crisp timbre of the drum. Snare drums were played with a pair of wooden sticks similar in size and shape to those employed today.

The bass drum was virtually identical to the side drum in construction, with a body about two feet deep and up to three feet in diameter. Most bass drums were constructed with a wooden body and hoops, though metal drums—including novel collapsible models, ideal for the traveling band—were introduced in the late nineteenth century. The large drumheads provided a perfect surface for publicity, and most bands painted their name, town, and perhaps a decorative emblem on the head. Prior to the 1880s bass drumsticks were made of wood, sometimes with buckskin-covered heads. Later, drumbeaters with leather-covered cotton gained acceptance.

Cymbals are concave disks of brass that provide a brilliant clashing accent to band music. Cymbals, depicted in the earliest illustrations of American bands, continued to be an essential part of these ensembles. The manufacturing source of many of the cymbals in American bands is not certain, but it is known that some expensive instruments were imported from China and Turkey. As shown in contemporary photographs, the instruments used in America through the 1890s appear to have averaged about a foot in diameter, somewhat smaller than those commonly employed today. Only the largest bands could afford the luxury of a separate cymbal player. In small bands of no more than fifteen or twenty players, the bass drummer usually doubled on cymbals. One cymbal was firmly affixed to the body of the bass drum, while the other was held by the percussionist. In this way two bandsmen could play all three essential percussion instruments.

A few other percussion instruments are occasionally seen in photographs of pre–1920 American brass bands. Pairs of kettle drums, which have large, hemispherical copper bodies and a single drumhead, are evident in some horse-mounted U.S. Army bands of the late nineteenth and early twentieth centuries. The triangle provided a bright, tinkling highlight to some concert bands while marching bands were occasionally preceded by a jingling johnny or "Turkish crescent." Several feet in length, this ornate instrument consisted of a vertical shaft that supported several brass crosspieces or inverted brass bowls. Each brass device was fringed with small bells that produced the characteristic rhythmic, jingling sound. Traditional jingling johnnies were crowned with a brass crescent, but American versions sometimes featured an eagle or other patriotic symbol. In addition to kettle drums, triangle, and the jingling johnny, it is probable that concert bands took advantage of such exotic percussion instruments as castanets, chimes, and bells for novel effects. But for most bands, most of the time, the snare drum, bass drum, and cymbals provided an ample battery of sound.

The Strings
The majority of American bands were content with a complement of brass, woodwinds, and percussion, but a number of ensembles, both large and small, incorporated one or more string instruments as well. John Philip Sousa favored the use of a harp for its unique quality, and he featured a violin soloist in many of his performances. As early as the 1850s the string bass was introduced into Dutch bands and although Sousa deplored its use, the

Members of this British juvenile band possess an unusual assortment of band instruments, including a circular alto horn or ballad horn (second from left), E-flat baritone sarrusophone (third from left), and jingling johnny (far right). Without additional instruments this band would have produced an odd sound.

instrument did eventually gain a foothold in such large American concert groups as the Goldman Band.

The use of string instruments was not restricted to large bands. The nine-piece Beaver Island (Michigan) Band of 1910 relied on a string bass to provide the lowest voice in an otherwise all-brass band. Photographs also reveal plucked-string instruments associated with bands. Musicians holding guitars, banjos, and mandolins are all occasionally found standing beside the wind and percussion players in nineteenth-century band images. Acceptance of these nontraditional band instruments testifies to the flexibility and vitality of the band in America.

The Beaver Island (Michigan) Band incorporated a string bass along with a typical complement of brass and percussion. The unusual instrumentation may have been influenced by Dutch settlers on the Lake Michigan island or simply by the lack of a local tuba player. Beaver Island Historical Society.

INSTRUMENTS IN COMBINATION

Woody Allen's movie *Take the Money and Run* contains a memorable scene in which Allen courageously tries to play the cello in his school's marching band. Intent upon making music with the ensemble, he settles in his chair and prepares to play, only to have to jump up and run ahead in order to keep up with the rest of the band. It is a ridiculously funny moment, the image an exquisite exaggeration of historical truth. With the seemingly endless variety of instruments available in the nineteenth century, American bandsmen had the opportunity to cast their bands in myriads of configurations. In theory, any number of brass and woodwind instruments, in any combination, with or without percussion and the odd string instrument, could be put together to form a band. Photographic and documentary evidence reveal that in practice, the possible combinations of these instruments were almost limitless. A number of other types of ensembles, including drum corps, fife and drum corps, and drum and bugle corps,

achieved local popularity prior to World War I, but these groups are not generally thought of as bands.

Themes and Variations

A few historical examples demonstrate the wide range in instrumentation embraced, by choice or by necessity, in American bands. In 1824, for instance, the Easton (Pennsylvania) Union Guards Band assembled three flutes, nine clarinets, two horns, one bassoon, one serpent (a bass wind instrument with side holes and a tubalike mouthpiece), triangle, cymbals, and drums to furnish music for the Easton Union Guards.[6] This diverse mixture was a common blend of instruments for the period and was well suited to the rendition of both patriotic airs and quicksteps. With new instruments available a quarter century later, the New Bedford (Massachusetts) Guards formed a different sort of band, consisting of two E-flat keyed bugles, one B-flat keyed bugle, one trumpet, two post horns, two tenor trombones, one bass trombone, one trumpcello (or trombacello, an early valved tenor horn), two B-flat and two E-flat ophicleides, two drums, cymbals, and a fife.[7] Despite the inclusion of a fife, this ensemble was appropriately referred to as a brass band. With exception of the percussion, these two ensembles had completely different instrumentations, yet both groups were typical bands.

In 1883, the citizens of Russell, Kansas, also formed a brass band, but they employed an instrumentation of well-matched brasses that differed completely from the New Bedford band of around 1850. Pairs of E-flat and B-flat cornets, a solo alto, two B-flat tenors, a B-flat baritone, and E-flat tuba, plus the usual drums and cymbals, gave this group a uniformity of sound not found in the Easton, Pennsylvania, or New Bedford, Massachusetts, ensembles.[8]

Touring concert bands featured more performers and a wider range of instruments than most other types of bands. The unidentified band—possibly a visiting European group—had forty-six instrumentalists, including performers on bassoon, oboe, and French horn.

The first band in Battle Creek, Michigan, was formed in the 1840s and included a combination of keyed and valved brass instruments. The ensemble began with only five musicians in 1848, but by the mid–1850s the band boasted a complement of thirteen. Keyed bugle player Lewis B. Clapp was the band's first leader. This image is one of the earliest known photographs of an identified American band; the original daguerreotype is apparently lost, but copies are preserved in the Willard Library, Battle Creek, Michigan.

In contrast to these modest bands of twelve to twenty players, the marching unit of the Seventh Regiment of New York in the 1880s boasted more than sixty musicians and a correspondingly rich instrumentation. Bandmaster Carlo Alberto Cappa chose the following instruments for his military band, so-called because the prominence of woodwind instruments made it similar to many European military bands:[9]

2 E-flat cornets	4 baritones	3 E-flat clarinets
12 B-flat cornets	1 euphonium	16 B-flat clarinets
2 E-flat altos	6 basses	2 snare drums
4 French horns	1 piccolo	1 bass drum
6 trombones	1 flute	cymbals

The factors governing size and instrumentation of these and other bands were many. To some extent, there was an orderly evolution in instrumentation as a result of technical improvements. Just as keyed brass had replaced woodwind instruments in many bands during the 1830s and 1840s, so they were gradually replaced by the more reliable and easier to play valved brass. Attitudes towards the ideal sound of brass instruments also evolved. Thus, by 1890 cornet soloists had almost universally adopted the B-flat cornet in preference to the E-flat cornet, whose popularity had peaked in the 1860s and 1870s. The B-flat cornet was largely supplanted by the B-flat trumpet as the lead brass instrument about the time of World War I. Many other examples of orderly instrumentation changes as a result of technology and fashion could be cited.

Brass *versus* Woodwinds

With respect to the biggest single issue of band instrumentation—the proper balance between the brass and woodwind families—the situation was neither orderly nor particularly evolutionary. Lacking the government directives often issued to European bands, American bandmasters were generally free to develop brass-to-woodwind ratios according to the resources available and their own aesthetic taste. The composition of many bands was consequently determined by a haphazard combination of local attitudes and the available personnel.

Almost as soon as the first all-brass bands were created, critics railed against their shortcomings, generally perceived to be an inability to play softly and a monotonous homogeneity of sound. In 1835, less than a year after Dodworth's band in New York had switched to an all-brass instrumentation, a contributor to the *American Music Journal* protested, "Brass bands when they play in tune are good things to march after; but it is not in the nature of things that they can produce the beautiful effects of the old bands."[10] Ever at the forefront of musical discussion, J. S. Dwight agreed. Writing in 1856 he complained that "all the brass bands sound alike" with the "same essential quality of tone, the same family type through all its seeming variations; the same aggravating increase of force, without increase of meaning."[11] For these critics, as for many others, a band required the contrasting voices of clarinets, bassoons, flutes, and French horns to sustain melodic and harmonic interest and to tone down the brashness of the ensemble.

Such views on instrumentation were put into practice by a few large ensembles. Even in the heyday of brass band conversions before the Civil War, the Marine Band and the Seventh New York Regiment Band staunchly maintained a liberal use of woodwinds in combination with their brass. Patrick Gilmore did much to publicize the artistic possibilities of a judicious instrumental mix when, in 1859, he added woodwinds to the celebrated all-brass Boston Brigade Band. Following this lead, most professional and military bands, as well as many of the larger amateur ensembles, favored some combination of brass and woodwind instruments during the latter third of the century. Gilmore's instrumentation for the Twenty-second Regiment Band of New York achieved a ratio of thirty-five reeds to twenty-seven brass to four percussion in 1878. Thirteen years later, Gilmore's Band was fully two-thirds woodwind.[12] John Philip Sousa, with many years' experience in orchestral playing, labored hard to achieve a symphonic sound in his band. By about 1898 he settled upon an instrumentation in which woodwinds outnumbered brass two to one. Sousa's balance, which he claimed achieved a "oneness of tone," is commonly reproduced in school bands today.

On the other hand, there was something to be said for

*Most small-town American bands prior to 1900 had about a
dozen members, with two percussionists and the rest brass
players. The band of Barnet, Vermont (population about fifteen
hundred when this photograph was taken ca. 1890) exemplifies
the typical American brass band of the time. Vermont Historical
Society.*

an all-brass band, and Allen Dodworth said it with conviction. Writing in *Message Bird* in 1849, Dodworth called the effect of a band of saxhorns "far superior to any other class of instruments in use." If well balanced, noted the New York bandleader, a ten- or fifteen-piece band could deliver a "very fine effect."[13]

The dark, rich sound of a group of saxhorns evidently appealed to many musicians. Such all-brass ensembles were prominent in many towns during the 1840s and 1850s, and they could be found by the hundreds leading or following countless regiments during the early phases of the Civil War. The earlier version of an all-brass band, which featured keyed bugles, horns, trumpets, and ophicleides, had been very popular, too—so popular, that it virtually redefined the popular concept of a band when it burst upon the scene in the 1830s. For the projection of sound outdoors, brass bands had no rivals.

The all-brass band was especially well suited to America's boisterous postbellum gilded age. Easy to play, acoustically reliable, and inexpensive, the valved brass instruments were ideal for the small amateur bands that appeared throughout the country. Patton urged an all-brass instrumentation for such groups in his guide to band formation. So did many instrument companies, some of which published recommended combinations for anywhere from six to eighteen brass instruments. The photographic archive at the Smithsonian Institution provides evidence that these parameters were taken to heart by thousands of bandsmen. The archive includes more than seven hundred photographs of American amateur bands for which the instrumentation is clearly visible. Of approximately one hundred and fifty photographs of eight- to twelve-piece bands from the period 1865 to 1915, only eleven have more than one woodwind instrument. The average instrumentation for these small

FORMATION OF BANDS.

Band of Six.	Band of Seven.	Band of Eight.	Band of Nine.
1 Eb Cornet.	1 Eb Cornet.	1 Eb Cornet.	2 Eb Cornets.
2 Bb Cornets.	2 Bb Cornets.	2 Bb Cornets.	2 Bb Cornets.
1 Eb Alto.	2 Eb Alto.	2 Eb Alto.	2 Eb Alto.
1 Bb Tenor.	1 Bb Tenor.	1 Bb Tenor.	1 Bb Tenor.
1 Bb Bass.	1 Bb Bass.	1 Bb Baritone.	1 Bb Baritone.
		1 Eb Bass.	1 Eb Bass.

Band of Ten.	Band of Eleven.	Band of Twelve.	Band of Thirteen.
2 Eb Cornets.	2 Eb Cornets.	2 Eb Cornets.	2 Eb Cornets.
2 Bb Cornets.	2 Bb Cornets.	2 Bb Cornets.	2 Bb Cornets.
2 Eb Alto.	2 Eb Alto.	3 Eb Alto.	3 Eb Alto.
2 Bb Tenor.	2 Bb Tenor.	2 Bb Tenor.	2 Bb Tenor.
1 Bb Baritone.	1 Bb Baritone.	1 Bb Baritone.	1 Bb Baritone.
1 Eb Bass.	1 Bb Bass.	1 Bb Bass.	1 Bb Bass.
	1 Eb Bass.	1 Eb Bass.	2 Eb Bass.

Band of Fourteen.	Band of Fifteen.	Band of Sixteen.	Band of Seventeen.
2 Eb Cornets.	3 Eb Cornets.	3 Eb Cornets.	3 Eb Cornets.
2 Bb Cornets.	3 Bb Cornets.	3 Bb Cornets.	3 Bb Cornets.
2 Eb Alto.	3 Eb Alto.	3 Eb Alto.	3 Eb Alto.
2 Bb Tenor.	2 Bb Tenor.	3 Bb Tenor.	3 Bb Tenor.
1 Bb Baritone.	1 Bb Baritone.	1 Bb Baritone.	2 Bb Baritone.
1 Bb Bass.	1 Bb Bass.	1 Bb Bass.	1 Bb Bass.
2 Eb Bass.	2 Eb Bass.	3 Eb Bass.	3 Eb Bass.

Drums and Cymbals to be added when so small a number as six, seven, or eight players are obliged to play music for marching. Two Eb Cornets and one Bb Cornet are preferable to 1 Eb and 2 Bb, as given above; but for Concert, Serenade and In-door Music, the latter classification would produce the best effect.

The New York music firm of Slater and Martin, one of the first companies to issue illustrated brass instrument catalogs, included this table in publications of the late 1860s. The all-brass instrumentation suggested for bands of six to seventeen members was gradually modified. By 1900 most dealers recommended three or four clarinets in a seventeen-piece band.

bands—the great majority town bands—was one snare drum, one bass drum with cymbals, and perhaps one clarinet, with the remaining players on brass. Many small groups had no woodwind players at all. The evidence is clear: if a band was small, it was likely to be predominantly brass.

This incarnation of the brass band differs markedly from the more formalized British-style brass band. Whereas American brass bands of the period 1840 to 1920 were variable in size and woodwind use, the British brass band is strictly a brass ensemble with a standardized instrumentation that includes E-flat and B-flat cornet, B-flat flugelhorn, E-flat altohorn, B-flat baritone, B-flat euphonium (i.e., bass), B-flat and G trombone, and E-flat and BB-flat tubas. Percussion is optional, and a full complement includes at least twenty-four musicians. The British approach has been championed by the Salvation Army, which sponsors many staff and citadel bands as well as thousands of smaller corps brass ensembles worldwide.

Modulations

In spite of the relatively unchanging complement of the smallest American bands prior to World War I, the average town band did undergo at least two significant changes during the half-century from 1865 to 1915. First, the size of bands increased. Prior to 1885 amateur bands depicted in photographs averaged twelve to fourteen players. In the 1890s the average size had increased to sixteen to eighteen players, and by 1910 most town bands exceeded twenty musicians. With the increase in band size came a corresponding increase in woodwind usage.

A second gradual trend, evident from approximately two hundred photographs of sixteen- to twenty-piece amateur bands, is the inexorable increase in the woodwind-to-brass ratio. Prior to 1880 most bands of this size

The Georgetown (Colorado) Cornet Band was a typical brass and percussion ensemble ca. 1885. The band posed in front of mine workings where most of the members would have been employed. Denver Public Library.

The transition from almost all-brass to mixed-brass-and-wind instrumentation is evident in photographs of Martland's Brockton (Massachusetts) Band, which also served as the Fifth Massachusetts Volunteer Regiment Band. In the first image of 1879 (top), only two of twenty-two players hold woodwind instruments. In photographs of ca. 1890 and May 1900 (not reproduced), four of twenty-five bandsmen play clarinet or flute. By ca. 1910 (bottom), seven of twenty musicians have woodwind instruments.

MARTLAND'S BROCKTON BAND, OCT. 1879.   HOWARD, Photo.

had no woodwinds at all. In the 1890s the great majority of these town bands included one or two clarinets, and by 1910 the average band of sixteen to twenty players boasted three or more woodwinds. The evolution of American bands is thus characterized by slow but steady shifts to larger ensembles with ever-greater proportions of woodwinds.

The changes in relative importance of brass *versus* woodwinds in American bands, as deduced from photographic evidence, is borne out by sales records of major American instrument manufacturers. The C. G. Conn

Many small-town bands persisted in using brass and percussion instrumentation well into the twentieth century. The sixteen members of the Ashland (New York) Cornet Band, ca. 1905, purchased a new set of Conn instruments, including a double-bell euphonium, but incorporated only one clarinet to balance thirteen brass and two percussion.

Company, one of the nation's most prominent instrument companies, dealt exclusively in brass from its beginnings in 1876 until 1895, when the first woodwinds were sold. Brass instruments continued to account for more than half of Conn's sales until about 1915, when the woodwinds first outsold the brass. By the early 1920s woodwinds dominated the firm's business by a margin of almost two-to-one.

It might be argued that the production records of Conn, along with dozens of other nineteenth-century instrument makers, reflect more the specialized skills of individual artisans than any commercial trends. This argument, however, cannot be extended to the giant music houses that dealt in a full range of supplies, from winds, strings, and percussion, to banjos, pianos, and harmonicas. One such firm, Bruno and Sons of New York, published massive catalogs of more than two hundred pages. In 1888 they devoted fifty-four pages to brasses but only sixteen to woodwinds. In the 1920s, on the other hand, brasses and woodwinds were illustrated on thirty-eight and twenty-two larger pages, respectively. Given the fact that woodwinds, which are mostly long and slender, take much less space to illustrate than tubas or cornets, these latter numbers represent a parity of woodwind and brass advertising.

The Chicago-based instrument company of Lyon and Healy, reputed to be the largest Midwest importer and manufacturer of musical supplies in the late nineteenth century, produced lavishly illustrated catalogs of musical merchandise. In the early 1880s more than forty pages were devoted to brass, while only four displayed woodwinds, a ten-to-one ratio. In the 1891 catalog, there were thirty-one brass and eight woodwind pages, for about a four-to-one ratio. In the early twentieth century, the relative importance of woodwind instruments increased,

The Osceola (Florida) Cornet Band, ca. 1890, combined new-style uniforms and recent piston valve cornets with obsolete rotary valve, over-shoulder models in their twelve-piece brass band. Smaller towns that were remote from major instrument supply centers often had to rely on older equipment. This phenomenon has been called the law of peripheral survival.

though the predominantly small-town, midwestern patrons of Lyon and Healy seemed to favor brasses through the century's first decades.

By the turn of the century the trend toward mixed wind instrumentation had unquestionably achieved momentum. In 1903, the C. G. Conn Company noted in its monthly advertising periodical, *Musical Truth,* that "as each new musical season opens up for amateur bands, the necessity of increasing the reed corps of the organization

becomes more and more apparent. The day of the brass band has passed."[14] This benediction for brass may have been a bit premature, but business records demonstrate that the market for woodwind instruments in American bands increased significantly in the last decade of the nineteenth century. By World War I, brass and woodwinds for the first time achieved numerical equivalence in sales.

But the debate was far from over. In 1934, Ohio State University eliminated its traditional woodwind, brass, and percussion band to become, in the words of their publicist, the "first college all-brass marching band."[15] A few years later, the noted orchestral conductor Leopold Stokowski, in bold defiance of prevailing opinion, suggested that the United States service bands restore the high brass instruments and eliminate their woodwinds altogether.

The all-brass and the mixed-wind bands coexisted in a relationship that was probably much more comfortable for the contemporary bandsmen than it is for latter-day historians who attempt to find a logical transition from the brass bands of the 1830s to the standard wind bands of today. All-brass bands, brass bands with one or two clarinets, and mixed-brass-and-reed bands could be found in abundance during the last half of the nineteenth century. The size and instrumentation of the "average" American band may have changed in a gradual and logical way, but most American bands were not average.

THE LAW OF PERIPHERAL SURVIVAL

The variety of instruments and instrumentations found at any one time in America's bands can be explained, in part, by the so-called law of peripheral survival, which states that the most remote populations are the last to change. Bands in the big cities were constantly exposed to the latest types of instruments, styles of uniforms, and tastes in music. These organizations had to adopt new fads and fashions quickly in order to make the best impression. Rural bands in remote areas, on the other hand, had less incentive—and often less capital—to change instruments, uniforms, or music. If an old instrument worked, it was very likely used until worn out. Obsolete instrument types, such as one-key flutes, ophicleides, and rope-tension drums were used by some American musicians well into the twentieth century, in spite of the dramatic technological improvements that were widely available. Over-shoulder tubas are occasionally seen in postcards of the 1900s, and rotary valve cornets were used in many bands long after instrument companies ceased to sell them. Thus, it is not surprising that many old photographs of small-town bands reveal a range of instrument styles—spanning a thirty- or forty-year period—all in use at the same time.

This lack of standardization may be confusing to the student of American band history. Yet the effect of this lack of standardization is perfectly clear. With the decisions about instrumentation resting largely on local preference, American bands of the nineteenth century not only offered audiences a rich variety of musical textures and sonorities, but also contributed significantly to the vitality of the art form.

6.

DISCOURSING SWEET MUSIC

Can you contemplate anything more edifying, elevating
and lasting in its influence than a daily sermon in the
universal language—music?

—Chicago Band publicity brochure, ca. 1911

If bandmasters had a variety of instruments to choose from when forming their bands, they had a veritable smorgasbord of musical morsels to consider when creating their programs. There was no need to concentrate on the few European compositions written expressly for wind band when hundreds of other melodies, both popular and classical, were readily arranged for a variety of band instrumentations. Supplementing this vast repertoire were the many original pieces devised by American bandmasters and soloists to show off their musical skills and daring. Such music conveyed a wide range of moods, encompassing, as one advertisement put it, "the gay, humorous, pathetic, patriotic and serious."[1] But, as a whole, this music can be characterized as lighter in mood than that generally performed by chamber music groups.

112

And it was much more easily understood. As John Philip Sousa once said, his band music was "direct" and "simple," "a music to be grasped at once."[2] There were many types of band music and each type had its particular charm for the listener.

TYPES OF MUSIC

Marches

"A military band concert would not be complete without a stirring march," claimed a program for one of Patrick Gilmore's band concerts in the late 1880s. Most audiences would have agreed. This popular musical form originated as a stimulant to the orderly movement of troops, but made an easy transition to the world of art as early as the sixteenth century when battaglias (compositions simulating battles) came into vogue. By the mid–1800s, American concertgoers were often treated to the pulsing rhythm of such spirited works as the classic "Washington's

The epigraph at the head of this chapter is from Chicago Band Association Papers, Chicago Historical Society.

March" and Grafulla's "Grand March." Though well crafted, such early marches were simple compositions of regularly phrased melodic lines underscored by a strong, steady beat. Interest was often heightened by the inclusion of an introductory fanfare or separate lyric trio sections alternating with the march proper.

During the last quarter of the nineteenth century, however, the American march underwent a dramatic stylistic transformation as a result of the creativity of such composers as David Wallis Reeves and John Philip Sousa. Among the many innovations of these bandsmen were the use of a countermelody or melodies (pioneered by Reeves in 1876),[3] the development of a more complex march form, the increase in tonal range, and the development of more driving and more interesting rhythmic patterns that were not necessarily confined to the percussion instruments. Taken together, these elements revitalized the American military march, which was accorded international acclaim.

Sousa tried to describe how he went about creating his rousing and enormously popular marches. "I turn my imagination loose among scenes of barbaric splendor," he wrote. "I picture to myself the glitter of guns and swords, the tread of feet to the drum beat, and all that is grand and glorious in military scenes."[4] Vivid as this imagery is, one has to listen to the music to appreciate its stirring qualities. Fortunately for audiences in the late nineteenth and early twentieth centuries, there was ample opportunity to do so. As surviving printed concert programs indicate, bands from all over the country eagerly incorporated marches by the March King, Reeves, Gilmore, and many lesser-known composers into their programming.

The fact that marches were easily adapted to concert audiences in no way precluded their use in actual marching situations. Although the Sousa Band was a concert band

As bandmaster of the U.S. Marine Band, John Philip Sousa put his famous marches to regular use. In 1889, for example, Sousa led the band for Benjamin Harrison's inaugural parade. After forming his own touring band in 1892, Sousa continued to write marches but rarely employed them while marching.

and is said to have marched only seven times in its long history,[5] Reeves's American Band was primarily a marching unit with the more than one hundred marches composed by Reeves channeled to this purpose. Most amateur bands played a mixture of concerts and parades, and for them, too, the versatile and ever-popular march was a staple. They used quicksteps and other fast marches (played at 120 beats per minute) on the concert stage and saved their slower parade marches for actual processions.

Patriotic Songs

"May they never forget the tune of 'Hail, Columbia.'"[6] With these ardent words bandsman George H. Gundt toasted the independent bands of America in 1824, and he could hardly have hoped for better results. For decades afterwards, American bands played a variety of arrangements of "Hail, Columbia," along with other patriotic songs such as "The Star-Spangled Banner," "Yankee Doodle," and the French "La Marseillaise." With the advent of the Civil War, there was a burst of songwriting that resulted in such nationalistic pieces as "The Battle Hymn of the Republic," "The Bonnie Blue Flag," and the "Battle Cry of Freedom," all of which were easily adapted to band instrumentation. It was at this time that "Dixie," a popular minstrel song written in 1859 by Daniel Decatur Emmett, took on its secessionist overtones and became one of the most popular band pieces in the Confederacy. Although fewer war songs were inspired by the Spanish-American War in 1898, bands of the period hardly lacked suitable patriotic music. They simply adapted Sousa's stirring marches, particularly "The Stars and Stripes Forever" and "El Capitan" (both written in 1896), as fitting musical tributes to the flowering of American power and purpose.

By text and by temper this music was obviously suited to Fourth of July and Decoration Day celebrations, Grand Army of the Republic reunions, and political gatherings. But the music was also popular for concert presentations, as the many surviving concert programs and reviews indicate. "Dixie," "America" ("My Country 'tis of Thee"), and "Hail, Columbia" were particularly promi-

nent among the patriotic pieces played at band concerts during the last decades of the nineteenth century. Long before "The Star-Spangled Banner" became the American national anthem in 1931, various versions of the work appeared regularly on concert programs, and between 1890 and 1920 the piece was widely favored as a concluding work. Most bands simply played these patriotic songs, but occasionally, as at a concert presented by John C. Weber's Military Band in Cincinnati in 1900, the words to all the national airs to be played during the performance were printed on the program, and the audience was encouraged to sing along with the band.

Popular Songs

Vocal music was immensely popular in the United States during the nineteenth century. From sacred hymns to popular ballads to operatic airs, songs challenged the abilities of amateur and professional singers alike. Songs also contributed greatly to the earnings of music publishers. Between 1770 and 1820, American presses issued more than five hundred songsters.[7] Three decades later, Stephen Foster's hugely successful "My Old Kentucky Home" reputedly sold over ninety thousand copies within the first year of publication. In such an environment the Swedish soprano Jenny Lind scarcely required the promotional genius of P. T. Barnum to achieve a successful American concert tour.

America's enthusiasm for song profoundly affected band concert programming. Like the classical orchestras of the day, bands typically scheduled one or more vocal selections along with the purely instrumental pieces. Bands also played instrumental renditions of such popular songs as "Auld Lang Syne," "Jingle Bells," the "Doxology," "Annie Laurie," and numerous Stephen Foster favorites. Medleys of Irish and Scottish folksongs, as well as plantation songs, were featured regularly.

America's enthusiasm for song may also have had an influence on the popularity of the cornet as a solo instrument. It can be argued that the lyric tonal quality of the cornet and the obviously songlike passages customarily written for it were two significant factors in the phenomenal popularity of this instrument during the second half of the nineteenth century.

Programmatic Pieces

Americans greatly enjoyed art works that told a story. For example, painter Thomas Cole's *Voyage of Life* series, which allegorically traces the stages of man's life, was distributed in popular prints during the 1840s and 1850s. The story-pictures made widely available in later decades by lithographers like Currier and Ives enjoyed even greater acclaim. Similarly, it was sculptor John Rogers's ability to create vivid and detailed scenes in plaster that accounted for the enormous popularity of his sculpture groups, some one hundred thousand of which were sold between 1860 and 1890.

Although music was a less tangible art than painting, lithography, or sculpture, purely instrumental pieces could also be constructed to tell stories. In the late eighteenth century F. Kotzwara's "Battle of Prague" and J. Hewitt's "Battle of Trenton" were performed frequently, and similar pieces were eventually composed or arranged specifically for bands. Depictions of military encounters, such as "Custer's Last Charge," were readily accomplished by the incorporation into the music of trumpet calls, booming drums, and real cannon shots. But even less dramatic subjects could be described musically. The immensely popular "Wood-Up Quickstep," written by John Holloway and introduced in 1834, supposedly depicted the refueling of a steamboat. Later, the accomplished composer and conductor David Wallis Reeves wrote a number of successful descriptive pieces, including "The Night Alarm" which tells the story of a fire company's energetic response to a fire and "The Evening Call" which describes a young man's visit to his girl friend—complete with a kiss and the ensuing scurrying about when the lady's father intrudes upon the scene. Even brass bands themselves became appealing subjects for programmatic music as composers created tonal passages utilizing brilliant fanfares and the inharmonious sounds of two bands playing together. "The Passing Regiment," popularized by Patrick Gilmore at a grand concert held in St. Louis in 1886, conveyed—through the skillful use of dynamics—the idea of a parading band.

As suggestive as musical tones might be, there was always the possibility that the composer's interpretation might elude the audience. Hence, printed programs often supplied verbal explanations of the "true" meaning of the music played. At a concert held in Cincinnati's Music Hall in May 1889, Gilmore's Band presented "An Alpine Storm" by Charles Kunkel. The following summary of the descriptive idyll was offered to listeners and gives some idea of the range of "real-life sounds" that a band tried to imitate.

Shepherds salute each other at day-break on their lutes, while the tinkling of bells indicates that the flocks are being driven to pasture. Soon the rumbling of distant thunder foretells the approach of a storm. Rain begins to fall, and the shepherds signal their dogs to bring the herds under shelter. The wind whistles through the mountain pines, continually increasing until at length thunder, lightning, rain, and wind combine, the tempest rages in all its fury, and the storm-king reigns supreme. Gradually the brighter side of nature asserts itself, and the storm subsides. Shepherds resume their lute greetings, birds fill the air with melodious warblings, flocks hie to their pastures, and the sun bursts forth in all its golden splendor.[8]

For those who found it difficult to listen to music without words, such program notes, and the meaningful musical themes they described, afforded a comfortable introduction to the abstract world of instrumental music.

Solo Pieces

Musical selections designed to show off the virtuosity of skillful musicians were staples of the American band repertoire. The Grand Concert that introduced the Boston Brass Band in 1835 featured as many as five instrumental solos—for trombone, flute, violin, clarinet, and keyed bugle—as well as numerous vocal selections. Showman that he was, Patrick Gilmore recognized the appeal of such flamboyant entertainment and regularly incorporated appreciable amounts of soloistic music in his own programs. A typical Gilmore concert, presented in Oberlin, Ohio, in 1879, included works for piccolo, cornet, violin, and voice solo, along with a piece featuring a quartet of French horns. Eight years later, promising the "best soloists in the musical profession," Gilmore offered an audience in Bloomington, Illinois, an evening's entertainment that highlighted, in turn, the talents of Raffayolo on euphonium, Fred Lax on flute, Ben Bent on cornet, Herr Matus on E-flat clarinet, soprano Letitia French, and, finally, E. A. Lefebre on the "comparatively modern instrument," the saxophone.

For Sousa, too, talented soloists were essential to round out concert programming, and the names of his outstanding virtuosi—Herbert L. Clarke, Frank Simon, Walter Rogers, Arthur Pryor, and Simone Mantia—were widely recognized by an enthusiastic public. Smaller bands had

Louise Shaffer, "Musical Artiste," was one of the few women solo cornetists in late-nineteenth-century America. This broadside is evidence that she achieved some success, but no details of her performance career have been found.

fewer and less talented musicians to draw on, but they tried to include one or two virtuoso showpieces on each band concert program.

While any instrument in the hands of a master could inspire admiration, it was the keyed bugle and its successor, the cornet, that produced the nineteenth century's musical superstars. When first introduced, the Royal Kent Bugle offered musicians an unprecedented opportunity to play both delicate and bold melodic passages on a brass instrument. Among the able musicians to thrill the public with this novel horn were Richard Willis, who was called a "perfect master" of the instrument,[9] the distinguished Black virtuoso, Francis Johnson, who so impressed Queen Victoria with his playing that she gave him a silver bugle as a gift,[10] and, of course, Edward Kendall, whose technical expertise and musical sensitivity earned "Ned" a solid reputation as the best keyed bugler in America.[11]

Around midcentury, with the perfection of the valved cornet, a whole new crop of performers burst upon the scene. Among these outstanding players were the sensitive and popular Matthew Arbuckle and his great rival Jules Levy, often described on publicity posters as the "greatest living cornet player." There was also David Wallis Reeves, who as a young man learned the art of double and triple tonguing in Europe and displayed these sensational techniques to admiring American audiences. Other outstanding cornetists who established careers as solo performers were Patrick Gilmore, Alessandro Liberati, Giuseppe Creatore, and Herbert L. Clarke.

Occasionally cornet soloists enhanced their reputations by capitalizing on personal idiosyncracies. Bohumir Kryl cultivated a distinctive moustache, and Arthur Amsden promoted his unusual ability to play two melodies on two cornets at one time. From time to time Amsden would also hum while playing, thus producing a remarkable

triad effect. Contests between accomplished performers were often devised for dramatic reasons. The best known "play-off" occurred in 1856 when Edward Kendall pitted his keyed bugle against the more modern valved cornet of Patrick Gilmore. From time to time there were other highly publicized competitions, including the informal duels between Levy and Arbuckle and the remarkable battle held in 1834 in New York—and repeated in New Orleans—between John T. Norton on slide trumpet and Alessandro Gambati on the "new valved trumpet."

Despite this periodic tendency to highlight performances with hoopla, the reputations of most well-known performers on soprano brass rested solidly on their extraordinary musical ability, which they demonstrated by playing hauntingly beautiful themes followed by striking variations of ever-greater technical complexity. Almost any melody, from "Yankee Doodle" to opera arias, could be employed in these showy theme and variation or *air varie* solos. Melodies of Auber, Bellini, Donizetti, and Meyerbeer were especially popular among cornet soloists of the nineteenth century. Curiously, in spite of the popularity of wind soloists and classical transcriptions, band versions of classical orchestral concertos were rarely performed.

Classical Transcriptions

Although the propriety of including orchestral transcriptions on band concert programs had become a matter of heated debate by the second decade of the twentieth century, the issue was rarely raised during the nineteenth century. Amateur and professional bandsmen alike enthusiastically included excerpts from both symphonic and operatic works in their presentations. Overtures by Rossini and Wagner were especially popular, as were selections from the operas of Mozart and Verdi. Works by Mendelssohn, Massenet, Weber, Liszt, Meyerbeer, Bellini, and even an occasional composition by Bach and Haydn were also adapted to band instrumentation. Though not particularly revered today, Joseph Gungl and Keler Bela were symphonic composers whose works enhanced the repertoires of many bands. Verdi's "Anvil Chorus" from *Il Trovatore* and Von Suppe's "Poet and Peasant" and "Light Cavalry" overtures rank among the most popular transcriptions of the second half of the nineteenth century.

American bands played this music partly because it was entertaining, but for most bandleaders the inclusion of the classics had a higher, educational purpose as well. "The important part that military bands have taken in the development of musical knowledge in America cannot be overstated," wrote Victor Herbert in the 1890s.[12] John Philip Sousa agreed. In his view, by supplying the masses with "musical pabulum," military bands had made the works of the world's great composers familiar to the American public. Owing to the influence of military bands, "Wagner is less of a myth to the people at large than Shakespeare and [Wagner's] musical compositions are better known than the creations of the great poet," wrote Sousa.[13]

If the classics saved the public from musical ignorance, they also saved the bands from musical boredom. Orchestral transcriptions provided a pleasing alternative to the lightweight songs and dances that were typical concert fare. In furnishing such a contrast, transcriptions also went a long way toward redeeming the band as a musical entity in the eyes of serious critics. Nevertheless, the actual adaptation of symphonic pieces was hardly a simple matter. A typical symphonic score might include twenty or more separate parts whereas the average small band could cover only about a dozen without doubling. In addition, rapid string passages were not easily performed on brasswinds, and the wide range of orchestral tone colors was lacking. Individual bands had to work very hard to acquire and produce acceptable transcriptions.

Dance Pieces

In his autobiography, *A New England Boyhood,* author Edward Everett Hale records an interesting story concerning wind bands and dance music. According to Hale, there had developed an unseemly tradition of heavy drinking and rowdyism on Harvard's annual class day. In order to rectify this lamentable situation, university president Josiah Quincy sought the advice of his students who promptly suggested that he "get us the Brigade Band for the day." The request was honored, and thus it was that on Class Day of 1838, instead of the usual wild antics there was a university sponsored chapel service and a dance, both with music by the Boston Brigade Band. Hale recalls the day and the dance in his memoir.

> The assembly moved up to that shaded corner between Stoughton and Holworthy. The band people stationed themselves in the entry of Stoughton, between 21 and 24, with the window open, and the 'dancing on the green' . . . began. The wind instrument men said afterward that they never played for dancing before, and that their throats were bone dry.[14]

Convinced that the dance was novel for the ladies too, Hale then added, "I suppose there was no girl there who had ever before danced to the music of a trombone."

Hale obviously regarded the use of military bands at dances as something of an experiment but, if so, it was an arrangement that caught on. In time many brass bands came to rely on their dance jobs for income, although they frequently altered their instrumentation by adding strings as the Boston Brigade Band did when it played at Harvard's Class Day the following year. Some bands

Brass bands were often employed to provide dance music in the nineteenth century. Outdoor dances, such as the Class Day celebrations at Harvard University, were especially well suited to brass music. Library of Congress.

Second Annual

PROMENADE CONCERT AND HOP,

OF THE

RUTLAND CORNET BAND,

TOWN HALL, RUTLAND, VT.,

Friday Evening, Feb. 21, 1879.

Mr. _____

Yourself and Ladies are respectfully invited.

Committee of Arrangements.

W. A. HILL,   E. L. HATCH,   W. SIMPSON.

CONCERT AT 8 O'CLOCK.   DANCING AT 9:30.

Ticket Admitting Gentleman with Ladies to Concert and Hop, $1.00.

Concert Tickets, 25 Cents.   Tuttle & Co., Printers, Rutland, Vt.

The combination concert and dance was a popular form of entertainment in nineteenth-century America. Dances provided an important source of income for both amateur and professional bands. Richard Dundas Collection.

simply moved indoors, however, adjusted their tempi, and—*presto*—they were a dance band.

The music that was popular on the dance floor was sure to be popular in the concert hall too. Waltzes, quadrilles, polkas, and gallops were commonly included on American band programs in the middle of the nineteenth century and later, as new dances such as the Viennese waltz came into fashion, tunes in this rhythm became part of the concert repertoire. While some bandmasters composed their own dance melodies, it was more common to adapt the popular songs of the day to dance rhythms. In an extreme example of this, John Philip Sousa's "The Washington Post"—written in 1889 as part of the promotional campaign for an essay contest sponsored by the Washington newspaper—was so popular that it was not simply adapted to a dance tempo, but actually stimulated the creation of an entirely new dance called the two-step.[15]

The long-standing relationship between wind bands and dance music began to be questioned around the turn of the twentieth century. As Frederick Fennell has pointed out, the popular new dances such as the foxtrot, Charleston, and rag required a more jazzy sound than was customarily offered by traditional bands.[16] Versatile as bands were, most could not satisfactorily adapt to the instrumental requirements of modern dances without breaking from earlier traditions. For many bands, this dilemma ultimately resulted in the elimination of current dance music from their repertoire.

Grandiose Pieces

While small bands of from ten to twenty players could perform satisfactorily on most occasions, larger groups could generate more volume, more pageantry, and more excitement. Many Americans were first exposed to the sounds of larger ensembles during the nationwide tours made by such professionals as Gilmore's Band. The effect of this sixty-five-piece band on an audience accustomed to a fifteen-piece town band can be imagined. But such an effect was probably minimal compared to that generated by the many specially arranged monster concerts of the nineteenth century. Patrick Gilmore was a master at promoting such extravaganzas. In addition to his well-known peace jubilees of 1869 and 1872 (when about one thousand instrumentalists in 1869 and two thousand in 1872 were amassed in Boston), Gilmore united and conducted a total of two thousand bandsmen for the Triennial Conclave of the Knights Templar in St. Louis in 1886. Other huge band concerts were organized regularly at regional band competitions and festivals. As late as 1917 John Philip Sousa toured throughout the East and Midwest with a three-hundred-fifty-piece military band made up of re-

cruits from the Great Lakes Naval Training Station. Often these gargantuan band concerts featured large choruses and military sound effects—including cannon.

In a sense these grandiose band concerts were counterparts to the huge orchestras amassed by such romantic composers as Berlioz, Wagner, and Richard Strauss. They also have correspondences in the world of art. The huge canvasses of such painters as Benjamin West, Samuel F. B. Morse, and, in later years, Albert Bierstadt must have stimulated emotional reactions not unlike those elicited by the overpowering sounds of a two-hundred-man military band. Gilmore's massed band concerts in their specifically designed coliseums bear striking parallels to H. Lewin's remarkable landscape painting *Mississippi River*, a canvas that was 1,325 yards long and had to be rolled out in a specially planned building to be viewed. Like these art works, which transported viewers to places they might not otherwise be able to visit, huge band concerts had a practical as well as an artistic purpose. Before the age of amplified sound they enabled masses of listeners to hear music presented in an outdoor setting.

PROGRAMMING

Given such an assortment of band music, the problem confronting the average bandmaster was less a question of what to play than what to leave out. The selection process differed from band to band and from concert to concert, with such varied factors as the ability of the musicians and the temperament of the director coming into play. The purpose of the performance also had a direct effect on programming. A band playing for a ball, for instance, had to favor polkas, waltzes, and schottisches, whereas a band at the head of a parade would need a preponderance of quick marches. Funeral music, which had become fairly standardized by the middle of the nineteenth century, required several types of music—solemn, slow marches for the walk to the cemetery, a dirge or two for the lowering of the coffin, and several lighter quicksteps for the return of the funeral party. The choice of the quickstep was a serious matter. As one experienced bandsman warned, common jigs such as "Wait for the Wagon" and "St. Patrick's Day" were unquestionably "in bad taste."[17]

There were fewer inherent programming requirements for band concerts. Nevertheless, directors constructed their concert programs with care, and most adopted a number of standard programming conventions. It was customary to open and close each concert with rousing, dramatic music played by the full ensemble. Transcriptions of grand symphonic works, renditions of America's national airs, and flamboyant, upbeat marches were commonly chosen to serve as first and last selections. For the remainder of the the concert almost anything might be played as long as the program as a whole offered enough variety to sustain the interest of the audience. Directors usually achieved this diversity by alternating soloistic pieces with pieces for the entire band and by introducing lighter dances and marches between the more serious operatic and symphonic excerpts.

To augment the variety, the band itself might alternate with another performing group—a string orchestra or a vocalist. It was not uncommon for a band to share billing with such nonmusical performers as elocutionists, magicians, and tableau actors. In 1882, Cobb's Brass Band was joined onstage by a long succession of such supplementary acts. These performers included minstrels, a string orchestra, clog dancers, a comedian, and a performing dog. Promising less variety, but certainly no less enjoyment, the Burlington Route Band of Farmington, Iowa, joined

Prior to the Civil War most "band concerts" were actually a potpourri of instrumental, vocal, solo, and ensemble works. The April 14, 1858, concert of the "Talmadge" (i.e., Tallmadge, Ohio) Band and Orchestra was typical of the time. Programs of other American concerts from the 1840s and 1850s included orations, juggling acts, and even short plays in addition to the featured band music. Tallmadge Historical Society.

forces one December evening with a trio of Tyrolean
Warblers and Al Fichtemuller (also the tuba player) in his
inimitable club-swinging act.

Although the length of band concerts varied somewhat,
the average seems to have been from one and a half to
two hours, a period of time considered to be comfortable
for musicians and audience alike. Some of the Sousa Band
concerts were a little longer, approaching three hours in
length. There were exceptions to these generalizations. It
was not uncommon for special festival concerts to last
many hours. During one such Midsummer Festival held
at Point of Pines in Michigan, a group of bands presented
a Grand Concert that reportedly lasted a full eight hours.[18]
On the other hand, occasional presentations, particularly
those held in the morning or as preludes to other events,
could last less than an hour, and informal serenades were
much shorter than that.

Overarching all these details was the assumption that,
above everything, a band performance ought to please the
public. The great Gilmore proudly proclaimed this to be
his "first duty" and all but the most "artistic" bandleaders
agreed. Even the widely acknowledged educational function of bands was consistently subordinated to the all-
important mission of entertaining the people. The pri-
macy of this principle in the creation of band programs
cannot be overstated. It was almost as if Jeremy Bentham's
philosophy of utilitarianism had been modified for use in
the concert hall, where, throughout the nineteenth century, the "greatest happiness of the greatest number" was
virtually guaranteed.

In practice, of course, a crowd-pleasing program could
take many forms. A fairly typical program was presented
by the twenty-five-piece Currier Band during the Cincinnati Industrial Exposition in 1879. Having played a similar

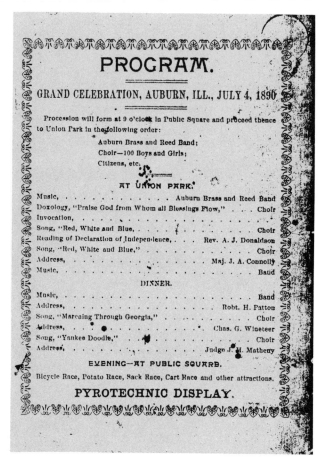

*The Illinois town of Auburn (population about twelve
hundred in 1890) enjoyed a varied program of activities at
the Fourth of July Grand Celebration. The Auburn Brass
and Reed Band probably provided music for the games and
fireworks at Public Square, as well as for the concert at
Union Park. Kurt Stein Collection.*

program earlier in the afternoon, they presented the following selections at their evening concert.[19]

March, "Girofle Girofla" by Lecocq
Overture, "La Dame Blanche" by Boieldeau
Waltz
Selection, "Bohemian Girl" by Balfe
Grand March from "Tannhauser" by Wagner
Overture, "William Tell" by Rossini
Potpourri from "Il Trovatore" by Verdi
Mosaique, "Chimes of Normandy" by Planquette
Fantasie, "Theme From Martha" by Flotow
Finale, "Fatinitza" by Suppe

A somewhat longer concert was offered by Dodworth's Concert Band at the Congregational Church in Brunswick, Maine, on August 5, 1856. One of the best bands in the country, Dodworth's Band of New York was competent to render this challenging program:[20]

Prayer from "Moses in Egypt" by Rossini
Fantazia from "Rigoletto" by Verdi
Caprice à la Polka by A. Dodworth
Lied, "Adelaide" by Beethoven
Duet, "Deh Conti," from "Norma" by Bellini (for two cornets)
Fantazia from "Il Trovatore" by Verdi
Wedding March from "Midsummer Night's Dream" by Mendelssohn
Scena et Aria from "Il Trovatore" by Verdi
Quadrille "Evening Bells" (with solos on bell harmonicon, flageolet, flute, oboe, clarinet and cornet) by H. B. Dodworth
La Serenade by Schubert
"Amelia" Polka by Thomas
Aria from "Don Giovani" by Mozart
Pot Pourie of College Songs, arr. by H. B. Dodworth

The concert programs of Gilmore's Band included an ambitious mixture of classical transcriptions, instrumental and vocal solos, and concert dances and marches. This program of 1877 took place when Gilmore was at the height of his fame and popularity.

Much in the tradition of the Dodworths, Patrick Gilmore invariably presented programs that were models of good balance and good taste. The following selections, which scrupulously alternated full band pieces with solos, were offered at a matinee performance given in Boston on Sunday, January 15, 1888. A solo for antoniophone—an uncommon, oddly wound type of saxhorn—was featured as the fourth selection.[21]

Overture, "William Tell" by Rossini (full band)
Solo for Clarinet, "Caprice Originale" by Stockigt
Paraphrase on Melody in F by Rubinstein (full band)
Solo for Antoniophone, "The Vacant Chair" by Root
Caprice Heroique, "The Awakening of the Lion" by De
    Kontski (full band)
Cavatina from Lombardi, "Non fu Sogno" by Verdi (for
    voice solo)
Concert Waltz, "Kroll's Ball Klange" by Lumbye (full band)
Solo for Cornet, "Polka Brilliante" by Demare
Echoes from the New South, "Pay Day on the Old
    Plantation" by Puerner (full band)
Piccolo Solo, "Fantaisie Lucretia Borgia" by Donizetti
Grand Fest March from "Tannhauser" by Wagner (full band)

Amateur bandsmen across the country were familiar with professional programs such as these and, as in matters of instrumentation and costume, were eager to emulate the practices of the prominent bands of the day. Nevertheless, hampered by a lack of accomplished players, many small, local groups had to settle for less ambitious musical offerings. Many town bands would not even have had printed programs, but the Cokato Cornet Band of Cokato, Minnesota, is typical of those that did present formal programs. For a concert held on March 18, 1890, the band played four selections:

"Westwood Grand March," by Southwell
"Pony Overture," by Southwell
"The Noss Family Quickstep," by Southwell
Polka for cornet and band, by Ramsdell

The remaining fourteen pieces of the so-called band concert were either choral or orchestral works.

It has been suggested that American band programming patterns changed over time. Specifically, it has been stated that great progress was made during the second half of the nineteenth century as a result of Gilmore's pioneering efforts to develop a more serious concert repertoire. Gilmore's own publicity made this claim, boldly stating that before the 1869 Peace Jubilee most bands played only marches, but that afterward there was "real improvement in American bands." Although Gilmore's influence was certainly a factor in the evolution of substantial programs, it is dangerous to place him too squarely at the vanguard of change. Dodworth and other professional bandleaders presented serious programs long before Gilmore's jubilees while other bands played light concert ditties long afterward. As late as 1911 a concert by the Michigan Agricultural College Cadet Band included two patriotic songs, two quicksteps, a waltz, a descriptive selection, a couple of romantic songs, and a duet from *Il Trovatore*. This was not an outrageous program for the time.

It is safer to say that although many bands, especially professional ensembles, moved toward the incorporation of classical transcriptions and serious concertos into their programs during the last decades of the nineteenth century, organizations limited in size, resources, and talent continued to present programs composed primarily of short songs, dances, and marches. Just as diversity was the hallmark of individual band concert programming, it was also the most salient characteristic of American programming practices.

Whatever the particulars, many bands found formulas that pleased their audiences. One reviewer, well satisfied with a performance in 1883 of Diller's Cornet Septet of New York—a group actually composed of three cornets, alto, tenor, euphonium, and tuba—reported, "Our Septet have shown themselves courteous and obliging gentlemen. They have invariably played pieces over again when the applause has seemed to justify their doing so. The selections, ranging from popular airs to the highest class of music, have been unexceptionable, and lovers of music in all its branches have had no reason to complain of the variety which has been offered."[22]

Other bands must have chosen their selections equally well. In 1914 the *American Musician* reported that one hundred times as many people heard band concerts as heard orchestra concerts. At approximately the same time William Hubbard claimed, justifiably, that the military or concert band was the "most popular form of concerted instrumental music in this country."[23]

Most bands prior to 1900 relied extensively on handwritten music. Daniel Cole, French hornist of the Hempstead (Long Island, New York) Band ca. 1835, included cues for keyed bugle, flute, and clarinet as well as his own part. Cole transcribed thirty-seven pages of music and embellished the covers of his book with sketches of his fellow bandsmen.

MUSICAL SCORES AND PARTS

The unstandardized state of band instrumentation in conjunction with the diverse nature of band programming seriously undermined the efforts of most bands to build up their music libraries.

The problem was particularly acute in the decades before the Civil War when the number of printed band parts was severely limited. Although wind band music is known to have been published occasionally in America during the eighteenth century, this was rare. It remained difficult to find printed scores or parts throughout the first half of the nineteenth century, despite the appearance in the 1840s and 1850s of a few collections such as Elias Howe's *First Part of The Musician's Companion* (published in 1844) and Allen Dodworth's *Brass Band School* (published in 1853). Lucky was the band whose leader could arrange piano music for his band or, better yet, could compose his own works. Unlucky were the bandsmen who had to copy out their parts by hand into band books. "We played manuscript music, written off for each man with pens," recalled Samuel F. Parcher, a musician active during the early days of the Portland (Maine) Band. "It was slow work writing music."[24]

Gradually, as bands increased in number, as publishing techniques improved, and as band business became big business with a variety of products, the acquisition of printed music became somewhat easier. By the last quarter of the nineteenth century a variety of music, ranging from simple pieces arranged for beginning bands to more challenging works of the masters, was available through instrument companies or directly from publishers. The Lyon and Healy Company listed hundreds of such pieces in their 1881 catalog and offered to acquire for customers any pieces not advertised. Recognizing the diversity of band instrumentation, many dealers supplied parts that were readily adaptable to either an all-brass or combined brass-woodwind ensemble. To accommodate their customers further, some companies allowed bandsmen the luxury of trying out printed music on approval before purchasing.

Despite these encouraging trends, bands had to depend on a wide range of sources for music. One alternative to buying music was to write the music oneself. Many bandmasters, especially those directing professional ensembles, did exactly that. Allen Dodworth, Francis Johnson, Patrick Gilmore, and John Philip Sousa all composed music for their bands to play. During the course of his illustrious career, conductor David Wallis Reeves reportedly wrote more than one hundred marches expressly for the use of the American Band in Providence.[25] Less commonly, but no less effectively, soloists wrote music to show off their own accomplishments. Jules Levy published a number of his own cornet pieces, and at a concert held in Cincinnati in 1889, Gilmore presented an unusual version of the "Carnival of Venice" in which each of the fifteen different soloists played variations that they had composed themselves. That some of these pieces eventually brought fame or fortune to the composers in no way alters the fact that they also brought repertoire to many bands.

In addition to composing their own music, many bandsmen successfully adapted to their own purposes music written by others. Suitable pieces were readily available as piano selections and in music journals such as *The Leader,* which occasionally published E-flat cornet parts for selected pieces. With the melody in hand, all that was needed were the harmonizing parts for the instruments contained in the band. If a band did not have among its members a talented arranger, interested bandsmen could purchase any of a number of tutors on the subject and teach themselves the art of arranging. Patton published his *Practical Guide to the Arrangement of Band Music* in 1875 expressly for the use of amateur bands that lacked the services of an experienced arranger. Other works, such as Henri Kling's treatise on *Modern Orchestration and Instrumentation* (published in America in 1905), and the many articles on arranging for brass band contained in *The Metronome,* augmented the information available to novices. In the absence of eager do-it-yourselfers, a band could always hire the services of a professional arranger. Lyon and Healy encouraged this option by advertising the services of various experienced technicians who, for from one to five dollars, would "carefully and correctly" arrange any music for brass bands.[26] New York bandmaster Claudio S. Grafulla, one of the most talented arrangers of his day, frequently prepared pieces for other bands. On one occasion he was able to write off a potpourri based on Fry's "Leonora" after simply hearing someone whistle the airs.[27]

Inasmuch as most ensembles shared the problem of acquiring music, it was also common for bands to beg or borrow music from each other. (Stealing was not unknown, but it was not recommended.) One old-time member of the Salem (North Carolina) Band recalled that his fellow bandsmen occasionally copied music from traveling circus bands. More formal exchanges of music were also negotiated by various organizations. The following letter, written on March 15, 1858, by a member of the Tallmadge (Ohio) Cornet Band, provides a vivid picture of such band cooperation.

Friend Wright

I re'ded your Letter & the music you returned. I have written you two other pieces and I think you will like them. You mention that you have received four new pieces from Graffula [i.e., Claudio Grafulla]. If you want to exchange I would be glad to do so. I have some very heavy pieces for Brass Band and they are first rate for Concert. They each occupy about 4 pages. One is from the Opera of Norma, one from the Opera of Sonnambula, one from the opera of Lucia DeLammermore and one From the Opera of Leonora. I have plenty of heavy Quick Steps. If you want to work I will send you some in exchange. I will mention some viz. Continentals Quick Step by Graffula, Constellation Quick by Graffula, Capt. Smith's Quick Step by Graffula, Ripvanwinkle Quick Step by Graffula, Wood Side Quick Step, Wood Up Quick Step, John Anderson and dozens of others that are rather difficult to perform so if you want some work to do I can accommodate you. Please remember me to all yours.

Truly, Isaac White[28]

For some bands the easiest way to acquire music was simply to ignore the printed page. Fragmentary documentary evidence indicates that a modest number of ensembles—white as well as Black, New Orleans-based and not—relied on "head-men" as well as "note-men" to render their programs. The nonreaders in the group simply memorized entire pieces of music or, less commonly, learned simple harmonic patterns and played ad libitum to support the melodic lines. Much more research should be done on these practices, especially since they relate so clearly to the evolution of improvisational jazz.

Not surprisingly, the disorderly patterns of borrowing and buying, arranging and rearranging music occasionally led to confusion about the origin of band compositions. In 1883, Patrick Gilmore took the unusual step of informing the public that, contrary to popular opinion, he was not the creator of "When Johnnie Comes Marching Home." As Gilmore explained in a statement published in *The Leader,* he had simply latched onto an existing tune— "a musical waif," he called it—and worked it up into the widely popular song.[29] Of more concern was the problem of composers not receiving proper credit for pieces that they had written. Although music published in America had been protected under the general United States copyright laws since 1790 and as a specific creative category since 1831, some pieces, through bandsmen's ignorance, carelessness, or intrigue, were reprinted or copied without proper credit to the composer. Music by foreigners was unprotected by law until 1891, and performance rights were not included in American copyright legislation until 1897.

Yet despite the problems, the rather chaotic approach to music acquisition also had benefits. It allowed many individuals to exercise their creativity in the fields of arranging and composition. More important, it allowed bands, however randomly, to build up their libraries. By 1889, Gilmore had built up a music collection of about ten thousand items.[30] Ellis Brooks's Chicago-based band boasted an outstanding music library of almost thirteen thousand numbers in 1910.[31] Although amateur bands had much smaller collections, they were also able to put music into the hands of the musicians and music into the lives of the people.

7.
BAND SUPPLIES OF EVERY DESCRIPTION

We are all very well pleased with the instruments we got
of you; after using them seven months we take the second
cake in our county.

—Willis H. Platt, Assistant Leader of Plainfield (Ohio)

Cornet Band, in a letter to Lyon and Healy Company

Francis Grund, a Viennese immigrant who studied American society during the vibrant days of the new republic, noted that Americans often seemed to confuse business with play. "There is, probably, no people on earth with whom business constitutes pleasure, and industry amusement, in an equal degree with the inhabitants of America," he mused in his commentary of 1837.[1] Had Grund returned to America fifty years later, he would have discovered that America's band instrument dealers had carried this national trait one step farther and had made a profitable business out of play as they sold hundreds of thousands of dollars worth of equipment to eager bandsmen across the nation. The effects of this commerce were profound. By retailing the requisite band supplies and by promoting the formation of bands with well-placed and effective publicity, enterprising businessmen not only stimulated the organization and growth of individual bands, but also helped to shape the evolution of the art form itself.

THE MERCHANDISE: INSTRUMENTS

"The first matter of importance in the formation of a Brass Band, is the selection of good instruments,"[2] claimed New York manufacturer Allen Dodworth in 1849. His assertion, not surprisingly, was echoed over the years by every major instrument maker and dealer in America. Bandsmen obtained their instruments from a variety of sources, ranging from European imports, to handmade productions of individual American artisans, to mass-produced instruments of the great American musical manufactories.

128

The epigraph at the head of this chapter is from the Lyon and Healy catalog *Band Instruments, Uniforms, Trimmings, &c.* (Chicago, 1881), 86.

Imports

Detailed records of musical instrument sales in nineteenth-century America are not available. Judging from the extensive selection of foreign-made instruments in early American musical instrument trade catalogs—as well as the abundance of British-, French-, and Central European-made winds that are found by antique dealers in the nation's attics—it appears that imports constituted the largest single source of band instruments prior to 1900.

In the late eighteenth and early nineteenth centuries, importing patterns were haphazardly dictated by the idiosyncratic practices of a few local dealers. The Boston merchants C. and E. W. Jackson, for instance, offered customers the following British-made inventory in October of 1821: keyed bugles for $45, trumpets for $22, violins for $7 to $30, clarinets for $9 to $20, flutes for $1.50 to $60, fifes for 50 cents to $2.25, and pianos for $200 to $400.[3] Other instrument importers diversified their stock, mixing nonmusical manufactures with bugles, flutes, and violins. Frederic Lane of Boston, for example, sold umbrellas, sword canes, and backgammon men, along with string and wind instruments in 1830.[4] Some musicians, including a number of Moravian bandsmen, opted to exercise more control over their purchases and ordered their instruments directly from European dealers. However, the delay in receiving goods from overseas could extend to a year or more, and may have counteracted any advantage in selection. Immigrants who carried their own instruments to this country provided yet another source of European-made musical goods. Whatever the method, obtaining a good band instrument was not a simple task in pre–1850 America.

By the mid-nineteenth century, many more American firms were advertising themselves as importers of musical

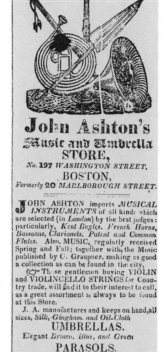

Boston music dealer and umbrella maker John Ashton offered a variety of imported goods in 1827. This advertisement appeared in the November 3, 1827, edition of the New Hampshire Statesman and Concord Register. *Kurt Stein Collection.*

St. Louis music dealers Balmer and Weber included a view of their 1840s music shop in the lithographed sheet music cover of "The Blues Quickstep" by J. W. Postlewaite. A wide range of merchandise, including pianos, banjos, brass, and woodwinds, are visible in the store's displays. Library of Congress.

merchandise, and while pianos and parlor reed organs often constituted the principal business, band instruments could be a welcome additional source of income. Every major American city appears to have had at least one such firm. The names of Klemm and Brothers, Philadelphia; Firth, Hall and Pond, New York; Meacham, Albany; Prentiss, Boston; and many other dealers are stamped onto dozens of extant, mid–nineteenth-century wind instruments that are apparently of European design and construction.

Musical instrument sales patterns of the pre–Civil War period indicate a seller's market. Most musicians had to accept whatever instrument was available to them or else wait many months for expensive, custom-made winds and brasses. The advent of mass production and mail order merchandising in the last third of the nineteenth century, however, radically changed the instrument selling business. By the 1870s a bewildering variety of band instrument makes and models confronted buyers. American musicians, for perhaps the first time, had a real choice in instruments. How was an intelligent decision to be made in this buyer's market? For many bandsmen the presence of a famous foreign maker's name was undoubtedly the deciding factor.

It is not surprising that America's almost total reliance on imported instruments in the early years fostered an overwhelming reverence for foreign wares later on. "Many are under the impression that a Brass Instrument that is not imported cannot be good," wrote Dodworth at midcentury.[5] Such widespread veneration of European instruments persisted, and American music dealers were quick to capitalize on this foreign mystique by garnering exclusive contracts with the best-known foreign firms. In New York City, both Louis Schreiber (from about 1873 to 1884) and later on the giant wholesaler Carl Fischer enjoyed lucrative "sole agent" relationships with the renowned London firm of Besson and Company. At the same time, William A. Pond in New York became distributor for the rival British maker, Boosey and Company.

French manufacturers, noted for their "perfection of the light piston valves," were also well represented by American band instrument importers. Lyon and Healy, a mammoth Chicago-based musical merchandiser, advertised an expensive line of top-quality Henry Gunckel brass and winds, as well as moderately priced instruments by F. Jaubert & Co. The Philadelphia firm of J. W. Pepper established import relationships with at least four French

130

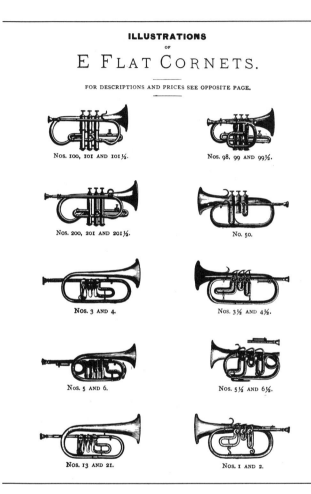

ILLUSTRATIONS

OF

E FLAT CORNETS.

FOR DESCRIPTIONS AND PRICES SEE OPPOSITE PAGE.

NOS. 100, 101 AND 101½.

NOS. 98, 99 AND 99½.

NOS. 200, 201 AND 201½.

NO. 50.

NOS. 3 AND 4.

NOS. 3½ AND 4½.

NOS. 5 AND 6.

NOS. 5½ AND 6½.

NOS. 13 AND 21.

NOS. 1 AND 2.

In 1881 Chicago-based Lyon and Healy offered twenty-five different models of E-flat cornets. Prices ranged from $23 for over-shoulder models (not illustrated here) to $94 for silver-plated imports by Henry Gunckel, Paris (models 98 through 101). Models 200 and 201 were less expensive imports by F. Jaubert & Co., Paris. All of these cornet varieties were "in stock at all times."

wind makers, including Buffet-Crampon and Jerome Thibouville-Lamy. Bruno and Sons in New York were exclusive agents for popular Pourcelle instruments from Paris, while Snyder and Hannold in Philadelphia marketed the relatively inexpensive brasses of A. Hilleron of Paris. Other low-cost Parisian instruments were sold in vast numbers through the great mail order houses of Montgomery Ward (Jules DeVere instruments) and Sears, Roebuck and Company (Dupont instruments until about 1905, Marceau instruments thereafter).

Winds and brasses of German and Central European manufacture were generally considered to be inferior versions of French and British models. Lyon and Healy reflected the common wisdom of the day in an 1881 advertisement:

Many . . . dealers are also practicing [a] stupendous fraud by selling cheap German instruments and styling them "improved piston, light valves," thus, while not stating positively that they are the *celebrated French piston valves, with improved light action,* they lead the public to so believe, and commit an unpardonable offense by palming this trash upon the unsuspecting as first-class instruments. This is a very clever trick, and bands can not be too careful in not getting caught.[6]

Rather than establish exclusive import deals with these less popular firms, Americans apparently obtained large numbers of inexpensive, unmarked German and Central European winds, which were stamped, if at all, with a local trade name such as "Eclipse," "Perfected," or "Superior." Many of these instruments may have come from the giant Bohland and Fuchs factory in Graslitz, Bohemia; hundreds of late-nineteenth-century "American" instruments bear the telltale *B & F* stamp.

The American prejudice against Central European brass was not entirely fair. The German and Bohemian factories produced some excellent brasswinds, while many of the French imports were actually of poor quality. Nevertheless, given the high quality of the best French and British productions as well as the vast numbers of serviceable and cheap imports, American wind instrument makers were faced with a great challenge. The success of these craftsmen in meeting that challenge parallels the nation's growth as a world industrial leader.

Early American Makers

The American branch of the band instrument industry may have begun as early as the 1760s when a few isolated craftsmen, primarily in New England, are thought to have applied their mechanical skills to the creation of woodwind and brass instruments. Demonstrating what Dodworth proudly called the "spirit of Yankee Enterprise," these pioneering makers and their successors set out to emulate their European counterparts, but in the end they developed their own unique artistry.

Many of the hundred or so known American wind instrument makers before 1860 were immigrant artisans who viewed musical productions as only one aspect of their livelihood.[7] German-trained John B. Dash, described as America's first wind instrument maker on the basis of a 1765 New York advertisement for French horns, was principally a tin- and coppersmith. Similarly, several early woodwind makers, including Jacob Anthony (of Philadelphia) and John Ashton, Henry Prentiss, and Ferdinand Schauffler (all of Boston), were turners, who applied their expertise in shaping wood and ivory to the manufacture of walking sticks and umbrellas, as well as flutes and clarinets. The first American drum makers commonly doubled as coopers or cabinet makers. Other musical instrument makers applied their skills to the manufacture of diverse articles such as telescopes, billiard balls, patent models, wagon wheels, watches, and gold pencils.[8]

There were only a few dozen American craftsmen who are recognized primarily as wind instrument makers prior to the Civil War. A few of these pioneers deserve special note. George Catlin (1778–1852), America's "first important maker of woodwind musical instruments,"[9] conducted his business in Hartford, Connecticut, from 1799 to 1815 and then transferred his shop to Philadelphia, where he worked from 1816 until his death. Unlike most other early American instrument makers, Catlin was born, and presumably learned his trade, in the United States. The nature of his early training is uncertain. He may have been apprenticed as a wood turner or a cabinet maker, but at some point he attained expertise in the design and construction of sophisticated woodwinds. In addition to the usual assortment of flutes and clarinets, Catlin's remarkable output included finely made bassoons and novel bass clarinets, instruments rarely attempted by other American makers until much later in the century. Though his Hartford-period instruments represent the American state of the art in woodwind design, Catlin was apparently unable to keep pace with rapid advances in woodwind fingering systems, and his Philadelphia business never enjoyed the success of his first years. Nevertheless, Catlin's impact on American woodwind making was great—because of his relatively large output of fine instruments and because of his influence, through example and apprenticeship arrangements—among the next generation of craftsmen.

One maker who was certainly inspired by Catlin's work was Samuel Graves (1794–1878), founder of Graves and Company. Usually designated the "first large manufacturer of wind instruments in the United States,"[10] the

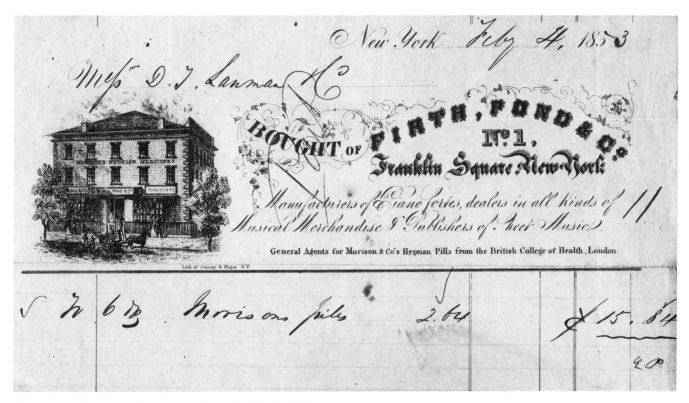

Like many other music instrument sellers, the New York firm Firth, Pond and Company supplemented their income with nonmusical merchandise. Judging from receipts of the 1850s, they did a brisk business in Morison & Company's "Hygeian Pills" imported from London.

firm was established in 1824 at West Fairlee, Vermont. Soon thereafter Graves moved his business to a larger, four-story building near the Ashuelot River in Winchester, New Hampshire. It was there that Graves's reputation grew, first for the manufacture of fine woodwinds, and, with the increasing popularity of keyed and valved brass instruments in the 1830s, for the fashioning of outstanding brasswinds as well. The output of Graves and Company was larger and more varied than any other American maker before the Civil War.[11] Keyed bugles, ophicleides, slide trombones, and a wide range of valved brass complemented an assortment of clarinets and flutes. In 1850 the firm moved once again, this time to Boston, which had become a center for instrument making and distribution. The woodwind line was apparently abandoned completely at about this time, reflecting the universal popularity of brass bands. Yet the beautifully made keyed bugles and cornets of the Boston years were among the finest instruments available to musicians of the day, and the dozens of surviving Graves and Company winds and brasses attest to the quantity and quality of this early American maker's instruments.

In the 1820s and 1830s American woodwind makers far outnumbered those specializing in brass, but the brass band craze quickly altered that situation. By the late 1840s the number of United States woodwind makers appears to have declined slightly, while brass makers enjoyed unprecedented growth. Brass specialists outnumbered woodwind makers by the mid–1850s.[12] Prominent among these metal craftsmen, most of whom worked in New England, were Thomas Paine (Woonsocket, Rhode Island), Isaac Fiske (Worcester, Massachusetts), and the Boston makers J. Lathrop Allen and E. G. Wright.[13] Each of these men capitalized on the brass band phenomenon and made unique contributions to the development and manufacture of brasswinds.

Thomas Paine (1812–1895) was an inventor and a machinist, and he has been credited with designing the string-activated rotary valve that characterizes so many early American brass. Paine's interest in the construction of valves probably began in the late 1830s when several Boston bands began converting to brass. Virtually all of his surviving instruments are novel in design, and may not have achieved widespread popularity. By the late 1850s Thomas Paine had abandoned brasses for the manufacture of clocks and violins.

Joseph Lathrop Allen (1815–ca. 1905) got on the brass-making bandwagon in 1839. Though his first instruments were probably keyed bugles, he soon devoted himself exclusively to valved brass. Allen is best known for his distinctive pinched rotary valve design, developed in about 1850. Allen reduced the diameter of each rotor and employed flattened, racetrack-shaped windways so that the valve was easier to turn and stop than conventional patterns. Allen enjoyed the endorsement of Harvey B. Dodworth, prominent New York bandleader, for whom a unique cornet with five Allen valves was constructed. The resulting business allowed Allen to expand his Boston operation to include a half dozen or more skilled craftsmen by the late 1850s.

Elbridge G. Wright (1811–1871) began his brass-making activities in Roxbury, Massachusetts, in the late 1830s, and shortly thereafter moved to Boston. Like Paine and Allen, Wright capitalized on the new fashions in band instrumentation and was quick to adopt new designs and technologies. But unlike his rival makers, who concentrated almost exclusively on valved brass, Wright continued to devote much time to the perfection of the keyed bugle. His spectacular presentation E-flat keyed bugles, constructed from sterling silver or gold—elaborately engraved with flags, eagles, and other patriotic devices—represent the pinnacle of the American instrument makers' art.

No early instrument maker was more closely tied to America's brass band movement than Isaac Fiske (1820–1894) of Worcester, Massachusetts. Fiske's operations began modestly in 1842, but he soon developed a reputation for outstanding workmanship and design. This renown, coupled with the rapid population growth of Worcester and other New England manufacturing centers, assured Fiske of a steady business. Fiske was probably the first instrument maker to enhance his image by sponsoring his own band. Fiske's Cornet Band, resplendent in fine uniforms and led by the brilliant young cornetist Matthew Arbuckle, achieved excellent results. The band, naturally, was outfitted with instruments by Fiske.

By 1860, the wind instrument making business in the United States was well established. Production was limited, with a total average American output of only a few thousand instruments per year. The more exotic wind instruments, such as bassoons, ophicleides, and keyed bugles, may have been attempted by only about a dozen individuals during this formative period. Yet brass and woodwind instruments of the highest quality were produced by skilled American craftsmen. The stage was set for the era of mass production.

Transition

It has been said that the Civil War cuts like a swath down the middle of the nineteenth century, and, in a sense, the conflict slices through the history of the band instrument business in the same way. Before the war, band instruments were manufactured primarily on a piece by piece basis. Because of the amount of handwork involved, it was difficult if not impossible to acquire a ready-made set of instruments. Instead, bandsmen had to place an order with the manufacturer and wait as long as six months for delivery. This situation changed radically after the Civil War. By the last quarter of the nineteenth century many large instrument companies, utilizing various methods of mass production, were offering musicians a dizzying array of ready-made instruments, both individually and in sets. If any one person can be credited with this revolution it would be John F. Stratton.[14]

John F. Stratton (1832–1912) was born into a musical New Hampshire family and became a gifted performer on trombone, keyed bugle, clarinet, and violin as a young boy. By the age of twenty he had become a bandleader in

The Civil War created an unprecedented American demand for brass instruments. Over-shoulder styles of the type used by the Seventh New York Cavalry, shown here camped near Washington, D.C., were manufactured in large numbers by John F. Stratton and others. Library of Congress.

Hartford, Connecticut, where he entered the musical instrument sales business. With an acute business sense, Stratton recognized the economic advantages of mass-producing band instruments. His first New York factory was established in 1860, just in time to capitalize on the unprecedented demands caused by the Civil War. Stratton was in a unique position in 1861 to fill government orders, which totaled more than sixty thousand field trumpets and bugles during the course of the war. His factory employed one hundred fifty to two hundred men, and at times produced an astonishing one hundred instruments per day. Other instrument makers may have benefited

135

from increased war production, but no one was in a better position to profit from it than Stratton.

Following the war Stratton continued to pursue an aggressive program of capitalization. He recognized that Europe could provide an ideal combination of skilled craftsmen and inexpensive labor. So in 1866 the first overseas Stratton factory was established in Markneukirchen, Saxony. Stratton's instruments, though not necessarily as fine as the individually handmade productions of New England makers, were sturdy, attractive, relatively inexpensive, and always in stock. Other wind makers were obliged to modify their operations accordingly.

A number of American firms took advantage of the Civil War to commence or expand their band instrument operations.[15] In Philadelphia the long-lived establishments of William Seefeldt, Ernst Seltman, and Henry G. Lehnert all began at about this time. With the commencement of operations by such New York–based manufacturers and dealers as Charles A. Zoebisch, Moses Slater, John Howard Foote, Louis Schreiber, and John F. Stratton, the city gradually overtook Boston as the largest wind instrument center in America. The Boston firms of David C. Hall and Benjamin F. Quinby also commenced production during the war years to supplement the expanded operations of Graves, Wright, and Allen. The early 1860s, furthermore, witnessed the beginnings of the great Chicago music dealership of Lyon and Healy. Each of these companies employed many workers and, one suspects, adopted at least some of the features of assembly line manufacturing. Thus, the turbulent decade between 1860 and 1870 saw a profound and irreversible change in the musical instrument business. Increased demand, coupled with increased production capacity, had transformed the wind instrument trade in America from a specialized craft to a major industry.

The Factories

With the advent of inexpensive, mass-produced wind instruments came the need for economical manufacturing methods and skillful marketing. Many smaller firms of the pre–1860 era were unable to meet these challenges. Others merged, reorganized, and developed new production and sales techniques. The distinguished Boston firms of E. G. Wright and Samuel Graves, for example, combined to form the Boston Musical Instrument Manufactory in 1869.[16] This company specialized in the production of a relatively few different models of the most popular, high-quality, valved brasswinds. Though several times more expensive than cheap imports, the Boston band instruments benefited from the outstanding reputations of the company's predecessors, and the firm prospered until after World War I.

During the 1870s and 1880s several important developments occurred in the American instrument trade. One notable event was the arrival in 1877 of the distinguished London brasswind maker and performer, Henry Distin, who worked first with Moses Slater in New York and then with J. W. Pepper in Philadelphia before building his own factory in Williamsport, Pennsylvania, in 1887.[17] Many other fine British and European instrument makers had come to America, but never before had a prominent foreign maker transferred his operations to this country. Shortly after the move to Williamsport, Distin retired, leaving the firm's management to Brua C. Keefer, who engraved his own name on subsequent Williamsport brass instruments.

The principal Philadelphia rival of Distin was his former partner J. W. Pepper (1853–1919), who began business in the Centennial year.[18] Pepper produced his own instrument brands, such as the "Artists Solo" and "Premier" brasses and the "Challenge" and "Standard" per-

The Philadelphia firm of J. W. Pepper often sold complete sets of band instruments. The Greenville (Rhode Island) Cornet Band purchased a set of eight brass for $166.20 in October 1888.

cussion. He also imported many other lines, including the "Surprise," "20th Century," and "Perfected" brands. Lavishly illustrated Pepper catalogs, which were widely distributed to bandsmen and other musicians, reveal an astonishingly diverse stock of band instruments. In one catalog of the 1890s cornetists could choose from ninety-eight different styles and models ranging in price from eight to sixty-five dollars. Also featured were ninety-six varieties of flutes and piccolos and more than one hundred thirty different snare and bass drums.

Of all the changes in America's band instrument trade during the 1870s and 1880s, the most notable relate to the westward expansion of the music business. Instrument wholesalers such as J. W. Jenkins (founded in Kansas City in 1884) and Sherman, Clay and Company (founded in San Francisco in 1879) provided important new outlets for a complete range of musical merchandise. The mail order houses of Montgomery Ward and Sears, Roebuck and Company also began their instrument sales activities in the Midwest. By the 1880s the Chicago-based Lyon and Healy Company boasted the largest band instrument business in the country.[19]

But increased sales were not the only contribution of midwestern and western businessmen. Just as Stratton transformed instrument making in the 1860s and helped shift the focus from Boston to New York, so C. G. Conn and others in subsequent decades established the states of Indiana, Illinois, Michigan, Ohio, and Wisconsin as leaders in the instrument making business.[20] The Centennial year of 1876—when Charles Gerard Conn (1844–1931) began mass-producing his novel, patented rubber-rimmed mouthpiece and, with the help of three or four employees, completed his first cornet—is a turning point in the history of American instrument making. From modest beginnings in his hometown of Elkhart, Indiana, Conn

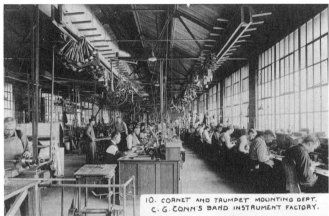

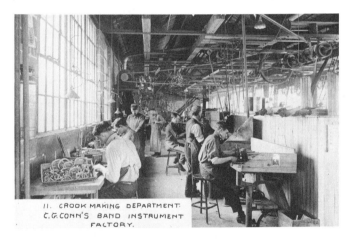

C. G. Conn's second factory, built in 1883 after a devastating fire destroyed the first, was itself destroyed by fire in 1910. In this 1905 postcard view, the railroad and streetcar lines that serviced the factory are visible.

Conn's factory in 1910 was efficiently organized and mechanized, but still relied on skilled handcraftsmen in each stage of instrument making. These postcards are part of a forty-card set that illustrates many aspects of the firm's operations.

created an unrivaled band instrument empire.[21] The business grew slowly, with fewer than eight thousand instruments completed at the time of a disastrous factory fire in 1883. Rather than quit, Conn within three months had built a new and larger factory. Operations expanded significantly in 1887, when Conn bought out the Worcester factory of Isaac Fiske. Production increased rapidly to two thousand units per year. At about this time the innovative Conn introduced the first American-made saxophone and double-bell euphonium, as well as early examples of the mellophone and sousaphone. Conn was willing to produce fine woodwinds as well as brasses, and was thus able to influence and profit from the growing popularity of the mixed brass and woodwind ensembles. By World War I, the C. G. Conn Company was producing about ten thousand brasses and five thousand wood-winds per year.

Other midwestern instrument companies followed Conn's example in short order. In 1882, James Warren York (1839–1924) founded his successful firm in Grand Rapids, Michigan.[22] He began as an importer, but within a few years he commenced manufacturing mouthpieces and later turned to brasses. Former Conn employee F. Q. "Gus" Buescher started his own Elkhart-based company in 1888.[23] By 1905 he enjoyed sales of $150,000 per year, representing perhaps two or three thousand instruments. The Buescher firm produced the popular "True Tone" brand of winds and was noted for its fine saxophones. Cleveland's Henderson N. White, founder of the H. N. White Company in 1893, was best known for high-quality "King" brand instruments.[24] Other famous midwestern company owners, all of whom first worked for C. G. Conn or one of his associates, include Frank Holton, whose Chicago operations began in 1898; E. K. Blessing, who worked in Elkhart after leaving the employ of Holton and Buescher in 1906; and Henry Martin, a former employee of both Conn and York, who established his own Elkhart factory early in the twentieth century.[25]

The reasons for the establishment of so many instrument makers in the Midwest are not entirely clear. Certainly the trend reflects a shift in the geographical center of America's population in general and the band movement in particular. It has also been suggested that instrument factories in Ohio, Indiana, Illinois, and Michigan avoided problems of unionization that were common in the East. Whatever the reasons, the pattern started by Conn and his musical neighbors persists to this day.

The growing popularity of mixed instrumentation in bands led to a resurgence of woodwind manufacturing in America. Several brass makers, notably Conn, Martin,

and Buescher, were successful in tapping this new market. Other makers, including Penzel-Mueller in New York and William S. Haynes and Cundy-Bettoney in Boston, devoted most of their energies to this aspect of the instrument trade.[26] Thanks to the efforts of the several major American brass and woodwind factories, the annual production of band instruments totaled many tens of thousands by World War I.

OTHER MERCHANDISE

Instruments alone were not enough to make a band. Musical merchandisers also did a brisk business in uniforms, music, and instrument accessories, as well as in such services as replating and repairing damaged instruments. These activities were an important part of the economics of the band movement and furnished employment for many American workers.

Uniforms

For many bands the acquisition of stylish military uniforms was only slightly less important than the acquisition of suitable musical instruments. In some communities, the bandsmen's finery generated even more interest and discussion than their instruments and music. Such a situation is conjured up in *The Music Man* when River City's unflappable bandmaster, Professor Harold Hill, faced with inquiries about his ability to form a band, quips lightly, "When the uniforms arrive they'll forget about everything else." It is a comic line but, as writer Meredith Willson knew from his many years with the Sousa Band, it bore a clear relationship to historical reality. The Cedar Falls (Iowa) Drum Corps, for example, boasted proudly in 1891 that they had been hired for several performances just "on the strength of our uniforms."[27] Other bands had similar experiences and, as surviving record books reveal, many amateur groups devoted large portions of their meetings to lively debates about uniforms and how to procure them.

Businessmen were quick to take advantage of this widespread interest in band fashion. By the last quarter of the nineteenth century, supply houses devoted exclusively to the sale of military-style uniforms and accessories could be found in every major city along the eastern seaboard. In Philadelphia alone there were at least nine uniform companies in the 1880s,[28] while New York and Boston similarly boasted multiple dealerships. There were also major uniform outlets farther west. The Pettibone Manufacturing Company, widely advertised as the "Leading House in the United States," maintained its uniform factories and business office in Cincinnati, Ohio. Although the Chicago area lacked a comparable outlet in the years immediately after the Civil War, Lyon and Healy, the city's premier instrument dealers, eventually entered the uniform business themselves and by the 1880s were offering their customers a wide range of band suits and accessories.

As far as the actual transaction of business was concerned, the geographical location of these businesses mattered little. Most companies actively solicited mail order customers to whom they mailed handsome printed catalogs depicting the available merchandise. And as these publications reveal, the world of band wear was extensive and elegant. Lyon and Healy's 1881 catalog offered customers four styles of uniforms, fourteen styles of caps, and numerous trimmings and decorations. By 1891 the uniform division of the business had expanded to the level that the company could afford to issue a separate band uniform catalog featuring thirty color illustrations of uniform styles.[29] Henderson and Company of Philadel-

In 1881, Lyon and Healy offered a variety of band uniform styles as well as different fabrics and colors.

phia published a similar catalog around the turn of the century; this fifty-two-page booklet depicted over sixty different jacket styles (each available in over twenty different fabrics) as well as matching trousers, capes, overcoats, and caps.[30] In addition to the basic uniform, merchants sold bandsmen a vast array of decorative extras that would enhance and personalize any outfit. These "equipments" included epaulets, shoulder knots, embroidered emblems, belts, buttons, and pouches. Gilt braid and decorative cord were available to add ornamentation to jackets, and band helmets could be enhanced by all manner of crests, pompoms, plumes, and spikes. These supplementary ornaments could be purchased separately and added, according to taste, to existing uniforms.

In spite of the obvious emphasis on style, the costuming of the band did not have to cost much. "Band uniforms cheaper than ever" was the motto of Jacob Reed's Sons Company of Philadelphia in the 1880s, and their claim seems amply justified.[31] For a mere ten dollars this company supplied a tasteful band suit consisting of a gold-trimmed band coat, a matching pair of trousers, and a flat-topped cap with brim. Not to be outdone, the Boston-based G. W. Simmons Company, which claimed to have ten thousand complete uniforms in stock at all times, offered a coat, a pair of trousers, and a cap for as little as seven and a half dollars. If bandsmen chose secondhand uniforms, the cost of outfitting the ensemble could be lower still. In the election year of 1884, G. W. Simmons advertised used cadet gray jackets and gray fatigue caps for just a dollar and a quarter per set.[32]

On the other hand, bandsmen with a taste for the flamboyant and with the requisite funds, could order custommade regalia of considerable splendor. A handsome outfit made up of a plumed hat (any color), trousers, and a cutaway coat decorated with epaulets, two rows of buttons, aiguillettes, and belt was available from Pettibone Manufacturing Company for twenty-two dollars in 1885.[33] For a few dollars more, the outfit could be enhanced by white duck leggins with gilt buttons (eighty cents), a pair of embroidered collar braids (one dollar and seventy cents), personalized cap ornament (thirty cents), and a black patent leather music pouch (one dollar).

Drum majors, for whom the "greatest possible amount of show [was] deemed desirable" might spend considerably more than other bandsmen. In 1874, M. Slater Company of New York promised to outfit these eye-catching officers with a splendid coat, gold belt, and gold-striped pantaloons for from fifty-two to sixty-four dollars.[34] The bearskin shako and wooden baton, without which the costume was considered incomplete, were extra. As listed in the Lyon and Healy catalogs of the early 1890s, these items in their most basic form cost nine dollars and seven and a half dollars, respectively. If a bandsman wanted an authentic bearskin shako and gold plating on the baton's decorative ball, he had to pay more than twice as much.

The most elaborate—and expensive—band uniforms for sale by Henderson and Company in 1900 were designed for the drum major, whose plumed shako and tasseled baton add an elegant aspect to a band on parade.

As contemporary photographs show, many bands did allocate the necessary funds for these items. Uniforms were so important to the Cornet Band of Orient, Long Island, that when it was discovered in 1889 that they could not get just what was wanted for twenty dollars per man, the band simply raised the expense limit to twenty-five dollars each. Some bands even ordered two uniforms, one for winter wear and a lighter weight outfit for summer performances.

To some extent, the fashion choices made by these groups changed over time. Just as there were styles and fads in everyday clothing, so there were trends in band fashions during the nineteenth century. The standard military jacket, replete with buttons, tails, and epaulets, was gradually replaced in many bands by the simpler and shorter jackets preferred by Sousa. Caps, too, changed over time, usually in tandem with styles of military uniforms. One sees a trend from high hats with plumes, to

Lyon and Healy illustrated many different styles of band hats, including these fancy designs, in sales catalogs of the 1880s.

keppies, to helmets with decorative spikes, to the soft cloth caps with visors typically donned by the professional bands in the 1890s. In addition to this wide range of military-style band uniforms, numerous novelty outfits came into vogue from time to time. When the Algerian-style Zouave units became popular during the Civil War, for instance, many bands adopted the colorful and exotic dress of these regiments. Cowboy bands, in which the players wore cowboy clothes, and kiltie bands, in which the musicians dressed in Scottish costumes, were both popular in the 1870s and 1880s.

It would, nevertheless, be dangerous to attempt to date a band photograph on the basis of the bands' uniforms alone. As late as the turn of the century, the Henderson Band Uniform Company carried an entire range of styles including Zouave outfits, traditional military jackets, and the most modern short coats. Bands continued to wear an assortment of styles, and the widespread use of secondhand clothing added to the variety. The vast divergence of personal taste always ensured that the appearance of each band would be somewhat distinctive.

Band Supplies

In addition to instruments and uniforms, enterprising merchants offered bandsmen numerous supplementary products. Most band companies carried a wide range of mouthpieces, mutes, reeds, and drumsticks. Dealers also sold springs, pads, keys, screws, and other instrument parts commonly used for repairs. Leaders in search of batons could find an array of styles, ranging from a simple holly stick that cost sixty cents to a handsome polished ivory artifact with engraved gold handle, leather case, and the princely price tag of sixty dollars.[35] Bandsmen requiring music stands had more choices. In addition to the standard folding metal racks, many merchants sold artistic wooden stands along with smaller music lyres that could be attached to the instruments or to the musicians' arms for playing on the march. There were polishing pomades to protect the instruments, and there were "embouchure restoratives" to protect the players' lips. Instrument cases, band lamps, and instrument cleaning brushes rounded out the list of supplies that were most commonly advertised.

Along with this band hardware, many companies carried printed music, score books, and related items. Introductory tutors and transposing manuals as well as a variety of published band music were widely available from the larger firms. Blank band books, music cards, portfolios, and music carrying cases were sold to bands so that bandleaders could copy out pieces to conform to their own instrumentation.

Bands could, thus, acquire a considerable amount of equipment. Groups that were limited in resources stuck to the essentials. But bandsmen who were limited in funds and unlimited in imagination could obtain fascinating two-in-one products that promised to cut down on the necessary purchases. One could acquire a marvelous portable music stand which just happened to double as a sword. Lightweight and handsome, the sword/stand could be worn decoratively on the belt or when needed, be unsheathed and extended sixty inches to serve as a sturdy music rack.[36] For the cornetist who needed both an instrument case and a music stand there was the versatile Acme Cornet Case. "A marvel of beauty and convenience," this contrivance successfully and elegantly combined both functions in one device.[37] There were, in addition, numerous crooks and key changers which, when added to existing instruments, would transform them to a new key, thus eliminating the musician's chore of transposing.

Bands in the Worcester, Massachusetts, area took advantage of Starkie's City Dye House for the maintenance of their uniforms. Specially printed trade cards such as this one testify to the large number of bands requiring such services.

Services

It is said that for every combat soldier in the army there are a half dozen auxiliary personnel backing him up. The ratio in the band world was not as high, but there were many individuals in the business of keeping bandsmen on the go. Professional arrangers supplied suitable music, and professional booking agents supplied suitable places to play. Given the fact that bandsmen often paraded in woolen coats and trousers in muddy streets or on hot summer days, it is hardly surprising that businesses sprang up for the purpose of cleaning and pressing band uniforms.

An entire industry developed around the care and repair of band instruments. Much of this work centered on the routine removal of dents and the replacement of broken valves, but experienced technicians also made major modifications that included the transformation of bell-up and

143

over-shoulder instruments into bell-front models. Similarly, cosmetic alterations were commonly offered by repairmen. By far the most popular of these services was the replating of brass instruments with a variety of nickel or silver finishes. During the heyday of the silver cornet bands in the last third of the nineteenth century, hundreds of bands paid from less than five dollars to more than forty dollars (depending on the type of finish and size of instrument) to turn their dull and dented brass-finish instruments into brilliant silver showpieces.[38] The engraving of cornet bells with florid designs was another common form of embellishment. Even the decoration of instruments with diamonds and pearls was not unknown, though this latter sort of work clearly belongs more in the realm of the jeweler than the instrument repairman.

SELLING TECHNIQUES

The manufacture of band supplies was only part of the band business. The economic success of a firm also depended on an effective marketing and distribution strategy. For small, localized companies, traditional advertising ploys such as the distribution of trade cards and the placement of advertisements in local newspapers and music journals generated sufficient publicity. But many music merchandisers dealt on a nationwide scale in the entire range of band merchandise. Among the large-scale businesses—such as Bruno & Son and Carl Fischer (New York), M. Slater, J. W. Pepper, and Charles Missenharter (Philadelphia), Rudolph Wurlitzer and Lyon and Healy (Chicago), and others—there developed a grand array of selling techniques. Many were forerunners of current practices.

Advertising was fundamental and took a variety of forms. Most large companies established a firm founda-tion of publicity through the judicious use of published notices and illustrated catalogs. Typical accompaniments to such basic advertisements were testimonial statements—generally touted as being unsolicited—from satisfied customers. These accolades were commonly published along with band news, biographical sketches of famous bandsmen, and new instrument advertisements in catalogs and company-sponsored periodicals. Conn's *Musical Truth,* H. N. White's *White Way News,* and J. W. Pepper's *Musical Times and Band Journal* are a few of the fascinating monthly magazines that published testimonial letters and capitalized on the close ties between bandsmen and their favorite musical instrument company.

Endorsements by famous bandsmen carried more clout than those of unknown amateurs, and companies tried to convince professional superstars to praise their products. Some firms achieved great success. Jules Levy gave favorable publicity to the Distin Company, and John Philip Sousa did the same for C. G. Conn. In fact, Conn carried this idea one step further by hiring distinguished virtuosi like cornetist Herbert L. Clarke and saxophonist E. A. Lefebre to test personally every instrument before it was sent to the prospective buyer. Accompanying each Conn cornet that left the Elkhart factory was a letter signed by Clarke stating:

> I have tested this Cornet and find it to be perfect in tune with an even scale, blows freely and the valve action is perfect, and it is an excellent instrument.[39]

Given such an enthusiastic endorsement by one of the world's greatest cornetists, it seems unlikely that many players would return an instrument as unsatisfactory or defective.

Supplementing these advertising efforts were additional tactics designed to arouse public interest and set one com-

Elegant Artist B♭ Gold Cornet

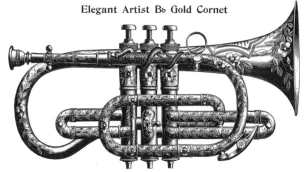

No. 18. B♭ Cornet, all gold-plated ; the whole instrument beautifully engraved and frosted ; gold snake with diamond eyes; pearl finger-buttons, two different mouth-pieces, valve cleaner, new and improved mute ; a fine rosewood Etui, containing oil-bottle and grease-box ; a most beautifully finished cornet, in new model satchel made of brown russet leather, and having the outside appearance of a traveling valise, handsomely fitted and lined with best plush and silk, nickel-plated trimmings and improved lock, ... $180.00

36. CORNET AND TRUMPET TESTING DEPT.
C.G. CONN'S BAND INSTRUMENT FACTORY.

Top: *The Elegant Artist Gold Cornet was a fabulous instrument at a fabulous price for 1890s soloists. The cornet was distributed by Harry Coleman of Philadelphia, who had recently acquired the New York factory of the Charles Missenharter Company where the instruments were apparently made.*
Bottom: *Hundreds of Conn cornets and trumpets await testing by virtuoso Herbert L. Clarke (seated), who signed a letter of examination for each instrument sold. This postcard, dated 1914, is one of the set of forty distributed by Conn to customers.*

pany apart from another. Some firms offered free lithographs of famous bands and bandsmen. Others offered free instruction manuals. One company active in the 1880s even offered free instruments, although if the customer read the fine print he discovered that what was free was the tone, not the instruments. The C. G. Conn Company, which was justly proud of its modern production facility, publicized its products through a series of forty fascinating postcards depicting various aspects of their music business. In what was one of the more dramatic publicity stunts of the period, Lyon and Healy promoted itself through its own company band.

In addition to good advertising, the large band supply companies developed highly efficient retailing procedures. With the exception of those firms devoted exclusively to wholesale trade, most companies maintained large and comfortable showrooms where knowledgeable salesmen demonstrated the merchandise to interested customers. Rudolph Wurlitzer had thirty such stores in operation by 1919, and Lyon and Healy's Chicago showroom was so magnificent that tourists reportedly dropped by just for a tour. Most companies also sought mail order customers from across the country. Taking advantage of vast improvements in transportation, America's music merchants, like other mail order retailers of the last quarter of the nineteenth century, were able to ship goods to the most rural and inaccessible regions. A liberal return policy and guarantees of satisfaction were common enticements to customers shopping at a distance. In yet another bid for sales, some companies commissioned "horse and buggy men" to hand-carry their products to rural Americans. A. J. "Bill" Johnson, who worked in this capacity for the York Company around 1900, recalled that the bulk of the business generated by these salesmen was to small community bands and to farmers.[40]

"There is satisfaction in a band where the instruments made by C. G. Conn, of Elkhart, Ind. are used. I am qualified to speak as I have used other makes besides the Conn, and I would quit the band business altogether if I had to use any other kind of an instrument."
A. B. Lowry, Bandmaster Fort Pierce Band, Fort Pierce, Fla.

Several major instrument makers, including Buescher, Holton, H. N. White, and C. G. Conn, issued advertising postcards with images of satisfied customers. More than a dozen different bands are depicted on cards endorsing Conn band instruments.

Underpinning these various selling techniques was a one-two punch of commercial genius that would have made Madison Avenue proud. First, music merchants made the notion of a town band irresistible. Then, when the public's interest had been piqued, they contrived to render band formation so easy that customers could hardly avoid jumping on the bandwagon. For their opening gambit, music merchants aimed at nothing less than the transformation of the band from a mere hobby into a pulsing symbol of patriotism, cultural achievement, and social refinement. In this endeavor music merchandisers generally had the enthusiastic support of newspaper editors, community leaders, and music teachers, all of whom favored anything related to artistic improvement. Drawing on this hospitable social climate, dealers had only to channel the public's interest into the band world.

Virtually every band instrument catalog and advertisement took advantage of the predisposition toward self-improvement. McCosh's *Guide,* the band handbook published as part of the Lyon and Healy catalogs of the late nineteenth and early twentieth centuries, linked bands directly with cultural advancement. "In small towns, where it is difficult to obtain good teachers, or where there are but few persons actively engaged in musical matters," wrote McCosh, "the most practical way of indulging a taste for the arts, is in the organization of a Brass Band."[41] Similarly, the Rudolph Wurlitzer Company reminded customers of the considerable benefits to be derived from bands. "By the very interest and enthusiasm which it arouses, the band is a tremendous influence for promoting the welfare and prosperity of a community. It is an asset and an advertisement—one which repays many times over for all time and money spent."[42] In fact, the Wurlitzer Company became the master of this not-so-subtle art of persuasion. One of the more clever Wurlitzer notices told the story of a certain midwestern town that was dead—"the joke of the county"—but somehow managed to become revitalized and prosper. Why? "Because," claimed the company, "a certain man saw the dire need of musical entertainment, and started a town band."[43] Propaganda, coupled with the obvious success of existing bands, did the job. And with public interest aroused, the companies could move on to phase two of their campaign—packaging the band.

When large firms such as S. R. Leland and Son of Worcester, Massachusetts, claimed to have "Band Supplies of Every Description,"[44] they meant it. A group of musicians could enter into negotiations with a number of companies and emerge with an entire band outfit. Instruments, the most important items, were conveniently sold in sets of about ten during the late 1880s for as little as one hundred twenty or one hundred thirty dollars—the approximate cost of a good bicycle at the time. For an extra fifty or hundred dollars, better instruments could be procured, but bands with limited resources could pay much less for used models. By offering payment through installments and by developing rental options, some companies made the financing attractive for many groups. Uniforms, music, and other accessories were offered with discounts and other incentives. Most companies also provided practical advice to beginning bandsmen. Published either as part of the catalogs, as in the case of McCosh's *Guide*, or separately in booklets like the J. W. Pepper Company's "The Town Band," these manuals covered such basic topics as how to organize a band, how to care for the instruments, how to line up for a parade, and how to achieve a balanced instrumentation. Many companies also aided in the tuition of new bands. Not only did they sell instruction manuals, but Rudolph Wurlitzer developed a correspondence course, and Leland

distributed lists of capable teachers available for hire. "[Our experts] will do all that [they] can to help you," promised one company, and the statement seems to have been more than an idle boast.[45]

SUCCESS OF THE INDUSTRY

That these sales techniques succeeded is beyond dispute. The large number of bands in existence at the end of the nineteenth century provide ample proof of marketing effectiveness. Myriad testimonials by bandsmen confirm the significant contributions and positive impact of the large band supply companies. One grateful customer of Lyon and Healy expressed his satisfaction in 1881:

> The instruments arrived in good shape, not a dent in them, which was certainly due to the fact that they were so carefully packed. To say they pleased us would not express it. We were more than pleased and surprised to find what a beautiful set of horns we could get for such a comparatively small price. We would recommend you to all band men, and say, "boys, give L. & H. a trial."[46]

This enthusiastic letter is but one of hundreds written to express similar sentiments. Henry Distin's brass catalog of 1906–1907 contains only twenty-four pages illustrating instruments but devotes forty pages to photos and testimonials of the many bands that used Distin instruments exclusively.[47]

But if business success is clear, the precise nature of the success is not because production records are incomplete. Lyon and Healy, which claimed to have three times as much band stock as any other American company in 1881, reported that during 1880–1881 they sold a total of one million dollars' worth of musical merchandise, one hundred fifty thousand dollars of which represented band instrument trade specifically. Ten years later, with a corre-

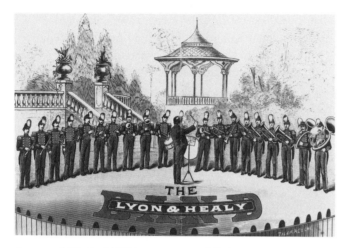

Lyon and Healy in Chicago sponsored their own company band, conducted by George W. Lyon. The band traveled widely and displayed the latest in instruments, uniforms, and accessories.

sponding increase in both the number of employees and the size of factory facilities, overall sales had risen to one and a half million dollars with, presumably, a comparable increase in band instrument sales.[48] Sears, Roebuck and Co., which had been active in supplying bands for at least two decades, claimed to have outfitted over five hundred complete bands in 1907 alone.[49] It has been conservatively estimated that, taken as a group, American manufacturers of brass instruments produced in excess of three hundred thousand dollars worth of merchandise in 1903. This quantity, in conjunction with the large numbers of imported band goods, contributed to a healthy development of the band trade. Though this branch of commerce represented less in dollar amounts than the piano trade, it

was nonetheless a major aspect of American musical commerce. Much more research needs to be done before a clear understanding of the extent of band merchandisers' profits can emerge.

It is even more difficult to document the breadth of the aesthetic influence of these companies on bands. To some extent music businesses supplied what bandsmen and their leaders wanted. But, to some equally immeasurable extent, bandsmen wanted what the companies supplied. The longevity of all-brass bands in small towns was partly a result of businesses rendering it so easy to establish this type of ensemble. The popularization of new instruments—such as the saxophone, the trumpet, and the sousaphone—at particular times was also partly due to business practices. When the experts at J. W. Pepper proclaimed that a "good band becomes a better band the moment the Trumpet Cornet is added,"[50] and when their brethren at Leland declared, "clarinets are *indispensable* in rendering modern compositions,"[51] players, especially amateurs, were likely to listen.

Musical purists may deplore the effect these instrument makers and distributors had on the artistic side of the band movement. However, most of these businessmen were motivated by more than just economic or self-serving objectives, and their influence was not necessarily bad. Many instrument makers like John F. Stratton, C. G. Conn, and George Lyon began as players and had strong emotional loyalties to bands as an artistic medium. Their interest in the art form was genuine and many-sided. Besides, it is probable that most businessmen in the band field knew as much, if not more, about musical excellence than the general public who, it will be seen, exerted a powerful influence of their own.

8.

THE OTHER SIDE OF THE FOOTLIGHTS: BANDSMEN AND THEIR AUDIENCE

The people came, from 'round the land,
To hear the band, the home town band.
Their music filled our hearts with joy,
The hometown band, when I was a boy.

—Carlton R. Lee, "The Home Town Band"

During the 1890s *The Birmingham News* published the following account of an outdoor band concert held one evening in the Alabama city:

> The first of Prof. Fred L. Grambs' band open air concerts took place last night in Capitol Park, at the head of Twentieth street. A good crowd of young ladies, young gentlemen, old men and old ladies and children were there and the delightful evening was made more pleasant by the sweet music.
>
> The programme as was printed in *The News* yesterday was carried out.
>
> The walks in the park were used by couples in sweet converse attuned to the music, and the fountain afforded a gathering place.

Mayor Van Hoose was present, and during one of the short waits, mounted on the curbing around the fountain and made a short speech, thanking Professor Grambs and his band in behalf of the city for the innovation.[1]

Although the writer of this article makes passing reference to the music played, his interest centers on the audience. Such an emphasis is entirely appropriate to a description of a nineteenth-century band concert because the bandsmen relied on their audience almost as much as the townsmen relied on their bands. Unlike a string quartet, which could perform satisfactorily for a handful of listeners or for the players themselves, a brass band expected the lively encouragement and spontaneous reactions of an audience. Without such support, the musicians might just as well pack up their horns and cease playing.

This actually happened in the town of Watsonville, California, in the mid-1870s. Stephen Martinelli, leader of one of the local brass bands, reported in the newspaper

149

The epigraph at the head of this chapter is from the beginning of a ten-stanza poem. Typescript in the Cokato Historical Society, Cokato, Minnesota.

that the ensemble had suffered for some time from a lack of "common courtesy and encouragements" from the people. Although the band was willing to practice hard and even donate its services on occasion, it found to its dismay that it was being "totally ignored." This was an intolerable situation. There was no alternative, declared Martinelli, but to disband until the town improved its attitude.[2]

Most amateur bandsmen of the time would have understood this reaction. It was not simply a question of a band's needing tangible rewards such as money, although money was certainly helpful. Equally important to the players was the stimulation provided by an enthusiastic crowd. This inherent dependence on the audience may explain why so many beginning bandsmen rushed out to play for neighbors before they were ready. In effect, a band performance was a musical conversation between the performers and the listeners. And although amateur bandsmen enjoyed the company of their fellow musicians, most players viewed performance in public as the final goal.

Professional bandsmen, for whom band performance was a business, had similar emotional ties to the people. Frank Simon, a successful professional band conductor and onetime cornetist with the Sousa Band, described this special bond between audience and players during an interview on the subject of radio broadcasting. When first introduced to this medium, Simon reported that he found the unresponsive walls of the studio to be repellent. "I thought the dead silence that follows the conclusion of each number was soul-crushing, to say the least," he said. "I could not feel my audience; I could not visualize them as I can now. For all the world, I might have been playing to a phantom audience, unseen spirits that were unable to whisper their appreciation, much less applaud approvingly."[3]

Simon eventually overcame his distaste for radio performance, and went on to conduct the famous ARMCO Band in its national radio broadcasts. For the bandsmen of the nineteenth century, however, and for John Philip Sousa and many other performers of the early twentieth century, a live audience was an essential component of any band performance. Consequently, bands put considerable time and energy into attracting and pleasing their public.

ATTRACTING THE CROWD

Publicity is a fundamental problem facing any performing organization. No band could expect to have an audience if people were unaware of its existence or its scheduled performances. Some thought had to be given to communicating with potential listeners. In small towns, word of mouth was often all that was needed, but most bands found that additional announcements in print were useful. They often discovered a welcome ally in the local newspaper editor who might be persuaded to publish announcements concerning the formation of bands, changes in personnel, and the locations and times of concerts. To supplement these community service messages, many bandleaders regularly inserted their own newspaper advertisements detailing the wide range of services their bands could offer. Large broadsides were always successful in calling attention to a band performance. Very active bands such as the Tallmadge Cornet Band of Tallmadge, Ohio, found it useful to print quantities of partially blank handbills on which specific concert times, dates, and prices could be inserted, as needed, by hand.

The town of Hopkinton in New Hampshire sponsored a gala benefit concert featuring noted soloists and the Hopkinton Cornet Band in April 1862. The original three-by-two-foot broadside is typical of advertisements for nineteenth-century band concerts.

The Six Counties Firemen Convention, ca. 1910, attracted large crowds in this unidentified American city. Similar scenes occurred regularly in towns across the nation.

The big professional bands handled publicity on a grander scale. These bands generally hired managers, such as Sousa's David Blakely, to arrange for the "papering" of a town well before the arrival of the band. Beautiful colored posters, elegant souvenir booklets, and collectible images of the musicians were all part of the publicity campaigns of these active, touring bands.

If the bands were eager to attract the public to their performances, they were equally eager to please the audience once assembled. To this end, bandsmen agreed to play in a variety of crowd-pleasing settings—even if this sometimes entailed discomfort to themselves. They played on diminutive bandstands in the middle of lakes, they played in cramped and unsteady boats, and they played in jolting bandwagons. Some bands accompanied holiday makers to sandy beaches where grit fouled their instruments' valves and slides. Others willingly trooped about town with cumbersome tubas and bass drums to give private serenades at the homes of prominent citizens. Most town bandsmen agreed to march in parades when needed, even though the sweltering heat of summer might cause the tar of the street paving to stick to their shoes and the blistering cold of winter might freeze their lips blue and their valves motionless. Every Easter morning at 2:00 A.M., the dedicated Moravian bandsmen of Salem, North Carolina, braved the darkness and the damp of the early morning hours to offer their fellow citizens the traditional predawn festival music.

In what was surely one of the most generous gestures ever made by performing artists, nineteenth-century bandsmen gave their blessing to the promenade concert, a new kind of musical setting which promised total comfort for the audience. As explained on an 1868 publicity poster for the Towler Brass Band, promenade concerts offered the "delights of the regular concert [without] that cramp-

Not all parades boasted huge crowds. A parade in Dolgeville, New York, honoring the Tryon Hook and Ladder Company appears to have had significantly more marchers than oniookers. Several bands marched in this parade, based on evidence of other photographs taken on the same day ca. 1885.

ing stiffness of body and weariness of spirit, which long sitting and want of conversational vent, commonly induces."[4] In other words, the audience was at liberty to walk about and talk during the presentation of the music.

Musical selections as well as musical settings were chosen with a view to pleasing the audience. The Chicago Band endorsed this accommodating philosophy so completely that the advertisement for its 1912 Ravinia Park concerts carried the sprightly motto: "A Modern Band for a modern Public . . . Stops at nothing to satisfy public taste." Most bands were less direct about their appeal to the audience, but by programming popular patriotic and romantic tunes, often in easygoing medley arrangements, they acknowledged the importance of pleasing the crowd. Exacting musician though he was, John Philip Sousa was extraordinarily conscious of the public's musical taste. He cheerfully incorporated popular new musical idioms such

In one of the smallest parades on record, the ten-piece Oswayo, Pennsylvania, band marched through town in May 1907. The audience of small children accompanying the band may have been on their way to a Sunday school picnic at which the band would have provided music.

154

as ragtime into his programming, and is known to have changed repertoire in midconcert if the mood of the audience seemed to require it. Sousa's biographer, Paul Bierley, writes of one occasion in 1889 when Sousa took the Marine Band to Fayetteville, North Carolina. Faced with an unresponsive southern crowd, the resourceful leader impulsively told the band to play "Dixie," whereupon wild cheers broke out and continued unabated for almost twenty minutes.[5]

Further enticements to the audience included half-price tickets for children, stunningly uniformed bandsmen, fully illuminated and decorated halls, and the booking of talented and attractive soloists. Special performances such as "gift concerts" were devised to lure an audience with the promise of a door prize. The fact that bandsmen could alter the direction of their instruments' bells according to the audience's position merely underscores the players' willingness to adapt to the people on the other side of the footlights.

Band organizers hoped that measures such as these might bring them an appreciative audience. They were not disappointed. Even average musicians, only moderately rehearsed, attracted loyal followings across America throughout the nineteenth century. In Oberlin, Ohio, the Saturday evening band concerts became so popular at the end of the 1880s that every hitching post in town was reportedly occupied during performances. People heard the music and they liked what they heard.

PROFILE OF THE AUDIENCE

"No matter how much we may differ in other ways, we are all alike when the band begins to play."[6] Such was the view of the Rudolph Wurlitzer Company, and, in a sense, it was true. The lively, measured beat of a brass band affected diverse people in the same emotional way. Nevertheless, the audiences assembled at band performances were certainly not all alike.

The size of the audience could vary considerably. Serenaders, for example, might play for one or two persons at a time. Some marching bands attracted such small audiences that there were more listeners among the marchers than there were along the parade route. On the other hand, bands commonly played for thousands. Burt's Band of Minneapolis entertained a crowd of more than thirteen thousand during a concert held in the summer of 1877.[7] And in the wilderness of Montana a crowd of over three thousand gathered to hear Fort Keogh's Fifth Infantry Band at the ceremonies marking the completion of the Northern Pacific Railroad in 1883.[8] As early as 1840, the Fourth of July band concerts on the Boston Common reportedly attracted an astonishing multitude of thirty thousand persons.[9] Years later, such a crowd could still be amassed when the Sousa Band played at Willow Grove Park in Philadelphia. Naturally, indoor audiences were limited by the size of the hall, but some of the larger buildings could hold assemblages of several thousand. The extraordinary concert palace built in Boston especially for Patrick Gilmore's mammoth National Peace Jubilee of 1869 accommodated over thirty thousand listeners and eleven thousand performers. For the International Peace Jubilee that was held several years later, Gilmore oversaw the erection of a coliseum capable of holding twice as many listeners and performers—a grand total of nearly a hundred thousand people.

In addition to the variability of size, there was great diversity in the kinds of audiences attending band performances. Industrial bands such as the Remington Typewriter Band and the General Electric Band played primarily for the enjoyment of the company workers, whereas

Band music enlivened outdoor activities such as picnics and excursions. Events like this croquet and basket picnic were probably a regular part of the Millersville (Pennsylvania) Cornet Band's activities during the summer of 1880.

the Chicago Band, for whom public service was a primary aim, often sought audiences among penitentiary inmates and settlement house patrons. The bands hired to play in the elegant bandstand located in the rotunda of the Emporium Department Store in San Francisco regaled milling throngs of shoppers with their music. The Ferris Wheel Band at the St. Louis fairgrounds, on the other hand, played expressly for the enjoyment of the merrymakers riding the giant attraction.

Military bands, especially in time of war, had built-in audiences among their fellow soldiers, most of whom found the music to be a welcome diversion. "I don't know what we should have done without our band," wrote a grateful soldier from the Twenty-fourth Massachusetts Volunteer Regiment, which enjoyed the inimitable musical services of Gilmore's Band during the Civil War. "Every

Brass bands were a standard feature at political rallies of the nineteenth century. Nighttime festivities with bands and banners, fireworks and military display, were commonplace during the 1860 election campaign of Abraham Lincoln.

The sun was setting in a cloudless sky as I reined in my horse in front of General Carr's headquarters. . . . The band, in their neat summer dress, were grouped around the flagstaff, while the soft strains of "Soldaten Lieder" thrilled through the soft evening air, and, fairly carried away by the cadence of the sweet music, a party of young ladies and officers had dropped their croquet mallets and were waltzing on the parade. Seated upon the parade, other ladies and officers were smilingly watching the pretty scene. . . .[11]

By contrast, a young schoolteacher named Henry B. Miller encountered a band in the midst of a raucous Election Day crowd in Carondelet, Missouri, in 1838. Miller, a staunch Democrat, recreated the scene in his journal:

The steam Boat St. Lawrance [sic] took a load [of voters] down in the afternoon; there was a band of music aboard playing up some lively airs, amongst the rest Yankee Doodle with great spirit; we had the Broad stripes & stars in the front of the Boat. The Whigs were down with a strong force and had possession of the Polls; when we came down there was a great excitement, the Whigs collecting round the Polls & crying out, "Whigs, Stick to the Polls, don't let the damned Democrats vote." The Democrats formed a procession from the Boat to go up to the town with their banner and music in front. When we came up to the house where the Election was held, [there was] great hurraing and noise.[12]

There was also a group of drunken men wielding bowie knives, clubs, and "handkerchiefs with stones in," but despite the hooliganism of the Whigs, the Democrats— and possibly the bandsmen as well—successfully cast their votes before leaving town.

Many audiences represented a heterogeneous cross section of the local population—women and men, children and adults, well-to-do and not. As newspaper editors of the time were fond of pointing out, band concerts attracted all classes of people including, as one put it, the

night about sun down Gilmore gives us a splendid concert, playing selections from the operas and some very pretty marches, quicksteps, waltzes and the like."[10] Such a scene was repeated in many Union and Confederate camps during the early months of the war.

Inasmuch as bands played in a variety of settings, they necessarily attracted a variety of people. Contemporary observers occasionally recorded the attributes of these audiences, and their words help bring the diversity of the crowds to life. Army Captain Charles King, for instance, came across a particularly genteel audience gathered on the parade ground at Fort Hays, Kansas, one pleasant June evening in 1876. He described the scene as follows:

*Promenade concerts were an extremely popular form of weekend
afternoon entertainment. The concerts in Central Park, New
York City, were as much social gatherings as musical events.*

NATATORIUM PARK, SPOKANE, WASH.

158

The band shell provided a concert environment fundamentally different from open-sided bandstands. The relationship between audience and musicians was more formalized by the one-directional band shell and the setting was less conducive to promenading and picnicking.

"rich and poor, grave, gay, lively and severe."[13] One lively and good-natured crowd gathered in Detroit in July 1859 to hear a band concert which the *Free Press* later described in some detail:

> Hundreds of people who have no other opportunity for recreation than such is afforded in the streets during the evening thronged the square, while the more accustomed and critical did not hesitate to mingle with the crowd, and enjoy the scene. Young America, which never neglects an opportunity to get near the big drum, was on hand, and rolled and tumbled about on the grass with particular zest. Nurses and baby wagons lined the margin of the street, and the people themselves filled up the sidewalks and the gutters to an extent seldom witnessed except on unusual occasions. Somebody sent up a paper balloon, which went off in fine style until it attained a high elevation, when it caught fire and burned up in a flash. The effort to establish this species of popular entertainment has been very successful, and cannot but be appreciated.[14]

Whatever the particulars, listeners by the millions flocked to hear the bands play. They paid admission fees when required and they tolerated pesky mosquitoes and adverse weather conditions during concerts. At the close of the performances, they rewarded the musicians with applause, enthusiasm, and promises of return visits. "When the last note was played, it was with reluctant steps that the people dispersed for their respective homes," claimed one southern journalist.[15] Surely other audiences in other places felt the same way.

Not infrequently, an audience gave even more tangible support to the bands. The town bands, in particular, received an enormous amount of encouragement from the local population. Believing in the band as an important cultural institution, citizens were willing to donate money, to sponsor fund-raising events, to provide a practice hall,

A small band could reach a large audience by playing from a boat in the center of a lake. This fourteen-piece ensemble entertained scullers on Bryant Pond in Maine, ca. 1865.

the company several fine selections of vocal music on the organ, which was followed by several songs and choruses by others, all of which were well received. During the evening Mr. Sutter gave the congregation several fine selections on the accordeon, in his masterly way, which was frequently applauded. During the latter part of the evening Miss Abbie Brandt presented the Band with an elegant cake. . . . The whole receipts of the evening were $150. The members of the Band authorize us to say that they feel deeply grateful for the many kind wishes of our people and the splendid manner in which they patronized the supper, and more especially to the ladies who contributed so nobly to make it a success. It is such acts as these that will give Russell one of the finest cornet bands in Western Kansas.[16]

It was "such acts as these" that also served to strengthen the bond between a band and its audience.

CONFLICT

The band-audience relationship was not always a happy one. Sometimes, as in the case of the band of Center Point, Pennsylvania, problems arose at the very outset. The local minister, hearing the brass band during its first marching practice session, declared that the music was entirely too worldly and should be discouraged. The townspeople in this instance disagreed and the band survived.

More common was the complaint that a band's music was too loud, particularly during rehearsals. Anticipating this problem, the noted bandleader and advocate G. F. Patton suggested that bands should practice on the outskirts of town or in the downtown business area in order to avoid annoying the citizens. "Music is all well enough," wrote Patton in his guide to the formation of bands, "but even the heavenly sounds that a party of ambitious and energetic beginners are capable of producing upon their

and in later years to allocate tax monies for the benefit of the bands. The following account of a public supper held in 1883 to raise money for the Record Cornet Band of Russell, Kansas, epitomizes the partnership between a community and its band.

The supper given at the Opera House for the benefit of the Record Cornet Band, last Friday night, was the grandest affair of the season, and was assisted, we might say, by every person in the city. At twilight the Band marched through the principal streets in town, playing a number of pleasing melodies, after which they halted in front of the Opera House, where they played several pieces. The ladies of town had made extensive preparations for the supper, and nothing was lacking, and nothing was forgotten, and although five large tables were spread, and each table was filled with customers from 6 o'clock until 11 P.M., yet the provisions or oysters were by no means exhausted. During the supper, and until its close, the Band played several of its finest selections, which were heartily applauded. During the evening Miss Riley gave horns cease to charm the ears when heard evening after evening from dark to midnight."[17] These were useful words of wisdom, and bands that did not follow Patton's suggestions often found themselves in unpleasant confrontations with citizens who objected to being forced into the role of audience. In Salem, North Carolina, in the 1830s the local band apparently alienated some citizens in the Moravian community by blowing too loudly in the streets during a church service.[18] Equally disturbing to its neighbors was a German beer garden band that played its "ooms" and "pahs" every Saturday night in New York City until midnight or one o'clock in the morning.[19] Bands may have been useful for accompanying many types of activities, but sleep was not one of them.

Despite the almost universal tendency among bandsmen to adopt codes of decorous behavior, musicians occasionally indulged in antics that drew criticism. Rowdyism at the conclusion of band meetings was not uncommon, and during performances there could be lapses in discipline. One experienced bandsman recalled an occasion on which a parading band had "no instruments in ranks but a Tuba, a couple of Cornets and a Bass Drum." The other musicians "could be seen rushing about among the crowd in search of Beer, cakes, oranges etc." Naturally, the overall effect of such antics was "most ridiculous."[20] Audience conduct, by the same token, was often far from ideal. Many were the musicians, professional and amateur, to be disturbed during a concert by the crowd's chattering, their overt girl-watching ("oogling" as their contemporaries described it), and by the "inharmonious noises made by the boys."[21] Bandsmen sometimes complained that the public bothered them at rehearsals by stopping to talk during serious work sessions. Some bands felt compelled to include in the organizations' bylaws certain prohibitions on visits during rehearsal time.

The list of minor grievances could be expanded. Audiences complained about the lack of seating at open-air concerts; bands complained about the lack of practice space in some towns. Listeners in Birmingham, Alabama, grumbled that the garish lighting on their bandstand ruined the mood of the concert, while the Elkhorn (Wisconsin) Band protested that the open-topped design of the town bandstand funneled much of their sound straight up to the heavens—and allowed the elements to reciprocate. But the bands and their audiences were most frequently at odds over the issue of money.

Musicians and listeners recognized only too well that the establishment of a band was an expensive proposition and, to its credit, the public was often liberal in its financial support of bands. Many town bands owed their uniforms, instruments, and sheet music to the generosity of the local citizenry. Bands reciprocated by playing for a variety of public celebrations at nominal fees, though this easy cooperation vanished as soon as a band demanded more pay than its audience was willing to give. Such a dispute arose in Detroit in March 1864. The city was sponsoring a celebration for the return of some Civil War regiments and invited the Detroit Light Guard Band to join in the festivities. The band agreed to play for its usual fee of twenty-five dollars, but this was not at all what the organizing committee had in mind. They had hoped that the band would appear on this patriotic occasion for free. In an emotional statement, which was published in the Detroit *Advertiser* on March 14, 1864, the band's spokesman provided a clear summary of the complaints bandsmen often had against their public:

Many people seem to think that the business of edifying music-loving people on all public occasions, is a mere pastime for our bands, and forget that the acquirement of skill in music is a matter involving a great deal of time and money. A good band cannot be maintained unless it is liberally patronized, and bands are dependent upon the pay they receive on these public occasions, to reimburse themselves for the time and labor spent in acquiring this art. Moreover, most of the members of the band have some other occupation, to leave which is a positive loss, unless they should receive some remuneration, a loss which the members of the Committee on Reception or many of the friends of our brave soldiers, could much better and should willingly sustain.

To ask the band to play for nothing in these public occasions would be like asking a member of the committee to take from his shelves divers articles of headgear and other goods and donate them to our soldiers.[22]

A similar quarrel erupted in Mankato, Minnesota, in 1868. The immediate cause of the dispute was the supposedly high fee charged by the Mankato Brass Band for providing music at a railroad excursion party. But the details of the argument were soon obscured by the accusations hurled back and forth in the *Mankato Weekly Union*. Voicing the town's opinion, the editor of the newspaper claimed that "music is a luxury, and poor people must take only what they can afford." A furious bandsman replied in the next week's issue:

You, Sir . . . like many of those who have the most to say against us, and who are not able to distinguish the difference between the softest tones of an E-flat cornet and the loudest rasp of a braying mule, seem to think that the expense of furnishing band music for a city, should be borne by the few members of a band, who furnish all the capital and do all the work, rather than by the citizens who stand back and enjoy it. . . . You certainly can have no just conceptions of what band instruments cost, or what an amount of labor, time and money it costs to learn to blow one correctly and after learning to blow and read music correctly that it is

impossible to play without meeting and practicing at least once in each week, which costs time, labor and money.[23]

The incensed writer went on to complain that the town seemed to think "they owned our instruments and ourselves too."

Disputes arose time and again. The role of the newspaper in airing such differences cannot be overemphasized, and in many communities the editor functioned effectively as an arbiter. Occasionally, as in the case of the Mankato Brass Band, the problems were insoluble, and the dispute ended with the disbanding of the discouraged musicians.

THE CRITICS

From time to time, bands attracted a special breed of listeners—the critics. In contrast to the general public, which expressed its reaction to a performance spontaneously with cheers, applause, and the occasional hurled missile, the critic deferred his evaluation until he could publicize it, presumably more rationally, in print. Such carefully considered opinions not only provide an interesting record of band competence, but also reveal the range of attitudes towards band music held by the more intellectual listeners of the day.

That many bands played abominably is indisputable. There are numerous reviews, still sizzling in their invective, to prove it. One critic who heard a performance by the band of Glen Cove, Long Island, in the summer of 1860 complained in the local paper that the group played the "most excreble [sic] music we ever listened to, sounding . . . a hundred feet off a good deal like the flapping of loose shingles on a tumble down barn, or a load of clapboards behind a runaway team."[24] No more polished was a German band in St. Paul, Minnesota. The attempt to serenade a newly married couple in 1852 received the following notice in the local newspaper:

> There is always a great deal said in favor of German music; but if the performance last Tuesday night, in front of Mr. Fuller's store, on St. Anthony street, is a specimen, we are not satisfied with it for their discords were horrible. They bored the ears of St. Paul for three hours, with a most villainous compound of offensive noises.[25]

It is said that the bride, equally displeased, threw water on the band during the performance.

One mercifully brief condemnation summed up an unfortunate Irish band's ability by simply saying, "No doubt these musicians may have very good ears for music, but the way they executed it, is like hangmen."[26]

Such notices notwithstanding, the local press tended to reward its local talents with good reviews. Following one of its concerts in the early 1880s, the Elkhorn Cornet Band of Elkhorn, Wisconsin, received the following notice in the town paper, *The Independent:*

> The band boys discoursed some very sweet music from the court house steps Wednesday evening and many and hearty were the compliments passed on the music by those who heard them. It is hoped that with the return of warm weather the boys will practice in the park frequently.[27]

Other laudatory reviews appeared in newspapers across the nation.

> Flagg's Brass Band accompanied the [Worcester (Massachusetts) City] Guards, and discoursed most eloquent music during the day after removal of the cloth at dinner.[28]
>
> Tuzzi's band [of Minneapolis, Minnesota] was out last evening . . . and at the corner of Harrison block, discoursed some very fine music.[29]
>
> The Pajaro [California] Brass Band were out in force on

Tuesday evening last, and sweet music enlivened the town till nearly eleven o'clock.[30]

> The Naperville [Illinois] Brass Band made a most excellent appearance in their uniforms, blue relieved with white, and their musical performances were admirable.[31]
>
> Prof. Fred. L. Grambs, assisted by the able members of his excellent band, inaugurated last night a movement which is both commendable and noteworthy. They assembled at Capitol Park at the head of Twentieth street, and for three hours discoursed delightful music for the benefit of a large and highly pleased crowd.[32]
>
> Our town was enlivened Tuesday morning by the music of the Timmonsville [South Carolina] Brass Band as it passed through on its way to the Fair Grounds. Timmonsville should be proud of its band, for there is no better in the State.[33]

If these notices seem almost indistinguishable from each other, it is because they conform to a standard editorial pattern of the nineteenth century. According to the formula used in newspapers all over the country, the critics focused less on the specifics of the music than on the overall impression of the performance, which was invariably taken to be meritorious. Even the vocabulary of the reviews became a ritualized encomium. These supportive notices indicate not so much that the bands were outstanding but that their place in the community was highly valued. The very existence of a band, regardless of its competence, was seen to be a social good.

Charles Ives, one of the most distinguished and original of American twentieth-century composers, was clearly in tune with these sentiments. Ives left his copyist special instructions prior to the preparation of orchestral parts to "Fourth of July," a symphonic movement that incorporates impressions of a small town band marching in a parade: "Mr. Price: Please don't try to make things nice!

All the wrong notes are *right* . . . Mr. Price: Bandstuff—they didn't always play right & together & it was as good either way."[34]

For most local critics it generally *was* as good either way. For a handful of sophisticated commentators, however, such tolerance was unforgivable. Lurking in the shadows of bandstands all over the country, these well-educated critics tested the nation's military bands on the touchstone of the fine arts and consistently found them unworthy. To these proponents of "high culture" the problem with bands was not merely the lack of expertise of most players but also the fundamental lack of musical value in the art form itself. J. S. Dwight, editor of the prestigious *Dwight's Journal of Music* in Boston for almost thirty years, was the most colorful of these judges. In his view, brass bands meant "war, brute force, threats, [and] defiance." While Dwight conceded their suitability for street parades and military displays, he preferred to "leave [them], for the most part, to the enemy, and cultivate a gentler music."[35]

Theodore Thomas, who formed his own symphonic orchestra in the 1860s and eventually became conductor of the Chicago Symphony Orchestra, was similarly offended by the bluster of brass. "At last the Summer programs show a respectable character and we are rid of the cornet!" he is said to have exclaimed in 1870 when Jules Levy was mercifully absent from the Central Park band concert programming.[36] Less renowned, but equally critical of bands, was Henry T. Finck who eventually became music critic of the *New York Evening Post.* Although Finck's father conducted the highly successful band of the Aurora Colony in Oregon, the younger Finck devoted his life to music of a "higher order." His opinion of bands was so low that he declared in his autobiography

The band's central role in small-town life is reflected in the composition of this photographic collage from the turn of the century. Vienna (pronounced "vyanna"), South Dakota, population of about four hundred in 1900, included the church, the school, and Main Street on its "photographic pillow," but the town band enjoyed the central position. Pillows of this type were popular souvenirs in the first decades of the twentieth century. Robert Multhauf Collection.

that most brass band music reminded him "of a threshing machine through which live cats are being chased."[37] Only the superlative professional bands of Gilmore, Sousa, and a few other exacting conductors could hope to earn the approbation of these "high culture" enthusiasts.

One could argue that these critics were evaluating America's wind bands by impossibly high standards. One could even argue, as did Mark Twain in 1889, that the standards were impossibly inappropriate. In a letter to Andrew Lang, who had severely criticized *A Connecticut Yankee in King Arthur's Court,* Twain points out the absurdity of judging a work of popular culture by "cultivated-class standards." Taken to its logical conclusion, intones Twain, this approach necessarily

> condemns the spelling book, for a spelling book is of no use to a person of culture; . . . it condemns all the rounds of art which lie between the cheap terra cotta groups and the Venus de Medici, and between the chromo and the Transfiguration; . . . and it forbids all amateur music and will grant sanction to nothing below the "classic."[38]

For his part, Twain rejected the "high art" critic's philosophy entirely and cast his lot with the masses. "I never cared what became of the cultured classes; they could go to the theatre and the opera, they had no use for me and the melodeon."

One suspects that Twain did care about the cultivated classes, but surely the majority of nineteenth-century Americans did not. Dwight's reviews, with a periodical circulation of a few hundred, reached only a small, elite readership and had questionable impact on American musical taste. Although the musical reviews by hometown journalists were probably read by most literate Americans, people ultimately decided for themselves what kind of music they enjoyed without the help of critics or the press.

This postcard, mailed in June 1910, depicts the large audience at a band concert at Asbury Park, New Jersey. The inscription on the reverse of the card reads: "Dear Elizabeth, / Don't believe you have as many folks in your town as are here represented."

Their verdict is clear. Bands were almost universally seen to provide a form of entertainment that incorporated cultural benefits as well as enjoyment. Although some individuals headed for refuge as soon as the band season began, the majority of Americans bought tickets to their dime concerts as enthusiastically as they purchased their dime novels. They hired bands to help them celebrate everything from dances and picnics to weddings and national holidays. They emblazoned images of their hometown band on everyday objects—cigar boxes, pillows, sheet music, chromolithographs. And when they went on holiday they sent back picture postcards of bands and bandstands by the tens of thousands.

Because most of these people were not among the more articulate Americans, they rarely left written records of their feeling about bands. Yet the brief messages scrawled on the backs of their picture postcards convey some idea of the genuine affection they felt for the bands:

Friend Beulah,
    I was surprised when I received [your] card. Thought you were dead. . . . Here is are band. is it not dandy.
                                        William Miller

Dear Sis,
    The Mooseheart Student Band of Mooseheart, Illinois is one of the best bands in the world.

And, from a sailor aboard the armored cruiser USS *Montana:*

Dear Dad,
    This is our band. Some class. We have music all the time.
                                        C. B. H.

9.
BAND PROFILES

The band represents the town on its gay days, when the
fair comes, when there is a celebration, Fourth of July,
any kind of jamboree, when every citizen becomes a boy
again. . . . What is a town without a good band?

—Sherwood Anderson, *Home Town*

One of the most striking characteristics of the American
band movement is its universality. Throughout the United
States, in rural areas and in cities, on the frontier and in
communities long settled, bands had strong and enduring
appeal. Instrument dealers often emphasized this phenomenon by publishing glowing testimonials written by
bandsmen from every state and territory in the country. It
was an impressive way to advertise their products but,
given the immense popularity of bands, it is unlikely that
the companies had to work very hard to document this
geographical spread.

In New England the band tradition began early and
became especially strong. Possibly owing to the prepon-

derance of instrument makers in the region, New England
supported many military and civilian bands before the
Civil War. The closely knit township system, which
united New Englanders both spatially and spiritually,
ensured that such organizations would continue to flourish
in the later decades of the century.

The South, with its well-developed appreciation for
military display, also promoted bands, especially in large
cities such as Richmond, Charleston, and, of course,
New Orleans. Although the South's county system of
government in combination with a plantation-based agricultural economy limited the widespread formation of
town bands, many small rural communities actively supported these popular musical ensembles. Staunton, Virginia, which in 1855 spawned the group that was to
become the Stonewall Brigade Band, is one of the more
famous of such towns, but there were numerous others.
In addition, plantation bands developed in isolated areas

The epigraph at the head of this chapter appears on p. 87 (New York:
Alliance, 1940), reprinted in John A. Jakle, *The American Small Town:
Twentieth-Century Place Images* (Hamden, Connecticut: Archon Books,
1982), 76.

throughout the region. Some of these country bands—most notably those sponsored by Henry Clay Warmouth at his Magnolia Plantation in southern Louisiana—provided training for the bandsmen who would eventually make the transition to jazz.

Any geographical region with a sizable German population seemed to develop brass bands almost automatically. Pennsylvania was one of the first states to demonstrate this trend, but in such midwestern states as Wisconsin, Minnesota, and Ohio, German settlers and bands thrived together. The large German emigration to Texas in the 1840s was instrumental in the development

of the strong band tradition in that state. In these areas the band movement received a boost not only from the many Germania bands, but also from individual German music teachers who introduced the art to aspiring musicians of various ethnic backgrounds.

In the far western sections of the country, bands were formed almost as soon as settlement began. In some cases bandsmen migrated together, as in 1854 when four members of the Hartford (Vermont) Band joined a Boston-based abolitionist emigration party headed for Lawrence, Kansas. Armed with a keyed bugle, a cornet, a post horn, and a baritone, the musicians played throughout the long

THE "OLDEST" BANDS IN THE UNITED STATES

STONEWALL BRIGADE BAND (Staunton, Virginia)	"Nation's oldest community band to be sponsored by local government and funded by tax monies"[1]
BELVIDERE CORNET BAND (New Jersey)	"Probably the oldest real, small town band in America"
ROYAL HAWAIIAN BAND	"Oldest municipal band in the United States"
ALLENTOWN BAND (Pennsylvania)	"Oldest civic band in America"
REPASZ BAND (Williamsport, Pennsylvania)	"Oldest band in America"
UNITED STATES MARINE BAND	"First organized band, military or otherwise, which has functioned without interruption since 1798"
BROWNINGSVILLE BAND (Maryland)	"Oldest rural volunteer band not supported by public funds"
SALEM BAND (North Carolina)	"Oldest existing wind band, civic or military, in the United States"
TEMPLE BAND (New Hampshire)	"America's first town band"
PURDUE UNIVERSITY MARCHING BAND	"First band to form letters, 1907"

train journey, and when they arrived in Lawrence they proceeded to organize the first civilian band in the territory.[2] Elsewhere the introduction of bands proceeded in a less orderly manner, but brass bands were common in many frontier settlements. Even in the stark wilderness, bands could occasionally be found. When Colonel Henry B. Carrington led seven hundred men through the desolate Wyoming Territory in 1866 to build Fort Phil Kearny, he consigned to one of his valuable supply wagons the instruments for a forty-piece band.[3]

Across the country, from town to town and from section to section, the band movement spread easily. Geographically mobile bandsmen carried their art with them, just as an equally transient public transported their respect and reverence for the band tradition. Zealously prodding the growth of the movement were instrument dealers, who made band supplies readily available, and newspaper editors, who held up "The Band" as a standard of civilization. "By the way," intoned an article in a Minnesota newspaper in 1859, "the band in this town [Owatonna] reminds us that we ought to have an institution of the same kind in Mankato."[4] Many towns tried to keep up with their neighbors by responding to such calls for culture.

But if there was widespread agreement on the overall value of bands, there was great diversity among the bands that were ultimately created. A newspaper correspondent from Aldridge, Montana, claimed that his town's band sprang "out of the grass roots,"[5] and so it was with most local ensembles. In the absence of rigid government standards, bandsmen could pick and choose their uniforms (piece by piece), instruments (also piece by piece), repertoire, and engagements according to their own tastes and the demands of their local public. They could, in effect, build their bands to highly individual specifications.

A number of entertaining band histories have already been published.[6] To these we add several selected band profiles. Focus on the growth and development of a few specific bands yields interesting organizational patterns and practices and, in the end, a better understanding of the band movement as a whole.

THE BANDS AT ECONOMY, PENNSYLVANIA

George Rapp, a Separatist preacher who emigrated from Württemberg with a small group of followers in 1804, searched long and hard for the perfect American site for his communal settlement.[7] Following an initial ten-year sojourn in Butler County, Pennsylvania, the Harmony Society, as Rapp's associates were eventually known, moved to Indiana. There, it was hoped, rudimentary industrial enterprises might augment the group's well-developed agricultural pursuits. Ten years later, owing to poor climate and difficulties with transportation, the Harmonists were on the move again. Having sold their Indiana property to Robert Owen (who would use the land to establish his own experimental community called New Harmony), Rapp's people headed back east—this time to Economy, Pennsylvania, a promising spot on the Ohio River several miles north of Pittsburgh. Robert Owen's son, William, who witnessed the mass departure of the Harmonists from Indiana during the winter of 1825, noted in his diary that Society members boarded steamboats to the lively music of their band. It was a fitting display, for bands would play an important part in the cultural life of Economy from the town's founding in 1825 until the formal dissolution of the Society in 1906.

At first the band was just one small element in the rich musical life of the town. Although the Harmonists were millennialists who ardently believed that the world could end at any moment, they also strongly believed that music was an important pursuit as long as the world was intact. Hence, instrumental and vocal music were nurtured in the first two Harmonist settlements. At Economy—where the development of successful silk and woolen industries provided the Harmonists with unprecedented prosperity—music in general and orchestral music in particular flowered as never before. Under the direction of Johann Christoph Mueller the orchestra presented numerous concerts that attracted appreciative audiences from many of the surrounding towns. If their performances were not as polished as those of the Moravians, the Harmonists nevertheless received critical acclaim during the late 1820s.

Simultaneously, a subset of the orchestral musicians supplied the town with outdoor wind music. Although military displays were of no interest to the brethren, the bandsmen did play to welcome visitors, to accompany harvesters in the fields, and to call the congregation to church. For Harmoniefest (February 15), the annual holiday to celebrate the formation of the Society, a band concert from the church tower became a traditional attraction. The instrumentation for these events was not constant but was taken from the wind instruments available in the orchestra. These instruments included two French horns, two flutes, two piccolos, two trumpets, two bassoons, and a drum. Two keyed bugles were also utilized in band performances at least by 1826.

With the ready availability of experienced wind players, and with George Rapp's avowed enthusiasm for *Gebrauchmusik* (useful music), there is every reason to suppose that as brass bands developed elsewhere in America during the 1830s, they might also have caught on in Economy. The evolution of the Harmonists' band and their more celebrated orchestra was suddenly cut short, how-

ever, when the community suffered a series of internal disturbances. First, there developed an ideological schism that resulted in the abrupt departure in 1832 of over three hundred community members (including the music director, Mueller) and the attendant loss of a large share of Economy's assets. Shortly thereafter, the death of the community's leading businessman, Frederick Rapp, exacerbated the organizational and financial disruptions. George Rapp sought to stabilize the community by drafting a new set of Articles of Agreement, but this was the beginning of the end of the Society. Although the community was not formally terminated until 1906 when the last surviving members sold out their interests, the original spiritual unity of the commune was never recaptured. Few new members were admitted after 1832, and by 1889 there were only about twenty-five Harmonists left. With its unconventional beliefs in the communal ownership of property and the desirability of celibacy, and with almost incessant internal quarreling, the Society was destined for extinction.

And yet, curiously, as the community became weaker and weaker, the Economy Band began, ever so slowly, to grow stronger and stronger. After the defection of Mueller, responsibility for the community's musical affairs passed to Jacob Henrici who lost no time in espousing the continued existence of the band. The very year after the schism Henrici carefully choreographed an Independence Day celebration which featured the band in a church tower concert. Thereafter, the band performed sporadically until a younger generation of musicians in the 1850s and 1860s gave it new life and spirit. Under the able direction of Benjamin Feucht, the town's doctor, these musicians performed a typical repertoire of waltzes, polkas, and marches for the community. On rare occasions they were invited to participate in patriotic and festive gatherings outside the village. The band's instrumentation had become predominantly, if not exclusively, brass by this time.

With the departure of Feucht and his cornet-playing brother in 1865, the future of the Economy Band seemed in doubt until suddenly, in about 1878, the Society's trustees reaffirmed the Harmonists' commitment to instrumental music by taking the unusual step of hiring a bandmaster from outside the community to revivify the flagging organization. The man chosen for this task was Jacob Rohr, an Alsatian bandmaster who had settled in Pittsburgh after serving in the Franco-Prussian War. Rohr traveled to Economy regularly to teach the musicians. In short order he had both the Economy Band and a juvenile band, the so-called "Cheese Band," well under way. Rohr composed and arranged prodigious quantities of music for the Economy Band to perform at the regular Sunday concerts and at other community functions. For the Harvest Home celebration in 1887 the band was provided not only with new music, but also with a new set of silver-plated instruments which prompted the band's new designation as the Economy Silver Cornet Band.

Instrumentation was set by the late 1880s at about twenty-four players as follows:

piccolo	solo alto	B-flat bass
E-flat clarinet	3 E-flat altos	E-flat bass
3 B-flat clarinets	3 B-flat trombones	2 E-flat tubas
6 B-flat cornets	baritone	drums

Well equipped and well drilled, the bandsmen slowly gained a reputation as an "admirable band." They were occasionally hired by neighbors for excursion parties and other events during the 1880s.

In a community that once eschewed militia duty and other things of a military nature, the hiring of an army bandmaster and the blossoming of a military-style band was a remarkable development. But the evolution of the band, extraordinary as it seems, was not complete. It fell to John Duss, a longtime resident at Harmony and cornetist in the band, to cast the group in its final configuration—that of a professional band.

John Duss had grown up in Economy and had received the musical instruction typically offered to children of community residents. After pursuing various careers outside the community, he returned to Economy in 1888 to take a job as a teacher and to play in Rohr's band. With the death of Henrici in 1892, however, Duss slowly began to wrest leadership of the band from Rohr. Once he had done so, he immediately set about improving the level of performance. First, he hired professional musicians from neighboring towns to augment the existing personnel of the band. Next, he required these players to attend rehearsals three times per week. With Society money that was available to him as a trustee, Duss went on to build a bandstand, publish his own band music, and hire professional soloists to appear with the group. By 1897 the band had grown to more than thirty players and comprised the following instrumentation:

piccolo	E-flat cornet	4 French horns
E-flat clarinet	6 B-flat cornets	B-flat bass
4 B-flat clarinets	2 B-flat tenors	2 E-flat tubas
oboe	B-flat baritone	BB-flat tuba
bassoon	2 B-flat trombones	4 percussion

Throughout the 1890s the group presented regular concerts at Economy. As a result of Duss's zeal, they per-

Jacob Rohr was leader of the amateur Economy (Pennsylvania) Band from 1878 to the mid–1890s, when John Duss gradually assumed control of the group. At the time of this photograph ca. 1885, Duss's influence was already evident, for he is standing in the central position with baton and cornet in hand. Old Economy Village.

A typical program cover of the Duss Band at Economy reflects the ambitions of its remarkable leader. John Duss employed his own considerable fortune to promote the band, hire professional members, and sponsor concert tours. Old Economy Village.

formed frequently for social gatherings and at municipal parks outside Economy. Duss recalled in his memoirs that these musical offerings gradually netted him a reputation as a "sort of musician-in-chief of a most musical Western Pennsylvania Community."[8] It was perhaps fitting that the name of the band slowly evolved from the Economy Band to Duss's Economy Band and finally to the Duss Band.

Yet even this success was not enough for Duss, who seems to have imagined himself another Patrick Gilmore.

Through some clever maneuvering, Duss and his wife had risen in the leadership of the Society and had managed—some say quite deviously—to acquire a fortune from the Society as it divided up assets prior to its formal termination. This money Duss spent lavishly to promote his band in New York City. Taking thirty local musicians with him and hiring thirty additional players in New York, Duss presented a concert in the Metropolitan Opera House in May 1902. This performance was followed by a series of concerts elsewhere in the city. The band apparently performed quite admirably, but the concerts were marred by Duss's annoying remarks between pieces and by an unending barrage of tasteless publicity that critics often compared to P. T. Barnum's stunts. Despite discouraging reviews, Duss persevered in his bid for stardom by spending exorbitant amounts of money on his band. For two seasons he even took a detour into the world of orchestral music and hired the Metropolitan Opera House Orchestra to help him show off his talent.

Duss was certainly not an inept musician, but he was never able to buy the fame he desired. In 1907, he gave up and returned to Economy. The Society had been officially dissolved the previous year. Although people continued to live in Economy, 1906 marked the end of the formal Harmonist involvement in the town and, consequently, the end of the Harmonists' band.

The evolution of this ensemble between 1825 and 1906 was far from typical. But in its uniqueness, the Economy Band and its flamboyant leader, John Duss, serve to demonstrate the phenomenal importance of bands in American society in the nineteenth century. Here was a town that produced a superb classical-style orchestra when most American towns had nothing of the kind and, in its later troubled days, actively turned its resources and enthusiasm to the support of a band. And here was an extraordi-

narily rich man who could do almost anything he wanted with his money and chose to use his millions to become a bandmaster.

JILLSON'S CORNET BAND OF HOPE VALLEY, RHODE ISLAND

Nestled in the gently rolling hills of western Rhode Island lies the picturesque mill town of Hope Valley.[9] Deriving its power and prosperity from the waters of the Wood River, the town had become a bustling machine and iron producing center of more than twelve hundred people by the middle of the nineteenth century. As in other manufacturing towns across America, the residents of Hope Valley sought to temper their commerce with culture, and townsmen eagerly inaugurated, among other organizations, a brass band.

The fledgling musical ensemble, initially called the Mechanics' Brass Band, was organized in the summer of 1867 by fifteen public-spirited citizens who together raised more than two hundred fifty dollars for instruments, music, and the tutelage of a band instructor. Most of these founding members were evidently associated with the Nichols and Langworthy Machine Company, a thriving local enterprise that manufactured steam boilers and engines, Hope Valley's most important industry. The participation of Henry C. Nichols, son of the company owner, and Joseph H. Potter, son of the local banker, did much to ensure public acceptance and financial stability of the band.

The first task of the band's organizing committee was to elect the officers. Amos P. Barber and Charles D. Chase were chosen as president and secretary-treasurer, respectively, while the responsibilities of musical director were taken up by George H. Brown. James D. Jillson, the

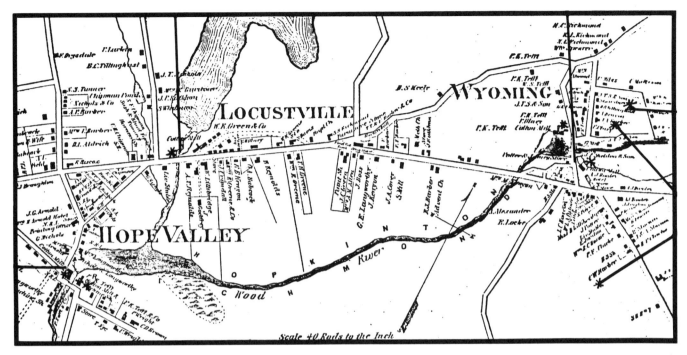

The towns of Hope Valley (including the section known as Locustville) and Wyoming, Rhode Island, formed a continuous settlement along the Wood River. Water power lured factories and mills to the area as early as the 1770s, and by the mid-nineteenth century there were dozens of industrial sites in the southwestern part of the state. Langworthy Public Library.

town dentist, served as the first E-flat cornetist and band-leader. It is not known what previous musical achievements qualified Jillson and Brown for these positions, but it is quite possible that they had served as bandsmen in the Civil War.

With officers appointed and funds in hand, it was the responsibility of George Brown to acquire the necessary instruments and music. A set of brass instruments was purchased for one hundred fifty dollars in Boston, after the musical director made an unsuccessful buying trip to Washington, D.C. The band's bass drum was obtained from a dealer in nearby Westerly, Rhode Island, for nine-teen dollars, and additional expenditures for music stands, music, and travel expenses were approved.

Each bandsman was assigned an instrument according to his interest and ability. The experienced musicians, Jillson and Brown, accepted responsibility for the difficult E-flat cornet parts, while Henry Nichols, who had received some training on cello and played in the Hope Valley String Band, was given first B-flat cornet. The other would-be musicians were allotted the remaining two B-flat cornets, three E-flat altos, two B-flat tenors, B-flat baritone, two E-flat tubas, bass drum, snare drum, and cymbals. The band members soon realized that musi-

BARBERS' HALL!
LOCUSTVILLE,
SATURDAY EVENING, MAY 23, 1868.

GRAND CONCERT
BY THE
MECHANICS'
Brass Band!
(J. D. JILLSON, LEADER,) ASSISTED BY

J. C. GREENE
AND OTHER EMINENT MUSICIANS OF PROVIDENCE.
AND THE
HOPE VALLEY ORCHESTRA,
(G. H. BROWNE, LEADER.)

PROGRAMME.
Part First.

1. HAIL COLUMBIA
2. CHARLESTOWN QUICKSTEP   Brass Band
3. ADELAIDE POLKA—Torrey   Orchestra
4. COMIC SONG—Joseph Baxter   Brass Band
5. VIOLET WALTZ. TWILIGHT DEWS   Brass Band
        Cornet Solo by J. C. GREENE.
6. SOMERS' WALTZ   Orchestra

Part Second.

7. SONG OF SPRING, WALTZ—H. B. Dodworth
8. GRAND MARCH   Brass Band
9. COMIC SONG—Wreck off Charleston Bridge   Orchestra
10. WOOD UP—Holloway   Brass Band
        Bugle Solo by J. C. GREENE.
11. WEARING of the GREEN and PAT MALOY   Brass Band
12. NAPPA QUICKSTEP   Orchestra
13. MOCKING BIRD QUICKSTEP—Volante   Brass Band

Part Third.

14. COLUMBIA GALLOP—Diethe   Brass Band
15. RAVENSWOOD WALTZ   Orchestra
16. COMIC SONG—Jessie the Belle at the Bar
17. IMITATION of the SCOTCH BAGPIPES
18. TRIO—Vocal—THE WATCHMAN   Brass Band
19. KELLER'S CELEBRATED AMERICAN HYMN—M. Keller   Brass Band

Admission, - - - 25 Cents.
Children under Twelve years, 15 Cents.
Doors open at 7 1-4.   Concert commences at 8.

L. W. A. COLE, Job Printer, Hope Valley, R. I.

During the Mechanics' Brass Band's first season of concerts in 1868, the distinguished bandmaster and keyed bugle virtuoso Joseph Greene served as the band's instructor as well as soloist in several concerts. Though known principally for his skill on the keyed bugle, Greene's first selection was a solo on valve cornet. Later in the program, however, he favored the audience with the rousing "Wood Up Quickstep," the most famous of all keyed bugle solos. Langworthy Public Library.

cal instruments were of little use without the skills to play them, so an additional one hundred dollars was appropriated to hire as instructor Dudley Brown, a professional music teacher from a nearby town. The band's treasury was exhausted before a note had been played, and it became necessary to tax each band member an initial two-dollar assessment plus fifty cents per week until the organization's debts were cleared.

There followed weeks of hard practice, both individually and with the entire ensemble. Through the long, hot summer months the band labored. The novelty of band membership apparently wore off quickly, for at least one founding member resigned and several others were fined fifty cents for missing rehearsals. The band's efforts eventually paid off, however, and by the fall of 1867 plans were being made for its first public appearance. The grand debut of the Mechanics' Brass Band took place at a fair held at Barber's Hall on January 1, 1868. By all accounts the performance was a success, both financially and artistically. The band grossed more than six hundred dollars and began the new year with a healthy bank balance. Concerts at Barber's Hall became a regular feature of Hope Valley life.

The Mechanics' Brass Band almost immediately became the object of considerable public interest. William A. Boss was one of the many townspeople to revel in the existence of the new cultural organization. At the New Year's Day Festival, Boss honored the musicians with an original and revealing literary endorsement:

Oh! come one and all, who love music and pleasure,
In the Mechanics' Brass Band, you'll find a treasure.
The first is their leader, his name it is Jillson,
Then Wood and there's Morton, there's Chase and there's
  Wilson;
There's Clay, and there's Griffith, and Jimmy the drummer,

And Amos and Jason, both jolly as summer:
And then there's one Henry, and also a Josie,
And when all together are pleasant and cosy.
  Then hail to the Band, all lively and jolly,
  They'll scatter the blues, drive off melancholly.
If you wish a tune played, you have only to choose,
And if they can play it, they will never refuse;
Oh was ever such music heard in creation,
Old Yankee Doodle they will play like the nation;
The Red, White, and Blue, the Star Spangled Banner,
The Poor Old Slave and Oh Susianna;
  Cease then ye grumblers, oh cease then your fretting,
  They'll play at your suppers, your socials and weddings.

As poetry, the ode falls short of perfection, but as history it has its merits. The band members were certainly known to the residents of Hope Valley on a first-name basis. The band pleased its audience with patriotic airs and popular songs. And, as Boss points out, the energetic musicians played at any number of suppers, socials, and weddings. The success of that winter band season was such that the ensemble was able to hire as its new instructor Joseph C. Greene, onetime conductor of the American Band in Providence and noted keyed bugle soloist. Greene appeared as a featured soloist in a number of the band's concerts later that spring.

Jillson was also prominent in the band's presentations. His popularity as a performer is evident from printed programs as early as 1869. Solo selections rendered by Jillson are commonly noted "by request." In 1872 Jillson's central role as soloist and leader of the band prompted the members to propose a formal name change, and by June of that year the ensemble became known as Jillson's Cornet Band.

As the group improved, they expanded their range of activities to include funerals, serenades, and flag raisings,

*Jillson's Cornet Band ca. 1880 posed in front of the home of
George H. Nichols. Four members of the mill-owning Nichols
family played in the band during its twenty years of activity.
Hope Andrews Collection.*

as well as Decoration Day and Independence Day celebrations, agricultural fairs, temperance rallies, and open-air
concerts. During the acrimonious presidential campaign
of 1884, Jillson's Cornet Band was extremely accommodating and played for both the Cleveland-Hendricks supporters and the Blaine-Logan camp. In the absence of
interesting engagements, the band often promoted their
own entertainments, including ice cream parties, festivals,
and excursions. For these many band-sponsored social
events the enterprising musicians did more than simply
furnish the music. Taking on the additional roles of im-
presario and caterer, the bandsmen made all the necessary
preparations. Thus, for a promenade concert held on
April 13, 1876, individual musicians were commissioned
to procure the following items: a suitable hall, publicity
posters, ice cream, oysters, fruit and confectionary, gro-
ceries, waiters, and tables. The band needed ice cream so

often that they eventually decided to buy their own ice
cream freezer.

Like most amateur bands with acceptable musical skills,
Jillson's Cornet Band was paid for performances. However, money-making was never the primary goal, and the
fees were highly variable. If the men had to miss work
to take an engagement, they generally requested at least
one and a half dollars per player (with double for the
leader), but beyond that there were no rules about recom-
pense except that a majority of voting members approve
the job. Because the band was in many ways a social
organization, such approval was typically based as much
on the potential for good fellowship as on the promised
financial rewards. For the three-day Washington County
Fair in 1875, the band required seventy-five dollars plus
expenses, but around the same time they voted to accompany the Masons' excursion to Providence, presumably a
more enjoyable occasion, for merely expenses. Sometimes
the band's activities netted them respectable profits—they
earned $199.53 in 1883—but their money was almost
always plowed back into the organization to pay for music, new instruments, instrument repairs, printed concert
broadsides, the leader's honorarium, and band lamps.
These expenses could mount up quickly. In 1876 when
the men decided to replace their worn-out uniforms with
fancy new outfits consisting of matching pants and coats
decorated by white vulture plumes, black belts, and
pouches, the band was forced to take out a bank loan of
two hundred and fifty dollars.

In many ways, the band functioned like a club, alter-
nately raising and spending money for the benefit and
enjoyment of the members and the community at large.
Like any respectable fraternal organization, it had officers
and rules, the latter posted conspicuously on the rehearsal
room wall. There were penalties for tardiness, absence

from meetings, and breaches of the conduct code. Although the bandsmen appear to have been on good terms with each other generally, the band is known to have expelled at least one member for misbehaving.

Much time and energy was devoted to the maintenance of the clubhouse or band room. Lacking better arrangements, the bandsmen had to rent a room which they usually hired from the Odd Fellows for about fifty dollars a year. This was a hefty expense and, when one added the cost of firewood and janitorial assistance, the total expenses seem burdensome. The members discussed the idea of building their own band room, but this project never materialized.

Finally, like any good club, they needed members. A significant number of musicians stayed with the band for many years, but not one of the founding members was present at the band's final meeting in January 1887. New players had to be recruited from musicians in the Hope Valley area. Approval by a four-fifths majority of members was required before acceptance into Jillson's Cornet Band, so the desire to join was a necessary, but not sufficient, qualification. One way to increase chances of acceptance was to be related to a member. During the twenty-year life of the group there were multiple memberships among the Avery, Briggs, Brown, Crandall, Dockery, Nichols, Perry, Potter, Rathbun, Spencer, Watrous, and Wood families. Overall, more than half of the band's members had relatives as fellow alumni. In spite of the group's success in attracting new players, it was not always possible to cover every part by regular band members. As a result, guest musicians, particularly on trombone and clarinet, were occasionally hired for specific engagements.

The band members generally met one night a week for business and practice. There were times when the meet-

All town bands marched in parades and Jillson's Cornet Band was no exception. Decoration Day and the Fourth of July were the most important outdoor band appearances of the year, but numerous excursions, picnics, socials, and weddings also filled the band's summer schedule. Langworthy Public Library.

ings expanded to two nights a week, and just before demanding performances the group often scheduled three rehearsals. Practice was held in the band room, but marching drills were usually conducted on the streets.

Although disagreements over seating arrangements and discipline policies occasionally arose, the group operated fairly smoothly for more than a decade under Jillson's guidance. In 1878, however, the leader resigned his position to become a mining stockbroker in Milwaukee, Wisconsin. The band accepted his resignation as inevitable, but the loss was keenly felt. Retaining the name Jillson's Cornet Band, the musicians tried to carry on, but the group lost much of its momentum. When several prominent bandsmen moved to Taunton, Massachusetts, in 1879, the band ceased operations for more than a year.

The return to Hope Valley of several former band members caused a resurgence of interest in Jillson's Cornet

Band. Thirteen bandsmen met and elected George Avery, a B-flat cornetist and the local undertaker, to be leader in 1881. For the next six years the band enjoyed a revival, maintaining a busy schedule of concerts, excursions, and picnics. But the demanding rehearsal and performance schedule must have taken its toll, for in 1886 the group was once again discontinued for "lack of interest." This time the musicians were serious about disbanding. Much to the chagrin of the townspeople, who felt that the town owned the band's equipment, the bandsmen decided to divide it all up—every instrument, band uniform, and piece of equipment down to the last cuspidor. On January 4, 1887, the band officially ceased to exist.

But could any reasonable town endure for long the lack of a band? Apparently Hope Valley could not. On April 19, 1887, the ex-bandsmen met to discuss reorganizing for Decoration Day, and although it is not certain that they actually played on that date, a year later Jillson's Cornet Band did appear, evidently for the last time, as about a dozen Republican members of the band reassembled for a concert to celebrate the election campaign of 1888.

The demise of Jillson's Cornet Band left in Hope Valley a void that was only partially filled in 1891 by the founding of the Columbia Fife and Drum Corps. It was not until 1893 that a new town band, the Columbia Brass Band, reestablished the tradition that had begun with the Mechanics' Brass Band a quarter century earlier. Demonstrating the element of continuity that is characteristic of so many American towns and their bands, the new Columbia Brass Band counted among its members a number of alumni of Hope Valley's first band. The new band also counted among its supporters numerous former fans of Jillson's Cornet Band.

A panoramic view of Hope Valley, ca. 1910, reveals a town that had changed little in fifty years. One notable addition was a small, square, two-story bandstand in the center of the picture. The first story of this dual-purpose structure was the town jail. Langworthy Public Library.

THE MINERS' BAND AT ALDRIDGE, MONTANA

Many towns formed bands in their early days, but Aldridge, Montana, a little mining camp perched beside a lake amid the seven-thousand-foot peaks of the northern Gallatin range, had a band even before the town had a proper name.[10] Although it existed only a short time, the band is a good example of the rustic musical ensembles that developed on the American frontier.

Settlement at Aldridge began in 1892, shortly after a rich deposit of coal was discovered beneath its rugged mountainous terrain. Coal mining had already been underway for several years in the neighboring settlement at Horr, but these new deposits, located some two thousand feet higher in the hills, promised to furnish a less expensive source for the mineral so vital as fuel for the state's copper-smelting industry. Under the auspices of the Park Coal and Coke Company, miners moved into the region, and by December 1894 they had tunneled seven hundred feet into the mountain. Aldridge was still just a raw mining camp, called variously Little Horr or New Horr or the Camp at the Lake, but it had a hotel, two boardinghouses, a blacksmith shop, and a number of saloons. It also had labor troubles and, in consequence, a band.

The unrest arose in November 1895 when mine workers, now in the employ of the larger Montana Coal and Coke Company, decided to demand a wage increase. Abruptly ceasing work, some two hundred workers gathered at the mines and then marched the three and a half circuitous miles downhill to Horr, where the management offices were located. To highlight their mission and strengthen their resolve, they placed a group of local brass players at the head of the impressive procession.

Despite such drama, the general manager refused to negotiate, but he did predict that a number of capital improvements (refurbishing of the flume that carried the ore from the mines to the coking ovens at Horr and an increase in the number of coking ovens that processed the ore before shipment to the copper smelters) would be made to bring about increased production and prosperity for everyone. Luckily for the miners, he was right. During 1896, production rose to about three hundred tons of coal per day thus rendering the mine, in one observer's estimation, "one of the greatest in the state." Such eco-

Residents of Aldridge, Montana, formed the Aldridge Silver Cornet Band ca. 1900. In size and instrumentation this typically American brass band (with the usual clarinet) was duplicated by thousands of other bands across the nation. Bill and Doris Whithorn Collection.

nomic stability, in turn, helped transform the camp into a lively town. More and more businesses, including a general store and numerous saloons, were built. A post office and a school were established in 1896 and in the same year, following the tactful intervention of W. H. Aldridge, a company director, in a labor dispute, the town finally adopted a formal name for itself.

In such an environment, Aldridge's band, which had made its dramatic debut during the labor dispute the previous year, also flourished. "Not an evening gives way to night," wrote the local correspondent to *The Livingston Enterprise* in July 1896, "without the boys' regular practice

The Aldridge Silver Cornet Band was closely tied to the local Miners' Union. Several bandsmen posed at a union gathering ca. 1897. Bill and Doris Whithorn Collection.

in the 'woods' to the delight of the inhabitants who hugely enjoy the treat thus offered." The "boys," numbering anywhere from about twelve to nineteen, were originally directed by a professional musician, but eventually the amateur first cornetist, an Englishman named Ed Wright, seems to have taken over. Often called the Aldridge Silver Cornet Band, the group sported four silver-plated cornets supported in the lower register by a blend of brass—trombones, baritones, alto horns, and tubas. One clarinet, plus the bass and snare drums, rounded out the instrumentation. Many of the instruments were owned by the town.

The Aldridge bandsmen did not have fancy military band uniforms but instead wore ordinary suits embel-lished by neckties and hats as distinctive as the men themselves. But whatever the musicians lacked in high fashion, they more than made up for in good-natured enthusiasm and merrymaking. It is claimed by an eyewitness that the bandsmen were always well organized, reportedly "marching up and down the streets of the camp, being stopped at each of the ten saloons and becoming more 'organized' as they went." At least one miner, in fact, joined the band "just for the drinks."[11]

Other musicians probably had other reasons but in this isolated town, whose population peaked at about eight hundred, the band was clearly one of the few recreational organizations available to townsmen. It attracted a cross section of the citizenry, including the school teacher, a saloon keeper, a pit foreman, and numerous miners. The Somerville brothers, who worked both as mule drivers and operators of the coal washers, were active in the band for many years. Although there was a large Austrian population among the Aldridge miners, they were not as prominent in the band as were Englishmen, Scots, and Irish. Also conspicuously absent from the band were the mine superintendent, the assistant superintendent, and the town constable. Although Aldridgites formed other social organizations, including a glee club and various lodges, only the baseball club seems to have enjoyed as much lasting support as the band.

The Aldridge Silver Cornet Band played in public on many occasions. Like other town bands, the group sere-naded newlyweds, provided music at dances, and escorted funeral corteges. It was with great pride that the band traveled the few miles to Fort Yellowstone (in Yellowstone Park) in 1896 to play for the gala celebration and dance marking Independence Day. Parading was more difficult for the band because Aldridge lay in a series of uneven hollows connected by a labyrinth of steep, winding paths.

With ingenuity and good cheer, however, the citizens developed a system whereby marchers were given cigars and refreshments at the steepest sections of the route. In so doing, they kept alive the classic band tradition of marching.

But the Aldridge ensemble was not just another town band. Just as the mountains looming over the tentative little settlement affected the layout of the town, so the mining company cast its shadow over the band. This is not to say that it was a company band, although the group did briefly take the name the Montana Coal and Coke Cornet Band. It was, rather, a workers group and was as often as not an anti-company band. By far the most frequent of the band's engagements were those played annually on Labor Day, Union Day (June 13), and after the Aldridge miners became unionized on April 19, 1897, Union Founding Day. The band also played for rallies during strikes and led delegations of miners in their many political activities. In 1901, the group underscored its commitment to labor by taking the name Aldridge Miners Union Band. Over the years many of the band's most active members were also among the most important union officials.

The band was as closely tied to the company as the town itself. When mine production was high and strikes only sporadic, the band, like the town, prospered. This was the case in the vibrant years between 1896 and 1904, a period when technical improvements in mine equipment and relatively calm relations between management and labor resulted in the economic and cultural flowering of Aldridge. The band was prominent throughout these years and, despite frequent personnel changes—caused primarily by the constantly roving population of the region—it maintained its existence without prolonged interruptions.

The Aldridge Silver Cornet Band possessed neither fancy military-style uniforms nor a dashing drum major. Marching was virtually impossible in the tortuous topography of the mining town's Rocky Mountain setting. Nevertheless, the band contributed a festive note to numerous events during its ten years of activity. Bill and Doris Whithorn Collection.

In August 1904, however, things began to change. This month marked the beginning of the "Long Strike" which halted mine production for a full year. Although operations eventually resumed, the company continued to wrestle with financial troubles, and life in Aldridge was never quite the same. The band played sporadically in 1905 and again for the annual Labor Day celebration in 1906, but it was a dying organization. The company held on a little longer, but by 1910 it, too, had ceased operations in Aldridge.

Aldridge's band was born with a mining town and died with it. During its ten-year existence, the band brought music, entertainment, and inspiration to the mining families in this remote section of Montana. Only "rarely," claimed the Aldridge newspaper correspondent with justifiable pride, was such enterprise "exhibited in a town of so small a population." [12]

THE ROYAL HAWAIIAN BAND

Many American bands relied on the musical expertise and guidance of foreign bandmasters during their formative years, but the Royal Hawaiian Band's leaders achieved an ethnic diversity that is probably unequaled. [13] Conspicuous among the many musicians hired to conduct this band during its long history were a Portuguese, a New Zealander, a German from Weimar, a Prussian, and an escaped American slave. These men, along with the native Hawaiians who also served in the post, contributed in varying degrees to the rich and vibrant heritage of this Honolulu-based musical organization.

As present-day band boosters are quick to point out, the Royal Hawaiian Band is the only American band to have been founded by royalty. The probable founder, King Kamehameha III, wanted a band early in the nine-teenth century, and at least as long ago as 1836 a small ensemble called the King's Band is known to have played for various parades and festivities sponsored by the government. For the funeral of Princess Nahi'ena'ena in 1837, the *Sandwich Island Gazette* reported the band to have been in full view, "decked in gorgeous comparisons, blowing, beating, and piping a solemn air." [14] Little is known about the band's first director, usually referred to simply as Oliver, but he was succeeded in 1845 by George Washington Hyatt, a Black man who had escaped slavery in Virginia and joined the Hawaiian band at its inception. Under Hyatt the complement of musicians hovered around ten players. Records indicate that the ensemble did not adopt the popular all-brass instrumentation at this time, but preferred instead a diapason consisting of flute, clarinet, bassoon, French horn, several brass instruments, and drums.

Hyatt's tenure came to an end in 1848 when he was replaced by a German musician named William Merseburgh. During the twenty-two years of Merseburgh's leadership the development of the band appears to have been slow and indifferent. Such was the conclusion of the local citizenry who were so dazzled by the extraordinary performance of a visiting Austrian naval band in 1870 that they immediately requested that their king, Kamehameha V, do something to improve his own band. Rivalry, once again, served as midwife to the birth of a band.

Kamehameha had to experiment with several potential bandmasters before he found a qualified and dedicated bandsman who could breathe new life into his organization. Following the short-lived and largely unsuccessful directorships of William Northcott (a New Zealander) and Frank Medina (a Portuguese), the king finally decided to ask the Prussian government for advice. Given the high state of development of German bands in the second

The Royal Hawaiian Band was unique in several respects. It is the only American band to have been founded by royalty, it is the first band to be composed of native Hawaiians, and it is said to be the oldest municipal band in the United States. By 1890 the band had adopted a mixed brass and wind instrumentation, with E-flat and B-flat clarinets, flute, and piccolo to complement the usual assortment of brass. Hawaii State Archives.

half of the nineteenth century, Kamehameha could hardly have chosen a better source of help. In due course the Prussians arranged to lend the Hawaiians the services of one of their own army musicians, a twenty-seven-year-old tuba player named Heinrich Berger. According to the formal arrangements worked out between the two governments, Berger was to live in Honolulu and work with the Royal Hawaiian Band for four years. In the end, however, Berger's commitment was much, much greater. Choosing to remain in Honolulu for the rest of his life, Henry Berger (as he was soon known) played a central role in the evolution of Hawaiian musical culture until well into the twentieth century.

Of necessity, Berger eased into his job slowly. He arrived in Honolulu in June 1872 to find a band of only ten young men at his disposal. He went right to work. "They had ears, and that is the principal thing in music," he recalled later. "I wrote them melodies within the range of a fifth, from F to C. Later we got to the octave. They made a great success and, within a month, they could play half a dozen melodies and a little waltz."[15]

From then on there was no stopping them. Recruiting new members, primarily from the local reform school where he developed an active junior band, Berger drilled his players regularly and gradually introduced more advanced repertoire. By 1885 the band had expanded to about thirty men with a typical mixed brass and wind instrumentation that included saxophones. They played at numerous official government functions as well as at public concerts in various locations in Honolulu. They also traveled to play at other sites in the Hawaiian Islands, and in 1883 they went to San Francisco where they won the honor place in a much publicized band competition. Besides presenting high-quality band music, the bands-

men, most of them Hawaiians, frequently sang Hawaiian songs during the middle of band concerts.

It has been estimated that Henry Berger conducted more than thirty-two thousand Royal Hawaiian Band concerts, as many as five per day, before he retired in 1915. In addition to this startling performance record, Berger had an enormous influence on musical development in general in the Islands in the late nineteenth century. His timely transcriptions of traditional Hawaiian songs, along with his creation of numerous new marches and other compositions in Hawaiian style, served to preserve the Islands' musical traditions and introduce them to the outside world. Simultaneously, Berger helped to advance the appreciation of Western music in Hawaii by transcribing orchestral pieces for the band as well as by organizing several orchestras and string quintets. The concerts of the Royal Hawaiian Band often reflected these two aspects of Berger's commitment to musical excellence by featuring Rossini overtures and Meyerbeer marches interspersed with such works as Berger's own "La Hanau o ka Moi" (Festival March) and the "Kamehameha Hymn."

As long as the Hawaiian monarchy endured, the Royal Hawaiian Band flourished. Subsidized by the government and officially categorized as a part of the Hawaiian Army, the band was often at the center of the glittering social and cultural events that marked the golden age of the monarchy in the 1880s. They played concerts at the palace bandstand, accompanied official ceremonies and royal parties, and serenaded incoming vessels in the harbor. Not infrequently the band was also hired by wealthy citizens for private balls. The fortunes of the band changed abruptly in 1893, however, when Queen Lili'uokalani was forced to abdicate her throne.

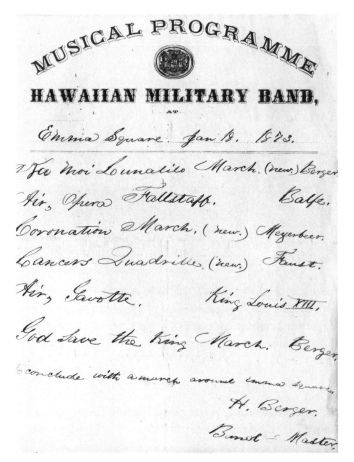

Handwritten programs of the Royal Hawaiian Band reveal its unique blend of the classics and native music. Several of the works on each program were composed or arranged by bandmaster Henry Berger to take advantage of Hawaii's musical heritage. Hawaii State Archives.

Under the ensuing provisional government and the republic that followed, the band was allowed to continue. As a matter of fact, President Sanford B. Dole relied on the band, still under the baton of Berger, to help maintain social order during a particularly troubled period in the mid–1890s. But the ensemble was now a changed organization. With the overthrow of their queen, all the Hawaiian bandsmen resigned, and Berger had to recruit new players—some from the local Portuguese band and many from as far away as San Francisco. The name of the band and even the uniforms were modified to reflect the new political climate. Not surprisingly, the Hawaiian Band, as it was now known, was discouraged from playing patriotic Hawaiian songs during the 1890s.

The problems facing the band during this period of political upheaval were numerous. The formation of a rival band by the displaced loyalist Hawaiian musicians was disconcerting, especially to Berger who had tried to remain removed from partisan politics. Even more troubling was the reluctance of the territorial government, which acceded to power when Hawaii was annexed by the United States in 1898, to shoulder the expense of the band. In 1905, when the House of Representatives voted to cut off the band's allocation, it appeared as if the group would have to be dissolved.

Fortunately this did not happen. The local county government willingly took over responsibility for the band and has maintained its financial support ever since. Although Berger resigned in 1915, he was followed by many other capable leaders who have preserved the traditions of the band. It was fitting that in 1909 the organization reclaimed its title as the Royal Hawaiian Band in recognition of the prestige and honor the ensemble enjoyed during the nineteenth century.

HELEN MAY BUTLER AND HER LADIES MILITARY BAND

"A woman of many distinctions is Helen May Young," proclaimed a newspaper headline as the versatile and energetic Helen May Butler Young launched her campaign for the U.S. Senate in 1936.[16] But, as the article went on to remind readers, candidate Young's first "distinction" had come many years earlier when, at the turn of the century, she organized and led a highly successful professional women's band. Generally referred to as Helen May Butler's Ladies Military Band, this group of dedicated musicians crisscrossed the country many times during the early 1900s and offered audiences a polished female version of the ever-popular touring concert band.

Helen May Butler was born in New Hampshire in 1873, but moved soon thereafter to Auburn, Rhode Island, where her father was a prominent railroad official. She pursued a variety of musical studies along with her more academic subjects and eventually became an accomplished performer on both violin and cornet. Her first serious experiment with conducting occurred in 1891 when she organized the Talma Ladies Orchestra, a group typically composed of several violins, viola, flute, clarinet, cello, cornet, and baritone.

The orchestra played locally on a number of occasions and received favorable reviews. But this was, after all, the height of the band era, and it soon became obvious that a ladies' band, especially one directed by a woman, had commercial possibilities. By 1898, Butler was actively drilling a female brass band in Providence, and two years later her twenty-five-piece U.S. Talma Ladies Military Band was well underway. Although its name and its personnel would change many times during the dozen or so years of its existence, the Butler Band was consistent in

Helen May Butler's Ladies Band varied instrumentation from a small, predominantly brass ensemble of fifteen to as many as fifty for major concert engagements. Butler's Band achieved artistic and financial success that was the envy of many all-male touring bands.

its high-quality musical offerings. "Music for the American people, by American composers, played by American girls" was one of the band's mottoes, and that is just what the public got.

In many respects, the band was modeled closely on the successful professional men's bands of the day. Instrumentation conformed closely to the standard practices already mentioned. When working with small ensembles of about fifteen pieces, Butler favored a mostly brass instrumentation supplemented by one or two clarinets. With her larger, forty- or fifty-piece bands, the woodwind complement was vastly increased with a corresponding enrich-

Helen May Butler owned a number of stylish band uniforms, each incorporating aspects of the well-known military-style band costumes of the day. Butler's use of feminine plumes and full skirts left no doubt about the gender of the leader and her performers.

ment of the sound. Like many male bandmasters, Butler maintained a close relationship with her instrument supplier. She and several of her soloists frequently made testimonials for the C. G. Conn Company, and for their performances at the Louisiana Purchase Exposition in St. Louis the entire band was equipped with Conn instruments.

Butler's ladies also played the same blend of popular and classical music as their male counterparts. Butler's programs, which encompassed the usual transcriptions, descriptive pieces, popular songs, and marches, were always, to quote a review, "refined, educating, elevating

and up-to-date." A composer as well as a conductor, Helen May Butler often featured her own works on her programs. The most famous of her compositions, "Cosmopolitan America," was designated the official campaign march of the National Republican Party in 1904, and soon thereafter it became a staple of the band's repertoire.

Even the uniforms, though feminine in cut, were derived from the military styles favored by men's bands. Braid trimming, plumes, Sousa-style caps, and even Continental three-cornered hats were all, at one time or another, donned by Helen May and her musicians. "Tights, or other appurtenances of the burlesque house," the ladies were quick to emphasize, were never "any part of our make-up."

These debts to bandsmen notwithstanding, Butler was intensely proud to be at the head of an all-female organization, and the band's publicity rarely allowed the public to forget the gender of the players and their talented director. "Only band in America independent of men's tuition or assistance," announced one advertisement. "First all women's brass band and female leader," reported another. And, once the band had become an established organization, the jaunty feminists confidently proclaimed that they were "equal in ability to any of the men's bands."

There was, however, one man who worked closely with this legion of females, and his name was J. Leslie Spahn. As band manager, his job was to make booking arrangements, a mission he undertook with enthusiasm bordering on fanaticism. "We are in our 30th week without a day off and have ten more weeks booked ahead," he wrote during the intensive tour of 1903. "I want to make it fifty-two weeks straight if I can."

Spahn's wish was fulfilled. That year the band, now based in Cincinnati, played day after day, sometimes two times a day, for thirteen months as it traveled through

New England, the middle Atlantic states, and extensively in the South. The Sousa Band, renowned for its many marathon tours, worked no harder than this.

Despite the rigors, there was never any shortage of young women eager to play in the band. Miss Butler claimed to have a steady stream of applicants from all over the country. Although each season a number of players left the band to be married, there was always a sizable waiting list from which to replenish the ranks. Band size varied considerably, depending on the job. For some engagements Butler used as few as fifteen or sixteen musicians, but more typically the group numbered from twenty-five to thirty-five players. Sometimes the band roster swelled to fifty musicians, rendering Butler's Band the largest female band "ever put on the road as a permanent organization."

The public also considered it one of the best women's bands ever put on the road. "This band unlike many so-called ladies' bands," claimed a letter published in the Denver *Times* in 1906, "is an organization of merit." Even more laudatory was a Nevada newspaper's contention in 1908 that the band was "without doubt the peerless ladies band of the world." On occasion, Butler was even dubbed the "female Sousa" and the tribute was probably not misplaced. At the famous summer concerts held at Willow Grove near Philadelphia, Butler shared the billing with such outstanding male bandleaders as Patrick Conway, Giuseppe Creatore, Herbert Clarke, and John Philip Sousa. The latter was not only a model for Butler, but also a personal friend.

The power and prominence of Butler's Band continued for more than twelve years. In addition to numerous

Lavish posters and other publicity efforts highlighted the Helen May Butler's Ladies Band tours in the first decade of the twentieth century. The band remained a profitable business until ca. 1912, when competing forms of entertainment eroded the popular support of many touring ensembles.

performances in towns and cities from coast to coast, the women appeared at many special celebrations. In 1902, they played at Madison Square Garden for the historic Women's Exhibition, a festive display of women's abilities and achievements. Butler's Band was also featured at the South Carolina Interstate and West Indian Exposition in 1902 and at the Louisiana Purchase Exposition in St. Louis in 1904. It was the only women's band to play at the Pan-American Exposition held in Buffalo in 1901. By one tally the Butler ensemble, with varying personnel and under various managers, played 203 times in Boston, 110 times in Buffalo, 126 times in St. Louis, and 130 times in Charleston. They never made a European tour, but they traveled the length and breadth of the United States.

Ultimately, like so many other bands at the time, the group began to lose support. Butler herself pinpointed 1912 as the year in which bands in general, and her band in particular, lost momentum. The rise of competing forms of entertainment and the corresponding decline in the popularity of amusement parks contributed to this obvious change in the fortunes of professional bands.

After 1913, it no longer paid to keep Butler's Band on the road.

Butler, still a young woman, went on to do other things. In addition to raising two children, she taught music and continued to play her cornet for solo engagements. She also developed an avid interest in politics and eventually decided to become politically active by seeking a Senate seat in 1936. She threw herself into the race with characteristic enthusiasm and commitment. Although she claimed at the time to have little hope of winning the election, she was, she said, inspired by the issues and by a strong desire to help pave the way for future women candidates.

Such a trailblazing spirit had been the hallmark of Butler's earlier band work as well. Although her band is little remembered today, it stood for many years as an exemplary ensemble that offered a unique blend of charm and musical expertise. As one handbill summed up the group's talent, "Helen May Butler and her Greatest American Ladies Band" were a "picture to the eye" and their music a "treat to the ear."

IO.

MODULATION: BANDS ON THE VERGE OF A NEW AGE

One must remember that in the 1890s, and even until the
first World War, nearly every community had at least
one band. Band music was as popular and competitive as
dance music is today, and bandmasters of outstanding
bands were nationally known and highly respected
figures. Those were the days. . . .

—John Duss

THE NEW CENTURY

Late in the night of December 31, 1899, a small band of
musicians ascended a balcony of the Boston State House
and took their positions. It was dark and cold as they
waited for the ceremony to begin. As midnight
approached, a brief trumpet fanfare and the strains of a
hymn marked the opening of the festivities. These musical
offerings were followed by the reading of a psalm, the
recitation of the Lord's Prayer, and a rendering of "America." Finally, the brass instruments had their moment of
glory. Huddling together in the chilly night, trumpeters
let loose a magnificent blast of brass that cut through the
icy air like brilliant starlight. The music was loud and

joyous and, as program planners hoped, provided a fitting
tribute to the advent of the new century.[1]

For this atypical occasion, the Twentieth Century Club
of Boston used band music in a very typical way—to
highlight an event, out-of-doors, with rousing and inspiring music. In the months and years that followed, other
organizations perpetuated the nineteenth-century band
tradition in similar ways. Between 1900 and 1910, in fact,
there were more town bands and more professional touring concert bands in existence in the United States than
ever before. Interest was so high that editors of the widely
circulated periodical *The Metronome* decided in 1907 to
reprint verbatim—and without direct acknowledgment—
the advice that George F. Patton had tendered to amateur
bandsmen over thirty years earlier. Ever the master of
band boosterism, the Rudolph Wurlitzer Company assured prospective customers during the 1910s that bands
were more important in American life than ever before.

190

The epigraph at the head of this chapter is from *The Harmonists: A
Personal History* (1943; reprint ed., Ambridge, Pennsylvania: Harmonie
Associates, 1970), 372.

The Mason City (Iowa) Band enjoyed the latest in transportation—a motorized Overland bandwagon. Automobiles transformed small-town American life and helped change the role of the town bands as well. Iowa State Historical Society.

As one of the Wurlitzer catalogs enthusiastically pointed out, "In every community that has not a band there is a demand now for band music. Every community that has bands wants bigger and more bands."[2]

In short, as the twentieth century commenced, it appeared that the popularity of bands, brass and otherwise, would persist unabated and that these musical organizations would continue to entertain the public in the customary ways. If this was the Age of Confidence for Americans in general, as writer Henry Seidel Canby has argued,[3] it was also the age of confidence for bandsmen in particular. Their ability to preserve earlier musical traditions seemed virtually assured.

Such complacency did not last long. Even as the Wurlitzer Company and others were advancing their time-

honored sales pitches, it was becoming increasingly obvious that the band movement was on the brink of momentous change. The stimulants to change were many and, as bandsmen themselves were quick to point out, included a blend of social and musical developments that coalesced around the time of World War I. Most notable was the large number of new amusements increasingly available to Americans during the second decade of the century. The phonograph, invented in 1877, finally began to become a popular diversion in the early 1900s. As the century began, some one hundred fifty thousand phonographs and three million records had been sold. Just twenty years later, an incredible two million phonographs had been produced with associated record sales nearing one hundred million annually.[4] The automobile enjoyed a similar surge in popularity during the 1910s. Between 1910 and 1920, the yearly output rose from fewer than half a million vehicles to about eight million cars, a production level that afforded millions of Americans vastly increased flexibility in their use of leisure.[5] Motion pictures, which had been shown publicly in 1896, reached an ever-widening audience by the late 1910s. Finally, radio broadcasting, which began in earnest in 1920 with the establishment of the first permanent commercial station in Pittsburgh, became so popular that it was listed as a favored amusement on virtually every study of the use of leisure in the twenty years before World War II.[6]

The effect of these inventions on society at large was profound—so profound that historian Marshall B. Davidson refers to the rise of radio broadcasting, phonographs, moving pictures, and automobiles as the "industrial revolution of recreation."[7] The effect of these new pastimes was close to revolutionary in the band world, too. Not only did these diversions lure audiences and musicians away from band performances but, in permit-

*Syncopated rhythms and improvisation brought a new jazzy
sound to the band. In spite of worn uniforms, ill-fitting shoes,
dented instruments, and broken cymbals, the Jenkins Orphan
Home Band created a joyous and dynamic scene in their
hometown, Charleston, South Carolina. South Carolina
Historical Society.*

ting and even promoting the segregation of leisured Americans according to age and cultural taste, these new activities severely undermined the intergenerational solidarity that had always been fundamental to the band movement. Furthermore, in carrying the polished sounds of professional bands to more people than ever before, the radio and the phonograph indirectly provoked negative feelings about amateur local talent. Faced with indifference or even hostility on the part of increasingly sophisticated audiences, many bands languished and lost momentum.

Even as changes in society at large impinged upon the band world, bandsmen were busy implementing radical changes of their own. The published literature of the 1910s and 1920s portrays this as a period of intense self-evaluation. As a questionnaire published in *The Metronome* in 1910 reveals, the issues ranged from questions of instrumentation ("Would you favor elimination of E-flat cornet parts?" "Would you favor the introduction of trumpets?") to problems of notation ("Would you favor a universal notation in treble clef?").[8] The rise of new dances, new dance music, and jazz contributed somewhat to this identity crisis, but at its heart lay the widespread conviction that bands had for too long been prey to the idiosyncrasies of inexperienced practitioners, and that it was time at last to impose some immutable standards on the art form. In addition to advocating standardized instrumentation for concert bands, crusaders of the early twentieth century campaigned actively for improved levels of performance and repertoire. The incorporation of these goals into the constitution of the American Bandmasters' Association, which was formally launched on July 5, 1929, ensured that band reform would be forthcoming.

Like the repeated rappings of a stonecutter's hammer upon a block of granite, these and other events slowly modified the shape of the band world. In time, the band movement as a whole took on a new, more modern configuration.

LOOKING AHEAD

School Bands

The most striking trend of the early twentieth century was the increase in the number of school and college bands. Although vocal music had been introduced into many schools following Lowell Mason's pioneering efforts in Boston in the 1830s, instrumental tuition was relatively rare throughout the nineteenth century. This situation began to change just after the turn of the century as instrumental programs were implemented in scattered American school districts, notably in Aitkin, Minnesota, where a school band was formed by a circus musician in about 1900; in Connersville, Indiana, where one of the first high school bands was founded in 1905; and in Dickinson County, Kansas, where the school band, formed in 1907, received wide recognition for stimulating school attendance.[9] Around 1920, the school band movement gained momentum, and the next decade saw bands established in hundreds of schools across the country.

The support for this crusade came from several quarters. Educators like Joseph E. Maddy of Rochester, New York, and A. R. McAllister of Joliet, Illinois,[10] firmly believed in the enriching value of music instruction and worked hard to put instruments in the hands of their students, many of whom would not otherwise have had such an opportunity. Instrument dealers were equally enthusiastic, and although they had obvious financial motives for their zeal, these businessmen also stressed the moral and social benefits of school bands—much as they

The Platteville (Wisconsin) Normal School Band, ca. 1910, followed the national trend toward larger ensembles and younger players. The predominantly brass instrumentation of this school band is augmented by five clarinets and a flute.

The Cornell University Band ca. 1900 was an unusually large amateur band, with more than forty members. The balanced instrumentation of woodwinds (with a quartet of saxophones) and brass is like that of the prominent professional ensembles of the day.

had stressed the same values to amateur adults years earlier. Often working together, music teachers and dealers sponsored contests and other incentives to publicize the merits of school and college band programs.

The success of the campaign is undeniable. As early as March 1920, the instrument dealer C. W. Osgood claimed flatly that "the school and college bands are our best customers now."[11] Other companies experienced a similar shift in sales. While the first national school band contest (held in Chicago in 1923) attracted thirty bands, by 1940 the local competitions that selected groups for the national finals were reportedly processing ten thousand bands, orchestras, and choruses per year.[12]

In contrast to high school bands, college bands were fairly common during the nineteenth century and provided popular extracurricular activities on such campuses as Cornell, Harvard, Ohio State, and others. But the

popularity of these organizations expanded greatly during the twentieth century, especially as skilled, professional bandsmen switched from performance to careers in college teaching. Wind ensembles are fixtures on many campuses today and throughout the land it is the inalienable right of football fans to enjoy a marching band performance during halftime.

Town Bands

Although many town bands suffered brief periods of neglect during the nineteenth century, most localities sustained genuine interest in the movement. It is clear, however, that overall interest in such ensembles declined noticeably in America after World War I. In some localities amateur bands yielded the stage to the emerging school bands in town. In others, the removal of the public bandstand in order to ease traffic congestion started a cycle of

The Square and Band Stand, Cornwall-on-Hudson, N.Y.

WATER STREET FROM THE SQUARE, EXETER, N. H.   1778

Top: *The bandstand at the center of Cornwall-on-Hudson, New York, like gazebos in many other small towns, became an unintentional target for automobiles. As traffic increased, bandstands were either moved or dismantled, thus symbolizing the shift of bands from the center of community life.* Bottom: *Architect Henry Bacon's elegant bandstand by the courthouse in Exeter, New Hampshire, lost much of its charm as the surrounding area became a paved street and parking lot.*

organizational problems from which the band could not recover. Elsewhere, musicians as well as their public found other ways to enjoy leisure and they simply allowed the bands to fold. Statistics are elusive, but there is little doubt that there were fewer town bands in America in 1920 than there had been in 1900.

Underlying this shift in the fortunes of the traditional town band was a gradual but decisive change in the character of small towns in America. Brass bands had thrived in the days when towns were both self-sufficient and similar to each other. Villages stood proudly separate from their neighbors, but at the same time promoted almost identical institutions and values. In such an environment it was only natural that bands—as well as dramatic circles, firemen's associations, baseball teams, and Main Streets—could be found almost everywhere, each locality providing the "best" rendition, of course. But challenges to such communal sameness developed, coming to a head in the 1910s.

The appearance of intertown connectors such as electricity, the telephone, automobiles, and national-brand products cut down on the independence of small towns and forced citizens to recognize their own unique strengths and weaknesses. Simultaneously, the movement toward more individualistic forms of entertainment such as the phonograph, radio, and mah jong seriously undercut the spirit of community that had fueled the civic organizations of the nineteenth century.[13] For many citizens it was no longer necessary or even desirable to congregate in central places for recreational activities. Bands and other local institutions suffered noticeably as a result of this decline in municipal chauvinism. Historian Lewis Atherton has identified the peak of disillusionment with small towns as occurring around 1920, the year in which Sinclair Lewis published his celebrated *Main Street*.[14] It

*Doylestown, Pennsylvania, with a population of about three
thousand, boasted a twenty-two-piece band in the first decade of
the twentieth century. Town bands gradually increased in size,
as well as in the number and variety of woodwind instruments,
between 1900 and 1920.*

is no accident that this literary landmark coincided with a decline in municipal bands.

Many communities continued to support bands, but the "modern" town band differed markedly from its forebears. In imitation of professional bands, modern ensembles tended to be fairly large, averaging around thirty musicians rather than the ten or twelve players that typically constituted nineteenth-century town bands. Modern community bands also tended to draw their personnel from larger geographical areas than formerly. Many local bands of the 1920s, 1930s, and 1940s were actually consolidated regional bands boasting a mix of players from many neighboring jurisdictions. In terms of instrumentation, there was a decided shift away from all-brass ensembles toward a well-balanced brass and woodwind instrumentation. The increased size of these bands, the gradual standardization of published band music, and the popularization of the Sousa-style band sound made this pattern in instrumentation—long endorsed by professional bands—inevitable for amateur bands as well. Finally, in stark contrast to their predecessors, many community bands after World War I began to admit female musicians to their ranks.

As the bands' demographics changed, so did their methods of funding. Although nineteenth-century town bands were notorious for their manifold fund-raising techniques, most depended heavily on donations. The idea of taxing citizens for their public musical entertainment had been tried in scattered localities, but the notion did not catch on until the twentieth century.[15] Kansas began to experiment with a band law in 1905 and by 1917 had produced legislation whereby a certain proportion of the taxes collected in cities of a stipulated size could be devoted to band support. Iowa's more famous band law was passed a few years later and served as a model for

ITHACA BAND CIGAR.
Manufactured by F. J. PRENTICE, ITHACA, N. Y.

The Ithaca (New York) Band epitomized the transition to larger complements with a variety of woodwinds. The reputation of this fine thirty-piece ensemble was enhanced in the form of illustrated cigar box labels for Ithaca Band Cigars.

similar legislation in other states. Band law proponents like George W. Landers and Karl King interpreted this trend in municipal music financing as indisputable evidence of the continuing strength of the town band movement. In reality, by rendering bands a part of local government, these statutes signaled change—both a decline in the public's enthusiasm for bands and the demise of the time-honored tradition of self-support.

Professional Bands

Musicians who sought to earn a living through band work found that the range of jobs available to them changed around the time of the World War I. The number of touring concert bands fell sharply during this period, as did the number of traveling circuses. A simultaneous decline in the popularity of vaudeville shows and amusement parks cut off other familiar sources of work. The final ratification of the Prohibition Amendment in 1919 meant that a year later, when the law went into effect, a majority of tavern and night spot jobs were eliminated. Owing to the rise of anti-German feeling during World War I, many of America's German beer garden bands curtailed their activities; a large proportion of these groups failed to resume their performances after the Armistice in 1918. It must have been small comfort to these displaced bandsmen that the tradition of military band music was enthusiastically preserved during the 1920s by the Wurlitzer Company and its "Military Band Organs," the most elaborate of which could simulate the sounds and songs of a twenty-piece band without employing a single bandsman!

On the other hand, new employment opportunities arose even as the earlier jobs vanished. Large numbers of bandsmen, for instance, exchanged careers in performance for careers in teaching. Dispersing across the country, these experienced musicians passed on their knowledge and love of band music to high school and college students who were joining bands in ever-increasing numbers. In addition, jazz, which emerged modestly enough in New Orleans in the early 1910s, soon captured the imagination of dancers and concertgoers across the nation and offered an enticingly novel field of work for many musicians.

The shift in musical taste from concert band to jazz band occurred fairly quickly and is epitomized by a scene from the 1941 MGM movie *Birth of the Blues,* which is set in the first decades of this century. In their search for a "hot" cornet player to fill out a new Dixieland group, Bing Crosby and friends visit a concert by the local mili-

tary-style band. The solo cornetist is portrayed as a supercilious prima donna with a large, waxed mustache, much in the tradition of Jules Levy. Crosby et al. reject this old-fashioned artist and manage to lure the bored drummer away from the traditional band. They eventually find their man—a dashing, suave, and totally American jazz cornetist—in the local jail.

The moviemakers obviously believed that by about 1920 traditional band music had become hopelessly old-fashioned and stuffy and that the bold, dynamic sounds of jazz represented the brave new music of the future. Their conception was not far from the historic reality. As early as 1915, Tom Brown and other musicians had carried the sounds of jazz to Chicago, New York, and San Francisco. By 1919, instrument sellers had reacted to the craze and were recommending suitable jazz combinations side by side with their suggested instrumentations for brass and wind bands. Before long many musicians crossed over to the newer sound.[16]

The United States service bands enjoyed a real boost during the 1920s. Although America's military bands were distressingly inferior to Europe's military bands during World War I, Walter Damrosch faced the problem head on and organized remedial training sessions for bandleaders serving in France.[17] Efforts to improve and publicize America's military bands continued when the troops returned home. What resulted was the formation of standardized tables of instrumentation, as well as the creation of official service bands—the United States Army Band, established in 1922; the United States Navy Band, organized on a permanent basis in 1925; and the United States Coast Guard Band, formed in 1925. The United States Marine Band, whose history extended back to the eighteenth century, continued its universally admired service in the nation's capital and on tour. Although the

World War I provided American military bandsmen with a firsthand look at fine European military bands. Bands of the U.S. Infantry, such as the one illustrated here on a postcard from France in the winter of 1917, soon adopted a standardized size and instrumentation based on the practices of their European counterparts.

In 1917 "jazz bands" were easily formed from larger, more formal ensembles. The Seventieth U.S. Infantry Jazz Band, probably composed of regimental band members, entertained troops at Camp Funston, Kansas.

number of professionals employed in these ensembles was relatively small, the influence of the service bands was great owing to the famous radio broadcasts and recordings that featured these groups. Many civilian bands carefully copied both military instrumentation patterns and repertoire.

Finally, as a result of the pioneering efforts of Edwin Franko Goldman and others, the modern symphonic band had its genesis at about the time of World War I and soon afforded new, more challenging employment possibilities for bandsmen.[18] Dr. Goldman was convinced that with proper training wind bands could perform on the same artistic level as the best symphony orchestras of the day. In 1911 he formed his own band, initially called the New York Military Band, to prove it. Dedicated to ele-

vating the band medium to new aesthetic heights, this group not only experimented with new patterns of instrumentation, but also championed the improvement of band repertoire through the performance—and even the commissioning—of serious new works for wind band. Other conductors during the 1920s and 1930s pursued similar goals and enthusiastically led the way for the Eastman Wind Ensemble and other distinguished concert wind ensembles of our day.

As a group, bandsmen of the postwar years generally found their profession to be more specialized and more standardized than formerly. Gone were the days when bandsmen flitted from dance orchestra to marching band to concert stage. Gone, too, were the days when a band could be whatever a bandleader said it was. The increased influence of unions, which regulated everything from wages to instrumental doubling to uniforms, and the logistics of band music publishing, a costly enterprise under the best circumstances, contributed to the process of standardization. Yet in the opinion of many musicians, the loss of spontaneity that these changes brought about was justified by the corresponding elevation of performance standards.

LOOKING BACK

Many bandsmen viewed the changing times with enthusiasm. Ever a champion of improved levels of musicianship and standardized instrumentation, John Philip Sousa looked ahead with optimism. "There is as great a future in America for the wind band as the symphonic orchestra," said Sousa in about 1910. "The public is here, the love of music is here, and I am confident that out of the talent of our country will come many fine conductors, fine players, and magnificent wind bands."[19] Victor Herbert echoed these sentiments in 1920 on the occasion of Goldman's landmark band music competition, which established the wind band, once and for all, as a serious musical entity. "The contest," claimed Herbert, "proves that a greater interest is being taken in bands and band music than ever before and also that we are developing a branch of that art that has hitherto been neglected."[20]

But if the years 1915–1920 served to launch the modern period of band history, they also marked the culmination of the vibrant traditions of earlier days. Bandsmen of the early twentieth century recognized the importance of their heritage and as the forces of change intensified about them, they frequently expressed a deep appreciation and fondness for the bands of the past. Sousa himself liked to emphasize the educational role of military bands and their

historical importance in elevating the cultural standards and musical tastes of the American people. As he saw the situation, "The influence of the band in the art development of the world is perhaps greater than that of any other musical force."[21] To John Duss of Economy, Pennsylvania, bands were memorable for the romance and joy they injected into the lives of ordinary people. In Duss's mind, bands meant "balmy days . . .[when] every barefoot boy whistled the newest band numbers from morn till eve, and young lovers sat dreamy-eyed under the

By 1915 the small-town band faced competition from radio, phonograph records, the automobile, and other technological advances that led to the growing sophistication and mobility of the American people. The town band of Lamoni, Iowa, population fifteen hundred, could still attract a small crowd on Main Street in 1915, but such ensembles faced increasing competition from new and varied forms of leisure activities. Iowa State Historical Society.

influence of the organ-like music of the best bands."[22] William Rannells, bandmaster of Rochester, Indiana, had yet another point to make. As he explained to a local journalist in 1910, it was the close friendships and companionship among bandsmen that, in retrospect, he appreciated most. Recalled Rannells, "There is no lodge fraternity as great as the fraternity which exists among band men."[23]

Much more could be said about the characteristics and contributions of pre–World War I bands, but no one has summarized the issues more eloquently than Frank Suddoth, Secretary of the Independent Silver Band of Mt. Vernon, Illinois.[24] Though inactive since 1889, the Independent Silver Band arranged to hold a grand twenty-fifth reunion in Mt. Vernon in September 1914. As Suddoth's detailed minutes make clear, almost every aspect of the five-day program was a joyous celebration of the customs and practices of the past.

The reunion began, in typical brass band fashion, with the local bandsmen welcoming the out-of-towners on the train platform. Shortly thereafter a parade was formed, and the men marched through town "to the strains of the sweetest music ever heard." The exhibition delighted the crowd, and no one seemed to mind that old Addison Fly played the wrong piece throughout the procession.

The next day, a Sunday, was devoted to a church service and a tour of the town, which had changed considerably since many of the bandsmen had departed. But on Monday and Tuesday the real celebrating began. The scheduled events included a concert at the Opera House, a concert at the First M. E. Church, a serenade at the Court House Square, and then a trip to the county fair, where the men had filled many engagements in years past. The climax of the reunion was an open-air concert held at 7:30 P.M. in the center of town. With an estimated eight thousand

The Independent Silver Band was photographed in front of the Mt. Vernon, Illinois, Court House in 1887, two years before the group disbanded. Frank Suddoth, who chronicled the band's twenty-fifth reunion in 1914, is the clarinetist seventh from the right. Thomas A. Puckett Collection.

people in attendance the band played the same pleasing mix of waltzes, marches, and cornet showpieces that they had presented during their farewell concert of 1889. Their efforts were "wondrously applauded."

Throughout the conclave the men traded stories and recalled events such as the time Professor Whiting's helmet blew more than forty miles to Olney during the cyclone of 1888. The uniform of Billy Chance, a two-hundred-pound wonder in 1914, was on prominent display during the festivities.

But soon, *too* soon, in Suddoth's opinion, the reunion came to an end. To conclude his formal record of the

201

The Independent Silver Band of Mt. Vernon, Illinois, celebrated its Silver Jubilee Reunion in September 1914. Here former bandsmen pose with their families in the same location that they had selected more than a quarter century earlier. Many of the band's members had left Mt. Vernon in the 1890s, but at least a dozen musicians returned to the town to renew old friendships, recreate the band's final concert, and reminisce about the once-famous ensemble. Thomas A. Puckett Collection.

events, Suddoth tried to describe what it had meant for these music-loving friends to meet again in the town they had held dear. Although his remarks centered on a small town in Illinois in 1914, they apply much more widely. Forthright and heartfelt, they seem a fitting eulogy for the nineteenth-century band movement:

> In our visions we have gone back to the days of our youth, . . . when our hearts were attuned to the infinite glory which was sure to come to the Independent Silver Band; only those who were an integral part of this organization know of that wonderful friendship that was inculcated in the hearts of its members as we met night after night in the little room in the Bond building with only a skylight above us and for hours practiced our several parts. On the occasion of this reunion, this great friendship is so manifest that words are but whispered eulogies as was our music the melody of the soul: such friendship is unmeasurable in silver and gold, and is surpassed only, in God's great love for us all. Members, their families and friends have been together nearly constantly during this great event, and as we part, each one to travel his way through the unfolded corridors of time, perfumed with the unforgetable joys at the hands of the people of our dear old home, tears of joy and of sorrow unrestrainedly trickle down our cheeks as we clasp hands in a last good bye. We all feel that we have been made better because of the renewal of this friendship of our youth; such friendship is the human dream of Heaven, the mystic tie which binds all mankind together and makes the whole world better, and there is none who have attended this great event but has been made to feel that it was a special privilege to be classed with this fine, honorable band of men.[25]

Bands would continue to exist. Even all-brass bands would be revitalized by the Salvation Army, historic performing organizations, and others. What is more, the memory of the movement would be preserved in such colorful expressions as "get on the bandwagon" and "strike up the band," and in the charming, evocative paintings by Grandma Moses. As a national symbol there is probably no image as widely recognized or cherished as the American small-town band parading down Main Street, flags flying, citizens cheering.

But the American band movement in its original phase was over. The simpler and supremely self-confident way of life that initially inspired and for decades sustained the art form had finally been supplanted by a more fragmented and less spontaneous modern age.

NOTES

1. MUSIC FOR THE PEOPLE

1. William Allen White, *The Autobiography of William Allen White* (New York: Macmillan, 1946), 58.

2. Elizabeth Leedom, "Brass Bands of the Mother Lode," *The Modesto Bee,* August 6, 1978, B1–2; citing the work of Kenneth Brungess.

3. Howard Mumford Jones, *The Age of Energy: Varieties of American Experience, 1865–1915* (New York: Viking Press, 1971), 122.

4. Joseph Barton, autobiographical sketch (ca. 1900), manuscript notebook in the library collections of the Church of Jesus Christ of Latter-day Saints, Salt Lake City, Utah.

5. David McCullough, *The Great Bridge* (New York: Simon and Schuster, 1972), 530–41.

6. Rudolph Wurlitzer Company, *Catalog No. 122* (Chicago, ca. 1919), 7.

7. Warren G. Harding played a number of different instruments in the Marion (Ohio) Cornet Band. Fiorello H. La Guardia learned to play both cornet and banjo from his father, and not only played in amateur bands in Prescott, Arizona, but also served as guest conductor in various New York City bands during his tenure as mayor. Orville Redenbacher played helicon tuba in the Purdue University Band in the 1920s.

8. For these and other details regarding the history of Moravian music, see Harry Hobart Hall, "The Moravian Wind Ensemble: Distinctive Chapter in America's Music" 2 vols. (Ph.D. dissertation, George Peabody College for Teachers, 1967).

9. Raoul F. Camus, "A Re-evaluation of the American Band Tradition," *Journal of Band Research* 7 (1970):5–6.

10. For more information on this subject, see Kenneth W. Carpenter, "A History of the United States Marine Band" (Ph.D. dissertation, University of Iowa, 1970).

11. James William Thompson, "Music and Musical Activities in New England, 1800–1838" (Ph.D. dissertation, George Peabody College for Teachers, 1962), 408–409.

12. Robert E. Eliason, *Keyed Bugles in the United States* (Washington, D.C.: Smithsonian Institution Press, 1972), 9.

13. New Orleans *Picayune,* August 2, 1838, quoted in Henry A. Kmen, *Music in New Orleans: The Formative Years, 1791–*

1841 (Baton Rouge: Louisiana State University Press, 1966), 212.

14. John Sullivan Dwight, *Dwight's Journal of Music* 9:18 (1856):141.

15. Leon Mead, "The Military Bands of the United States," *Harper's Weekly* (supplement for September 28, 1889), 785. In the same year there were an estimated 40,000 amateur bands in the United Kingdom.

16. William L. Hubbard, ed., *History of American Music,* American History and Encyclopedia of Music, vol. 8 (New York: Squire, 1908), 283–84.

17. William J. Schafer, *Brass Bands and New Orleans Jazz* (Baton Rouge: Louisiana State University Press, 1977), 8.

18. Schafer, *Brass Bands,* 56.

19. Charles Dickens, *American Notes* (Greenwich, Connecticut: Fawcett Publications, 1961), 107.

20. Robert E. Riegel, *Young America: 1830–1840* (Norman: University of Oklahoma Press, 1949), 367.

21. John Philip Sousa, *The Fifth String* (New York: Grosset and Dunlap, 1902), 96.

22. Quoted in Russel Blaine Nye, *Society and Culture in America, 1830–1860* (New York: Harper, 1974), 17.

23. Clayton Howard Tiede, "The Development of Minnesota Community Bands during the Nineteenth Century" (Ph.D. dissertation, University of Minnesota, 1970), 124.

24. Mary Evelyn Durden Teal, "Musical Activities in Detroit from 1701 through 1870," 2 vols. (Ph.D. dissertation, University of Michigan, 1964), 1:343.

25. For an interesting comparison, see Peter C. Marzio, *The Democratic Art: Pictures for a Nineteenth-Century America, Chromolithography, 1840–1900* (Boston: David R. Godine, 1979).

26. Quoted in Tiede, "Minnesota Community Bands," 145.

27. Chicago Band Association advertising brochure (ca. 1911), Chicago Band Association Papers, Chicago Historical Society, Chicago, Illinois.

28. Wurlitzer, *Catalog No. 122,* 7.

29. Quoted in Tiede, "Minnesota Community Bands," 125.

30. Lewis Atherton, *Main Street on the Middle Border* (Bloomington: Indiana University Press, 1984), 119.

31. Richard Franko Goldman, *The Wind Band: Its Literature and Technique* (1961; reprint ed., Westport, Connecticut: Greenwood Press, 1974), 11.

32. Howard Mumford Jones, *Age of Energy,* 17–19.

33. Samuel L. Clemens, *Speeches,* in Foster Rhea Dulles, *A History of Recreation: America Learns to Play,* 2d ed. (New York: Appleton-Century-Crofts, 1965), 191.

2. THE PROFESSIONALS

1. "The Autobiography of William Robyn," in Ernst C. Krohn, *Missouri Music* (New York: Da Capo Press, 1971), 255.

2. Robyn, "Autobiography," 266.

3. John Philip Sousa, "Music Becomes an American Profession," in *Sousa and His Band,* souvenir program (1925), 5.

4. William J. Schafer, *Brass Bands and New Orleans Jazz* (Baton Rouge: Louisiana State University Press, 1977), 35; Leon Mead, "The Military Bands of the United States," *Harper's Weekly* (supplement for September 28, 1889), 785; H. W. Schwartz, *Bands of America* (Garden City: Doubleday, 1957), 140–41.

5. "Musicians in New York," *Dwight's Journal of Music* 1:7 (May 1852):52. The quoted estimate of 2,685 is derived from *Music World.*

6. Paul Eric Paige, "Musical Organizations in Boston, 1830–1850" (Ph.D. dissertation, Boston University, 1967), 34.

7. Clayton Howard Tiede, "The Development of Minnesota Community Bands during the Nineteenth Century" (Ph.D. dissertation, University of Minnesota, 1970), 185.

8. U.S. Bureau of the Census, *Compendium of the Ninth Census (1870)* (Washington, D.C.: Government Printing Office, 1870), Table LXV, 604–607; *Compendium of the Tenth Census (1880)* (Washington, D.C.: Government Printing Office, 1880), Table CIII, 1368–69.

9. Katherine K. Preston, "Popular Music in the 'Gilded Age': Musicians' Gigs in Late Nineteenth-Century Washington, D.C.," in *Popular Music: A Yearbook* (Cambridge, England: Cambridge University Press, 1985), 26.

10. "A Mammoth Jubilee!," *Opera House Program* (Columbia, Missouri, April 13, 1888), 7.

11. *Opera House Program*, p. 9.

12. H. W. Schwartz, *Bands of America* (Garden City: Doubleday, 1957), 131.

13. Paul E. Bierley, *John Philip Sousa: American Phenomenon* (Englewood Cliffs: Prentice-Hall, 1973), 58–59.

14. Fred L. Grambs Scrapbook Collection, 1882–1938, vol. 4, Birmingham Public Library, Birmingham, Alabama. [Note: Clippings in this collection are not identified as to source or date.]

15. For more information on America's early military bands, see Raoul F. Camus, *The Military Music of the American Revolution* (Chapel Hill: University of North Carolina Press, 1976), and Raoul F. Camus, "A Re-evaluation of the American Band Tradition," *Journal of Band Research* 7 (1970):5–6. Camus makes the point in his writings that the U.S. Army regulation of 1834 was actually designed to *hold down* the size of bands to reasonable levels.

16. See Kenneth E. Olson, *Music and Musket: Bands and Bandsmen of the American Civil War* (Westport, Connecticut: Greenwood Press, 1981), 25. See also Robert Garofalo and Mark Elrod, *A Pictorial History of Civil War Era Musical Instruments & Military Bands* (Charleston, West Virginia: Pictorial Histories Publishing Co., 1985); William Bufkin, *Union Bands of the Civil War (1862–1865): Instrumentation and Score Analysis* (Ph.D. dissertation, Louisiana State University, 1973); Frederick Fennell, "The Civil War: Its Music and Its Sounds," *Journal of Band Research* 4:2 (Spring 1968):36–44, and 5:1 (Fall 1968):8–14; Jon Newsom, "The American Brass Band Movement," *Quarterly Journal of the Library of Congress* 36:2 (Spring 1979):114–39; William C. White, *A History of Military Music in America* (New York: Doubleday, 1957); Francis A. Lord and Arthur Wise, *Bands and Drummer Boys of the Civil War* (South Brunswick, New Jersey: Thomas Yoseloff, 1966).

17. Olson, *Music and Musket,* 72.

18. James Christie to Sarah Christie, August 6, 1862, Minnesota Historical Society, St. Paul, Minnesota.

19. Maurice Matloff, *American Military History* (Washington, D.C.: U.S. Army, 1969), 287.

20. Thomas C. Railsback, "Military Bands and Music at Old Fort Hays, 1867–1889," *Journal of the West* 22:3 (July 1983):28–35.

21. Loren Geiger, ed., "U.S. Navy Band," *Boombah Herald* 4:1 (1977):1.

22. Edwin H. Pierce, "United States Navy Bands, Old and New," *Musical Quarterly* 33:3 (July 1947):381–89.

23. Roger Pineau, ed., *The Japan Expedition, 1852–1854: The Personal Journal of Commodore Matthew C. Perry* (Washington, D.C.: Smithsonian Institution Press, 1968), 189.

24. John B. Dale, "Journal of a Cruise in Old Ironsides, 1844–1846," Diary entry for June 21, 1844, New England Historic Genealogical Society Library, Boston.

25. F. W. Jewett to E. Harrison, September 28, 1828, Litchfield Historical Society, Litchfield, Connecticut.

26. Grambs Scrapbook Collection, vol. 3, Birmingham Public Library, Birmingham, Alabama.

27. Hamlin Garland, *A Son of the Middle Border* (New York: 1917), 135–37, in Foster Rhea Dulles, *A History of Recreation: America Learns to Play*, 2d ed. (New York: Appleton-Century-Crofts, 1965), 286.

28. It has been claimed that Edward Kendall's circus performances corresponded to a decline in his ability and popularity. For a succinct rebuttal of this argument and for more information on Kendall's career, see Robert Kitchen, "Edward Kendall: America's First Circus Bandmaster," *Bandwagon* 21:4 (1977):25–27.

29. Bierley, *Sousa*, 33.

30. Nels Hokanson, "With Bosco's Circus in Northern Illinois," *Journal of the Illinois State Historical Society* 62:2 (1969):188.

31. Thomas T. Bennett, "Tours by a Musician with a Traveling Circus," Diary, 1838–1845, Harvard Theatre Collection, Harvard University Library, Cambridge, Massachusetts.

32. *Ellis Brooks Military and Concert Band* advertising pamphlet (Chicago, 1911).

33. Bierley, *Sousa*, 159–60.

34. H. M. Lewis, "Town Bands in Johnson County, Arkansas" (1985). Typescript.

35. Loren Geiger, "Fred Jewell," *Boombah Herald* 12:2 (1985):11–15.

36. Helen May Butler Papers, National Museum of American History, Washington, D.C.

37. Quoted in Tiede, "Minnesota Community Bands," 38.

38. Schwartz, *Bands of America*, 120.

39. Robert Garofalo and Mark Elrod, *A Pictorial History*, 106.

40. Leon Mead, "The Military Bands of the United States," *Harper's Weekly* (supplement for September 28, 1889), 785.

41. Sousa, "Music," 5.

42. The John Prosperi account book is in the Archives of the National Museum of American History, Smithsonian Institution. The estimate of Prosperi's annual income is taken from Katherine K. Preston, "Popular Music," 28.

43. William H. Neave to Edward Baxter Neave, October 25, 1867, Edward Baxter Neave Papers, William R. Perkins Library, Duke University.

44. "From Philadelphia," *The Leader* 13:8 (May 1888):6.

45. Bennett, "Tours By a Musician," entry for July 27, 1838.

46. Mead, "The Military Bands," 785.

47. William H. Neave to Edward Baxter Neave, October 4, 1867, Edward Baxter Neave Papers, William R. Perkins Library, Duke University.

48. Schwartz, *Bands of America*, 192.

49. *Artists of Gilmore's Jubilee Tour, 1889*, souvenir program (1889), 21.

3. THE BAND BOYS

1. Farr's Band Constitution, as contained in Minute Book, 1892–1895, Historical Society of Princeton, Princeton, New Jersey.

2. William W. Rannells, "History of Brass Bands from the First Organization in Rochester until the Present Time," in Marguerite Miller, *Home Folks*, 2 vols. (1910; reprint ed., Marceline, Missouri: Walsworth Printer, n.d.), 2:48.

3. Rannells, "History of Brass Bands," 2:46.

4. From *Mirror of Taste and Dramatic Censor* (1810) in H. Wiley Hitchcock, *Music in the United States: A Historical Introduction* (Englewood Cliffs: Prentice-Hall, 1969), 25.

5. Mark Twain, *Roughing It* (New York: Harper and Row, 1913), 2:12.

6. Lyon and Healy Company, *Band Instruments, Uniforms, Trimmings, &c* (Chicago, 1881), 32.

7. J. W. Pepper and Son, *Everything Musical for the Band, the Orchestra, the Home* (Philadelphia, 1918), 5.

8. G. F. Patton, *A Practical Guide to the Arrangement of Band Music . . . together with an Appendix Containing Practical Hints in Relation to the Organisation of Bands . . .* (New York: John F. Stratton, 1875), 175.

9. Union Brass Band of Marysville, Ohio, "Articles of Agreement" (1863), Ohio Historical Society, Columbus, Ohio.

10. Navarre (Ohio) Citizens Band, "Record of the Proceedings of the Navarre Citizens Band, incorporated July 28th 1888," Navarre-Bethlehem Township Historical Society, Navarre, Ohio.

11. Elizabeth Leedom, "Brass Bands of the Mother Lode," *The Modesto Bee*, August 6, 1978, B1–2; citing the work of Kenneth Brungess. It is possible that western bands in general attracted more professionals than bands in the older and more settled eastern communities. More research is required in this area.

12. Personal communication from Christina Dodds (Special Collections and Archives Assistant, Olin Library, Wesleyan

University, Middletown, Connecticut) to authors, January 28, 1985.

13. Personal communication from Ann C. Johanson (Librarian of the Historical Society of Princeton, Princeton, New Jersey) to authors, February 8, 1985.

14. Joyce Ellen Mangler, *Rhode Island Music and Musicians, 1733–1850* (Detroit: Information Service, 1965), 9, 10, 25, 34, 48.

15. William L. Hubbard, ed., *History of American Music,* American History and Encyclopedia of Music, vol. 8 (New York: Squire, 1908), 289.

16. Rudolph Wurlitzer Company, *Catalog No. 126* (Chicago, ca. 1922), 7.

17. Kenneth S. Clark, *Music in Industry* (New York: National Bureau for the Advancement of Music, 1929), 1.

18. Clark, *Music in Industry,* 49–50.

19. Clark, *Music in Industry,* 97.

20. Quoted in Paul Eric Paige, "Musical Organizations in Boston, 1830–1850" (Ph.D. dissertation, Boston University, 1967), 179.

21. James M. Trotter, *Music and Some Highly Musical People* (1881; reprint ed., New York: Johnson Reprint Corp., 1968), 57–58.

22. George S. Kanahele, *Hawaiian Music and Musicians: An Illustrated History* (Honolulu: University of Hawaii Press, 1979), 42.

23. One of the three Jacksonville, Illinois, bandstands was restored and transferred to Washington, D.C., where it now stands at the west end of the National Museum of American History, Smithsonian Institution. The dedication of this "national bandstand" occurred on July 4, 1984, with a recreation of a nineteenth-century band concert.

24. Sinclair Lewis, *Main Street* (New York: Harcourt, Brace and World, 1948), 304.

25. Paul E. Bierley, *John Philip Sousa: American Phenomenon* (Englewood Cliffs: Prentice-Hall, 1973), 163.

26. Louis Moreau Gottschalk, *Notes of a Pianist* (London: Lippincott, 1881), 202.

27. William J. Schafer, *Brass Bands and New Orleans Jazz* (Baton Rouge: Louisiana State University Press, 1977), 22.

28. Quoted in Schafer, *Brass Bands,* 31.

29. Paul Laurence Dunbar, "The Colored Band," in *The Complete Poems of Paul Laurence Dunbar* (New York: Dodd, Mead & Co., 1972), 286–87.

30. Annie E. K. Bidwell, "Rancho Chico Indians," Dorothy J. Hill, ed. (Chico, California: Bidwell Mansion Association, 1980), 14, California Historical Society, San Francisco, California. Typescript.

31. Bierley, *Sousa,* 85.

32. Trotter, *Highly Musical People,* 63.

33. H. N. White Company, *White Way News No. 5* (Cleveland, ca. 1932), 22.

34. Personal communication from Helen Ducommun, Laurens, Iowa, to authors, April 10, 1985.

35. Thomas Wentworth Higginson, *Cheerful Yesterdays* (New York: Arno Press and the *New York Times,* 1968), 41.

36. James H. Brown, "Some Pioneer Brass Bands Hereabouts," Battle Creek, Michigan, newspaper clipping, August 14, 1931, Willard Library, Battle Creek, Michigan.

37. From a transcript of an Ann Arbor newspaper article (ca. 1900) relating to Otto's Juvenile Band, Bentley Historical Library, University of Michigan, Ann Arbor.

38. Allen Dodworth, *Dodworth's Brass Band School* (New York: H. B. Dodworth, 1853).

39. Patton, *Practical Guide,* 175–93.

40. D. S. McCosh, *McCosh's Guide for Amateur Brass Bands,* in Lyon and Healy, *Band Instruments, Uniforms, Trimmings, &c.* (Chicago, 1881), 1–29. The *Guide* was also published as a separate pamphlet.

41. Patton, *Practical Guide,* 176.

42. Advertisement in *The Leader* 13:8 (May 1888):4.

43. Advertisement in *C. G. Conn's Truth* 5:8 (February 1904):34.

44. Heather S. Hatch, "Music in Arizona Territory," *Journal of Arizona History* 12:4 (Winter 1971):272.

45. Patton, *Practical Guide,* 183.

46. J. W. Pepper and Son, *Everything Musical,* 5.

47. "How to Improve the Band," *American Musician and Art Journal* 30:3 (February 14, 1914):10–11.

48. Bernard J. Pfohl, *The Salem Band* (Winston-Salem, North Carolina: Winston Printing Co., 1953), 14.

49. *The Leader* 10:12 (October 1885):1.

50. McCosh, *Guide,* 4.

51. Old Band Teacher, "Reminiscences of Ye Ancient Band-master," *American Musician and Art Journal* 29:1 (January 18, 1913):21.

52. Leon Mead, "The Military Bands of the United States," *Harper's Weekly* (supplement for September 28, 1889), 785.

53. Clayton Howard Tiede, "The Development of Minnesota Community Bands during the Nineteenth Century," (Ph.D. dissertation, University of Minnesota, 1970), 68, 115.

54. Lawrence B. Romaine, "A New England Town Band, 1843–1860," *Old Time New England* 43:3 (1953):80–83. The quoted payment of $200.00 is unusually high based on records and receipts of other bands. This detail may, therefore, be an exaggeration.

55. "Bandmen of Yesteryear Kept Battle Creek Music Conscious," Battle Creek, Michigan, newspaper clipping, ca. 1939, Willard Library, Battle Creek, Michigan.

56. Rannells, "History of Brass Bands," 2:41–42.

57. Henry A. Kmen, *Music in New Orleans: The Formative Years, 1791–1841* (Baton Rouge: Louisiana State University Press, 1966), 205.

58. *Trumpet News* (May 15, 1877), in James A. Keene, *A History of Music Education in the United States* (Hanover, New Hampshire: University Press of New England, 1982), 294.

59. "Band Tournament at Fremont, Ohio," *The Leader* 9:9 (June 1884), 4.

4. MUSIC FOR EVERY OCCASION

1. Lawrence B. Romaine, "A New England Town Band, 1843–1860," *Old Time New England* 43:3 (1953):80–83.

2. From the Boston *Post* (1882) in *The Leader* 8:3 (December 1882):1.

3. *The Grafton Cornet Band, 1867–1967* (Grafton, Vermont: Grafton Historical Society, 1967), 9.

4. G. F. Patton, *A Practical Guide to the Arrangement of Band Music . . . together with an Appendix Containing Practical Hints in Relation to the Organisation of Bands . . .* (New York: John F. Stratton, 1875), 185.

5. Jon Newsom, "The American Brass Band Movement," *Quarterly Journal of the Library of Congress* 36:2 (1979):118.

6. Romaine, "A New England Town Band," 80–83.

7. William W. Rannells, "History of Brass Bands from the First Organization in Rochester until the Present Time," in Marguerite Miller, *Home Folks,* 2 vols. (1910; reprint ed., Marceline, Missouri: Walsworth Printers), 2:40.

8. "The Autobiography of William Robyn," in Ernst C. Krohn, *Missouri Music* (New York: Da Capo Press, 1971), 264.

9. Frédéric Louis Ritter, *Music in America* (New York: Charles Scribner's Sons, 1890), 422.

10. James H. Brown, "Some Pioneer Brass Bands Hereabouts," Battle Creek, Michigan, newspaper clipping, August 14, 1931, Willard Library, Battle Creek, Michigan.

11. Patton, *Practical Guide,* 191–92.

12. "Sharps and Flats," *The Leader* 8:3 (December 1882):1.

13. "Serenade" (March 12, 1860), transcription of article in Garnavillo, Iowa, newspaper, Garnavillo Historical Society.

14. Horace Peaslee, "Park Architecture: The Bandstands," *Architectural Record* 51 (1922):269–74.

15. *Grafton Cornet Band,* 12.

16. The collection of band ephemera at the National Museum of American History, Smithsonian Institution, includes more than 250 images of American bandstands. Most of

these are postcards from the first decade of the twentieth century.

17. George Burnap, *Parks: Their Design, Equipment and Use* (Philadelphia: Lippincott, 1916), 136.

18. Peaslee, "Park Architecture," 271.

19. Mary Evelyn Durden Teal, "Musical Activities in Detroit from 1701 through 1870," 2 vols. (Ph.D. dissertation, University of Michigan, 1964), 1:232.

20. H. W. Schwartz, *Bands of America* (Garden City: Doubleday, 1957), 74.

21. Schwartz, *Bands of America,* 68.

22. "Plattsburgh N.Y., Tuesday, June 18, '95," excursion broadside, The Sheldon Museum, Middlebury, Vermont.

23. St. Albans (Vermont) Brigade Band Record Book (1869–99), Vermont Historical Society, Montpelier, Vermont.

24. George Thornton Edwards, *Music and Musicians of Maine* (1928; reprint ed., New York: AMS Press, 1970), 333.

25. Franklin M. Garrett, *Atlanta and Environs: A Chronicle of Its People and Events* (New York: Lewis Historical Publishing Co., 1954), 2:153.

26. Patton, *A Practical Guide,* 191.

27. C. G. Conn Company, *Catalog* (ca. 1900), 230.

28. Frank Simon, as told to William Errol McFee, "Audiences I Have Known," in H. N. White Company, *White Way News No. 5* (Cleveland, ca. 1932), 6.

29. Bernard J. Pfohl, *The Salem Band* (Winston-Salem, North Carolina: Winston, 1953), 11.

30. William Dean Howells, *A Boy's Town,* in Henry Steele Commager, ed., *Selected Writings of William Dean Howells* (New York: Random House, 1950), 777.

31. Rannells, "History of Brass Bands," 2:36.

32. Rannells, "History of Brass Bands," 2:36–37.

33. Rannells, "History of Brass Bands," 2:37.

34. *Grafton Cornet Band,* 5–6.

5. TOOLS OF THE TRADE

1. An introductory overview of the development of wind instruments is given by Adam Carse, *Musical Wind Instruments* (New York: Da Capo, 1965).

2. Carse, *Wind Instruments.*

3. J. W. Pepper Company, *Catalogue and Price List* (Philadelphia, 1900), 13–22.

4. William Carter White, *A History of Military Music in America* (New York: Exposition Press, 1944), 239. The "regulation" instrumentation was not universally adopted.

5. Robert Garofalo and Mark Elrod, *A Pictorial History of Civil War Era Musical Instruments & Military Bands* (Charleston, West Virginia: Pictorial Histories Publishing Co., 1985), 35–52. Nineteenth-century trade catalogs provide an excellent overview of the variety of percussion instruments available to bandsmen.

6. Harry Hobart Hall, "The Moravian Wind Ensemble: Distinctive Chapter in America's Music," 2 vols. (Ph.D. dissertation, George Peabody College for Teachers, 1967), 1:223.

7. Lawrence B. Romaine, "A New England Town Band, 1843–1860," *Old Time New England* 43:3 (1953):80–83.

8. [The Record Band], *Russell Record* (August 30, 1883), Kansas State Historical Society, Topeka, Kansas.

9. Leon Mead, "The Military Bands of the United States," *Harper's Weekly* (supplement for September 28, 1889), 785.

10. "The State of Military Bands in New York," *American Music Journal* (October 1835), as quoted by Robert E. Eliason, *Keyed Bugles in the United States* (Washington, D.C.: Smithsonian Institution Press, 1972), 26.

11. John S. Dwight, "Music in the Open Air—Brass Bands and Bands Non-military," *Dwight's Journal of Music* 9 (June 21, 1856):93–94.

12. Gerald Grose, "Patrick S. Gilmore's Influence on the Development of the American Concert Band," *Journal of Band Research* 6:1 (1969): 11–16; Frederick Fennell, *Time and the Winds* (Kenosha, Wisconsin: Leblanc, 1954), 37–39.

13. Allen Dodworth, "The Formation of Bands," *Message Bird* 1 (1849):9.

14. From *Musical Truth* 5:6 (1903):7, as quoted in Martin Kriven, "A Century of Wind Instrument Manufacturing in the United States: 1860–1960" (Ph.D. dissertation, State University of Iowa, 1961), 71–72.

15. George S. Bonn, *A History of the Bands of the Ohio State University* (Columbus: Eta Chapter of Kappa Kappa Psi, 1936), 31, 36.

6. DISCOURSING SWEET MUSIC

1. *O. C. U. Concert,* concert broadside (1881), Oberlin College Archives, Oberlin, Ohio.

2. John Philip Sousa, "Bandmaster Sousa Explains His Mission in Music," *Musical America* (April 16, 1910), as quoted in Paul E. Bierley, *John Philip Sousa: American Phenomenon* (Englewood Cliffs: Prentice-Hall, 1973), 119.

3. David L. Stackhouse, "D. W. Reeves and His Music," *Journal of Band Research* 5:2 (1969):15–28; 6:1 (1969):29–41.

4. Bierley, *Sousa,* 123.

5. Bierley, *Sousa,* 154.

6. Harry Hobart Hall, "The Moravian Wind Ensemble: Distinctive Chapter in America's Music," 2 vols. (Ph.D. dissertation, George Peabody College for Teachers, 1967), 1:227.

7. H. Wiley Hitchcock, *Music in the United States: A Historical Introduction* (Englewood Cliffs: Prentice-Hall, 1969), 25.

8. "Gilmore's Great Cincinnati Music Festival," program (1889), Cincinnati Historical Society.

9. E. A. Hitchcock, as quoted in Ralph Thomas Dudgeon, "The Keyed Bugle, Its History, Literature, and Technique" (Ph.D. dissertation, University of California, San Diego, 1980), 56.

10. James M. Trotter, *Music and Some Highly Musical People* (1881; reprint ed., New York: Johnson Reprint Corp., 1968), 307.

11. Dudgeon, "The Keyed Bugle," 75, 89.

12. From Victor Herbert, "Artistic Bands," originally published in Anton Seidl, *The Music of the Modern World* (New York: D. Appleton, 1895–97), as quoted in Richard Franko Goldman, *The Wind Band: Its Literature and Technique,* (reprint ed., Westport, Connecticut: Greenwood Press, 1974), 66.

13. John Philip Sousa, *Through the Year with Sousa* (New York: Thomas Y. Crowell, 1910), entry for February 25, originally from *The Band.*

14. Edward Everett Hale, *A New England Boyhood* (1893; reprint ed., Upper Saddle River, New Jersey: Gregg Press, 1970), 246.

15. Bierley, *Sousa,* 48.

16. Frederick Fennell, *Time and the Winds* (Kenosha, Wisconsin: Leblanc Company, 1954), 40.

17. G. F. Patton, *A Practical Guide to the Arrangement of Band Music . . . together with an Appendix Containing Practical Hints in Relation to the Organisation of Bands . . .* (New York: John F. Stratton, 1875), 191.

18. *Point of Pines Mid-Summer Musical Festival,* concert broadside (n.d.), Michigan State University Archives, East Lansing, Michigan.

19. *Currier's Full Band,* concert program broadside (1879), Cincinnati Historical Society.

20. *Grand Concert by Dodworth's Concert Band,* concert program broadside (1856), Pejepscot Historical Society, Brunswick, Maine.

21. *Gilmore's Grand Concerts,* concert program (1888), courtesy of Lillian Caplin.

22. *Diller's Cornet Septet of New York,* concert program (1883), Cornell University Archives.

23. William L. Hubbard, ed., *History of American Music,* American History and Encyclopedia of Music, vol. 8 (New York: Squire, 1908), 283.

24. George Thornton Edwards, *Music and Musicians of Maine* (1928; reprint ed., New York: AMS Press, 1970), 332.

25. Stackhouse, "D. W. Reeves," 5:15.

26. Lyon and Healy Company, "Arranging Band Music," in *Band Instruments, Uniforms, Trimmings, &c.* (Chicago, 1881), 92.

27. William Carter White, *A History of Military Music in America* (New York: Exposition Press, 1944), 61–62.

28. Isaac White to Mr. Wright, March 15, 1858, Tallmadge Historical Society, Tallmadge, Ohio.

29. "When Johnny Comes Marching Home," *The Leader* 10:12 (October 1885):2.

30. Leon Mead, "Military Bands," 788.

31. *Ellis Brooks Military and Concert Band,* advertising pamphlet (Chicago, 1911).

7. BAND SUPPLIES OF EVERY DESCRIPTION

1. Francis J. Grund, *The Americans in their Moral, Social, and Political Relations* (New York and London: Johnson Reprint Corp., 1968), xvi.

2. Allen Dodworth, "The Formation of Bands," *Message Bird* 1 (August 1, 1849):9.

3. C. and E. W. Jackson advertisement, *Euterpeiad* 2 (1821):127.

4. Robert Eliason, *Early American Makers of Woodwind and Brass Musical Instruments* (1976). Typescript.

5. Allen Dodworth, "Brass Bands," *Message Bird* 1 (June 15, 1850):361.

6. Lyon and Healy, *Band Instruments* (Chicago, 1881), 35.

7. The activities of many early American instrument makers have been described in the writings of Dr. Robert Eliason, formerly of the Henry Ford Museum in Dearborn, Michigan. Of special interest is his unpublished 200-page typescript: *Early American Makers of Woodwind and Brass Musical Instruments,* (1976). A useful review is found in his article, "The Road From Dash to Bach: Landmarks of Brass Instrument Making in the United States," *Selmer Bandwagon* 69 (1973)7–9. Published biographies by Eliason about specific makers include *Graves & Company Musical Instru-ment Makers* (Dearborn, Michigan: Greenfield Village and Henry Ford Museum, n.d.); *Early American Brass Makers,* (Nashville: The Brass Press, 1979); and "George Catlin, Hartford Musical Instrument Maker," *Journal of the American Musical Instrument Society* 8 (1982):16–37, and 9 (1983):21–52.

8. Eliason, *Early American Makers.*

9. Eliason, "George Catlin."

10. Eliason, *Graves & Company.*

11. Between 1837 and 1840 about 100 wind and brass instruments per year were sold by Graves to Marsh and Chase of Montpelier, Vermont. Robert Eliason, "Letters to Marsh & Chase from Graves & Company, Musical Instrument Makers," *Journal of the American Musical Instrument Society* 4 (1978):43–53. It is possible, therefore, that the total output of Graves & Company may have approached 1,000 wind instruments per year in the late 1830s and early 1840s.

12. Eliason, *Early American Makers,* records 30 active woodwind makers and 5 brass makers in the period 1825 to 1829. From 1835 to 1839 these numbers increase to 40 and 7, respectively. From 1845 to 1849 he notes 43 woodwind and 18 brass makers, and from 1855 to 1859 33 and 35 makers of woodwinds and brass, respectively.

13. Eliason, *Early American Brass Makers,* includes surveys of the life and manufactures on J. Lathrop Allen, Thomas Paine, E. G. Wright, and Isaac Fiske.

14. Biographical information on John F. Stratton is contained in anonymous articles entitled "John F. Stratton & Son," in *Music Trade Review for 1889* (1889):162 and Edward Lyman Bill, ed., *A General History of the Music Trades in America* (New York: Bill and Bill, 1891), 81. Additional information is contained in Martin Krivin, "A Century of Wind Instrument Manufacturing in the United States: 1860–1960" (Ph.D. dissertation, State University of Iowa, 1961), 31–36; and Lloyd P. Farrar, "Under the Crown and Eagle," *American Musical Instrument Society Newsletter* 12 (1983):2–3.

15. Eliason, "The Road," 8.

16. Christine M. Ayers, *Contributions by the Music Industries of Boston: 1640–1936* (New York: H. W. Wilson, 1937).

17. Henry Distin Manufacturing Company, *Descriptive Catalog "Highest Grade" Band Instruments* (Williamsport, Pennsylvania, 1907). See also Lloyd Farrar, *Chronologies and a Survey of Serial Numbers* (1983), 4–12, which contains a chronology of the Distin Company. Typescript.

18. J. W. Pepper, *Illustrated Catalogue and Price-List* (Philadelphia, ca. 1890); J. W. Pepper, *Catalog of Musical Instruments* (Philadelphia, ca. 1900). Much information on the company is also available in issues of *Musical Times and Band Journal*, which was published periodically by the company. A chronology of Pepper is provided by Farrar, *Chronologies*, 13–24.

19. Lyon and Healy, *Band Instruments*, 186.

20. Krivin, "Wind Instrument Manufacturing," 32f.

21. Krivin, "Wind Instrument Manufacturing," 55–83. Details of Conn's activities and history are contained in the Conn company periodical *Musical Truth*, which was published from about 1890 to the 1920s. Its name was subsequently changed to *Elkhart Truth*.

22. Krivin, "Wind Instrument Manufacturing," 84–90.

23. Krivin, "Wind Instrument Manufacturing," 90–96.

24. Krivin, "Wind Instrument Manufacturing," 100–103. The history and progress of the H. N. White Company is recorded in the firm's periodical *White Way News*.

25. Krivin, "Wind Instrument Manufacturing," 97–100 for Holton, 109–11 for Blessing, and 120–25 for Martin.

26. Krivin, "Wind Instrument Manufacturing," 104–108 for Haynes, 112–19 for Cundy-Bettoney, and 125–30 for Penzel-Mueller.

27. Lyon and Healy, *New Edition Lyon & Healy Band Instruments, Uniforms, Trimmings, &c.* (Chicago, 1891), 108.

28. Advertisements in the band periodicals *The Leader* (Boston) and *The Bands' Messenger* (Philadelphia) from the period 1884 to 1888 include the following Philadelphia-based uniform and band cap distributors: H. Bernhard, George Evans & Co., J. J. Fisher, Horstmann Bros. & Co., D. Klein & Bros., Joseph H. Lambert & Son, Jacob Reed's Sons, Wanamaker & Brown, and J. H. Wilson. Most of these merchants operated stores near Fifth and Market Streets.

29. No copy of this Lyon and Healy uniform catalog is known to us, though its existence is noted in the general band merchandise catalogs of the 1880s and 1890s.

30. Henderson and Company, *Band Uniforms Catalogue No. 120* (Philadelphia, ca. 1900).

31. "Band Uniforms Cheaper Than Ever," *The Leader* 10:12 (October 1885):8.

32. "G. W. Simmons & Co.," *The Leader* 9:9 (June 1884):5.

33. "The Pettibone Manufacturing Company," *The Leader* 10:9 (June 1885):8.

34. M. Slater, *Illustrated Catalog of Brass and German Silver Musical Instruments* (New York, 1874), 44.

35. Carl Fischer, *Carl Fischer's Reliable Band Instrument Catalog* (New York, ca. 1905), 79.

36. Lyon and Healy, *New Edition*, 99.

37. "The Acme Cornet Case," *The Leader* 9:9, (June 1884):8.

38. See, for example, "Silver Plating for Instruments," advertisement by H. G. Lehnert in *The Bands' Messenger* (Philadelphia, ca. 1884).

39. Herbert L. Clarke to the Clarke Music Company (no apparent relation) of Syracuse, New York, March 5, 1914, in the band ephemera collection, National Museum of American History, Smithsonian Institution.

40. Kriven, "Wind Instrument Manufacturing," 88.

41. Lyon and Healy, *New Edition*, 5.

42. Rudolph Wurlitzer Company, *Catalog No. 126* (Chicago, ca. 1922), 7.

43. Rudolph Wurlitzer Company, *Catalog No. 122* (Chicago, ca. 1919), 8.

44. S. R. Leland and Son advertisement in *The Leader* 10:12 (October 1885):5.

45. Wurlitzer, *Catalog No. 126*, 7.

46. Lyon and Healy, *Band Instruments*, 91. The testimonial was from E. Kitterer, leader of the Danville (Virginia) Cornet Band.

47. Distin, *Descriptive Catalog.*

48. Lyon and Healy, *Band Instruments*, 32; Lyon and Healy, *New Edition*, 26.

49. Sears, Roebuck and Co., *Catalogue No. 117* (1908), Joseph J. Schroeder, Jr., ed. (Northfield, Illinois: DBI Books, 1971), 248.

50. J. W. Pepper, *Everything Musical for the Band, the Orchestra, the Home* (Philadelphia, 1918), 4.

51. S. R. Leland and Son, *Illustrated Catalogue and Price List of the Eclipse Band Instruments . . .* 21st ed. (Worcester, Massachusetts, 1900), 3.

8. THE OTHER SIDE OF THE FOOTLIGHTS: BANDSMEN AND THEIR AUDIENCE

1. Fred L. Grambs Scrapbook Collection, 1882–1938, vol. 4, Birmingham Public Library, Birmingham, Alabama. [Note: Clippings in this collection are not identified as to source or date.]

2. Transcript of a Watsonville, California, newspaper clipping dated July 30, 1874, Pajaro Valley Historical Association, Watsonville, California.

3. Frank Simon, as told to William Errol McFee, "Audiences I Have Known," in H. N. White Company, *White Way News No. 5* (Cleveland, ca. 1932), 6.

4. *The Second Promenade Concert by the Towler Brass Band,* concert broadside (April 21, 1868), Rare Book Room, Duke University Library, Durham, North Carolina.

5. Paul E. Bierley, *John Philip Sousa: American Phenomenon* (Englewood Cliffs: Prentice-Hall, 1973), 50–51.

6. Rudolph Wurlitzer Company, *Catalog No. 126* (Chicago, ca. 1922), 7.

7. Clayton Howard Tiede, "The Development of Minnesota Community Bands during the Nineteenth Century" (Ph.D. dissertation, University of Minnesota, 1970), 155.

8. "An account of the celebration held in St. Paul, Minneapolis and along the line on completion of the main line to the Pacific in September 1883," Henry Villard Papers, Minnesota Historical Society, St. Paul, Minnesota.

9. Paul Eric Paige, "Musical Organizations in Boston, 1830–1850" (Ph.D. dissertation, Boston University, 1967), 208.

10. John Partridge to Fanny L. Partridge, April 19, 1862, Chicago Historical Society, in Kenneth E. Olson, *Music and Musket: Bands and Bandsmen of the American Civil War* (Westport, Connecticut: Greenwood Press, 1981), 162.

11. Thomas C. Railsback, "Military Bands and Music at Old Fort Hays, 1867–1899," *Journal of the West* 22:3 (1983):28–35.

12. Thomas Maitland Marshall, ed., "The Journal of Henry B. Miller," *Missouri Historical Society Collections* 6:3 (1931):262.

13. Quoted in Tiede, "Minnesota Community Bands," 125.

14. Mary Evelyn Durden Teal, "Musical Activities in Detroit from 1701 through 1870," 2 vols. (Ph.D. dissertation, University of Michigan, 1964), 1:223.

15. Grambs Scrapbook Collection, vol. 4, Birmingham Public Library, Birmingham, Alabama.

16. [The Record Band], *Russell Record* (December 27, 1883), Kansas State Historical Society, Topeka, Kansas.

17. G. F. Patton, *A Practical Guide to the Arrangement of Band Music . . . together with an Appendix Containing Practical Hints in Relation to the Organisation of Bands . . .* (New York: John F. Stratton, 1875), 183.

18. Harry Hobart Hall, "The Moravian Wind Ensemble: Distinctive Chapter in America's Music," 2 vols. (Ph.D. dissertation, George Peabody College for Teachers, 1967), 1:312.

19. "Saturday Walks in the German Quarter," *New York Times,* December 8, 1858, 5, in Tiede, "Minnesota Community Bands," 118.

20. Patton, *Practical Guide*, 189.

21. "The Concerts," *The Musical Magazine* 1:20 (September 28, 1839), 320.

22. Teal, "Musical Activities in Detroit," 1:225.

23. Quoted in Tiede, "Minnesota Community Bands," 65.

24. Alan C. Buechner, "Long Island's Early Brass Bands," *Long Island Forum* 45:6 (June 1982):106–11.

25. Quoted in Tiede, "Minnesota Community Bands," 112.

26. Tiede, "Minnesota Community Bands," 9.

27. Holton Company, *Concert Bands of Elkhorn* (Elkhorn, Wisconsin, n.d.), 4.

28. *Gleason's Pictorial Drawing-Room Companion*, October 4, 1851.

29. *Minneapolis Tribune*, May 30, 1868, 4, in Tiede, "Minnesota Community Bands," 123.

30. Transcript of a Watsonville, California, newspaper clipping September 14, 1871, Pajaro Valley Historical Association, Watsonville, California.

31. "Local Matters," *The Sentinel* (July 19, 1860), in Mary Lou Cowlishaw, *This Band's Been Here Quite a Spell . . . 1859–1981* (Naperville, Illinois: Naperville Municipal Band, 1981), 44.

32. Grambs Scrapbook Collection, vol. 4, Birmingham Public Library, Birmingham, Alabama.

33. *Darlington News*, August 1, 1878, Darlington County Historical Commission, Darlington, South Carolina.

34. John Kirkpatrick, "A Temporary Mimeographed Catalogue of the Music Manuscripts and Related Materials of Charles Edward Ives, 1874–1954" (New Haven, Connecticut: Yale University School of Music, 1960), 11.

35. John Sullivan Dwight, "Music in the Open Air—Brass Bands and Bands Non-military," *Dwight's Journal of Music* 9 (June 21, 1856):93–94.

36. H. W. Schwartz, *Bands of America* (Garden City: Doubleday, 1957), 111.

37. Deborah M. Olsen and Clark M. Will, "Musical Heritage of the Aurora Colony," *Oregon Historical Quarterly* 79 (1978):232–67.

38. Samuel L. Clemens, "Letter to Andrew Lang" (Hartford, 1889), in Henry Nash Smith, ed., *Popular Culture and Industrialism, 1865–1890* (Garden City: Doubleday, 1967), 398–402.

9. BAND PROFILES

1. The sources for the claims reproduced in this table are as follows: Stonewall Brigade Band: Frank B. Holt, "Stonewall Brigade Band, Continuous Since 1855," typescript (1982), 27; Belvidere (New Jersey) Cornet Band: Belvidere Cornet Band Association Inc., *Historical Souvenir Booklet, 1870–1964* (Belvidere, N.J.: Hicks Printing Co., 1964), [9]; Royal Hawaiian Band: George S. Kanahele, *Hawaiian Music and Musicians; An Illustrated History* (Honolulu: University of Hawaii Press, 1979), 335; Allentown (Pennsylvania) Band: William Carter White, *A History of Military Music in America* (Westport, Connecticut: Greenwood Press, 1977; reprint of 1944 ed.), 114; Repasz Band (Williamsport, Pennsylvania): *Repasz Band* publicity booklet in the collections of the Lycoming County Historical Society & Museum; see pages written by William Volkma; U.S. Marine Band: Frederick Fennell, *Time and the Winds* (Kenosha: G. Leblanc Co., 1954), 37; Browningsville (Maryland) Band: see clippings file on the band in the collections of the Montgomery County Historical Society, Rockville, Maryland; Salem (North Carolina) Band: Harry Hobart Hall, "The Moravian Wind Ensemble: Distinctive Chapter in America's Music," (Ph.D. dissertation, George Peabody College for Teachers, 1967), 293; Temple (New Hampshire) Band: Anne D. Lunt, "History of the Temple Band," typescript, 1983; Purdue University Marching Band: "Paul Spotts Emrick," in Shirley Willard, *Fulton County Folks* (Rochester, Indiana, 1981), 2:232.

2. Chris Banner, "The Community Band in Kansas: A Longstanding Musical Institution," *Journal of the West* 22:3 (July 1983):36–46.

3. Dee Brown, *The Gentle Tamers: Women of the Old Wild West* (New York: G. P. Putnam's Sons, 1958), 49.

4. Quoted in Clayton Howard Tiede, "The Development of Minnesota Community Bands During the Nineteenth Century" (Ph.D. dissertation, University of Minnesota, 1970), 62.

5. William Whithorn and Doris Whithorn, *A Photo History of Aldridge: Coal Camp that Died A-Bornin'* (Minneapolis: Acme Printing, 1966), 131.

6. Several American band histories have been compiled. These histories include: Viola Johnson, ed., *The First Twenty Five Years: The Watsonville Band* (Watsonville, California: Watsonville Band, 1972); Mary Lou Cowlishaw, *This Band's Been Here Quite a Spell: Naperville Municipal Band, 1859–1981* (Naperville, Illinois: Naperville Municipal Band, 1981); *Concert Bands of Elkhorn* (Elkhorn, Wisconsin: Holton Company, n.d.); Bernard J. Pfohl, *The Salem Band* (Winston-Salem, North Carolina: Winston, 1953); Thomas Carroll, "Bands and Band Music in Salem (Massachusetts)" *Historical Collections of the Essex Institute* 36 (1900): 265–87; *The Grafton Cornet Band, 1867–1967* (Grafton, Vermont: Grafton Historical Society, ca. 1970); Belvidere Cornet Band Association Inc., *Historical Souvenir Booklet, 1870–1964* (Belvidere, New Jersey: Hicks Printing, 1964); J. Stanley Lemons and F. M. Marciniak, *Strike Up the Band—the American Band* [of Providence] (Providence: Rhode Island College, 1979); Harry H. Hall, *A Johnny Reb Band from Salem: The Pride of Tarheelia* (Raleigh, North Carolina: Confederate Centennial Commission, 1963); Dorothy Ballantyne and Elin Christianson, "The Hobart (Indiana) High School Band" (Hobart, Indiana: Hobart Historical Society, 1985), typescript; "100th Anniversary Michigan City Municipal Band, 1869–1969" (Michigan City, Indiana: ca. 1969), typescript; Ernest A. Stolba, "A History of the Fitchburg Military Band of Fitchburg, Massachusetts" (Fitchburg, Massachusetts: 1945), typescript; Christopher Henry Banner, "The Manhattan (Kansas) Municipal Band, 1920–1980: An Ethnographic History" (B.A. dissertation, University of Hawaii, 1983); *1884–1959, Pictorial History of the Browningsville (Maryland) Cornet Band* (n.d.); Isaac Rob-

bins, "Some of the History of the Provo Marshall Band First Organized in 1849" (Provo: 1965), typescript; Marshall Moore Brice, *The Stonewall Brigade Band* (Verona, Virginia: McClure Press, 1967); Priscilla M. Harding, "McKinley's Own: An Ohio Band Plays the 'Splendid Little War,'" *Timeline* (October/November 1985): 10–22.

7. This history of Economy, Pennsylvania, and its bands is drawn from Richard D. Wetzel, *Frontier Musicians on the Connoquenessing, Wabash, and Ohio: A History of the Music and Musicians of George Rapp's Harmony Society, 1805–1906* (Athens, Ohio: Ohio University Press, 1976); and John S. Duss, *The Harmonists: A Personal History* (1943; reprint ed., Ambridge, Pennsylvania: The Harmonie Associates, 1970).

8. Duss, *The Harmonists*, 283.

9. Most of the historical information on Jillson's Cornet Band has been obtained from two manuscript record books of the band for the years 1873 to 1887, now in the authors' collection. Additional information, particularly on the formation of the band in 1867 and the formation of the Columbia Band in 1893, has been supplied from archival materials in the Langworthy Public Library, Hope Valley, Rhode Island, and in the personal collections of Mrs. Hope Andrews of Hope Valley. Historical information on the mill towns of southwest Rhode Island is contained in Gladys Segar and Betty Salomon, *Water Power Revisited: A Circle of Dam Sites Along the Wood and Pawcatuck Rivers* (Hope Valley, Rhode Island: Langworthy Public Library, 1980), and Betty Salomon and Tess Hoffman, eds., *Hope Valley Revived* (Hope Valley, Rhode Island: Langworthy Public Library, 1977).

10. The details of the history of the Aldridge Silver Cornet Band are included in William Whithorn and Doris Whithorn, *A Photo History of Aldridge: Coal Camp that Died A-Bornin'* (Minneapolis: Acme Printing, 1966). Quoted matter used here in the text is from this source.

11. Whithorn, *Photo History of Aldridge*, 134.

12. Whithorn, 131.

13. Most of the information contained in this profile is derived from George S. Kanahele, *Hawaiian Music and Musicians; An Illustrated History* (Honolulu: University of Hawaii Press, 1979).

14. Kanahele, *Hawaiian Music,* 336.

15. Kanahele, *Hawaiian Music,* 337.

16. This survey is based on the Helen May Butler Papers, National Museum of American History, Smithsonian Institution. All quotations used here in the text are from this source.

10. MODULATION: BANDS ON THE VERGE OF A NEW AGE

1. Howard Mumford Jones, *The Age of Energy: Varieties of American Experience, 1865–1915* (New York: Viking Press, 1971), 388.

2. Rudolph Wurlitzer Company, *Catalog No. 122* (Chicago, ca. 1919), 7.

3. Henry Seidel Canby, *The Age of Confidence* (New York: Farrar and Reinhart, 1934).

4. Jones, *Age of Energy,* 342; Irving Sablosky, *American Music* (Chicago: University of Chicago Press, 1969), 141.

5. Jones, *Age of Energy,* 7–8.

6. Foster Rhea Dulles, *A History of Recreation: America Learns to Play,* 2d ed. (New York: Appleton-Century-Crofts, 1965), 335.

7. Marshall B. Davidson, *Life in America,* 2 vols. (Boston: Houghton Mifflin Co., 1951), 2:78.

8. "A Letter of Inquiry, Regarding Possible Improvements in American Military Bands and a Number of Interesting Answers Thereto," *The Metronome* 26 (1910):18–19.

9. "New Uses for Brass Band," *The Metronome* 23 (1907):11.

10. Richard Franko Goldman, *The Wind Band: Its Literature and Technique* (1961; reprint ed., Westport, Connecticut: Greenwood Press, 1974), 94.

11. C. W. Osgood, Letter, March 29, 1920. Band ephemera collection, National Museum of American History, Smithsonian Institution.

12. James A. Keene, *A History of Music Education in the United States* (Hanover, New Hampshire: University Press of New England, 1982), 296–304.

13. Frederick Fennell, *Time and the Winds* (Kenosha, Wisconsin: G. Leblanc, 1954), 40.

14. Lewis Atherton, *Main Street on the Middle Border* (Bloomington: Indiana University Press, 1984), 109.

15. Chris Banner, "The Community Band in Kansas: A Long-standing Musical Institution," *Journal of the West* 22 (1983):36–46.

16. Wurlitzer, *Catalog No. 122,* 8. Wurlitzer suggested that a four-piece band should include piano, drums, saxophone, and banjo. Large ensembles should add, progressively, a cornet, trombone, violin, marimba, and clarinet.

17. Keene, *History of Music,* 291–292.

18. Goldman, *The Wind Band,* 84–92.

19. John Philip Sousa, *Through the Year with Sousa* (New York: Thomas Y. Crowell, 1910), quotation for December 20, originally from *The Bandsman.*

20. Goldman, *The Wind Band,* 88.

21. Sousa, *Through the Year,* entry for April 26, originally from an interview.

22. John S. Duss, *The Harmonists: A Personal History* (1943; reprint ed., Ambridge, Pennsylvania: The Harmonie Associates, 1970), 372–73.

23. William W. Rannells, "History of Brass Bands from the First Organization in Rochester Until the Present Time," in Marguerite Miller, *Home Folks,* 2 vols. (1910; reprint ed. Marceline, Missouri: Walsworth Printer), 2:48.

24. Frank Suddoth (March 15, 1915). Typescript. The original is in the band ephemera collection, National Museum of American History, Smithsonian Institution.

25. Suddoth, 4.

INDEX